ISSUES OF ARMS CONTROL LAW AND THE CHEMICAL WEAPONS CONVENTION

NOVA ET VETERA IURIS GENTIUM

PUBLICATIONS OF THE INSTITUTE OF PUBLIC INTERNATIONAL LAW
OF UTRECHT UNIVERSITY

SERIES A: MODERN INTERNATIONAL LAW
NUMBER 21

ISSUES OF ARMS CONTROL LAW AND THE CHEMICAL WEAPONS CONVENTION

Obligations *Inter Se* and Supervisory Mechanisms

Edited by

ERIC P. J. MYJER

MARTINUS NIJHOFF PUBLISHERS
THE HAGUE / BOSTON / LONDON

A C.I.P. Catalogue record for this book is available from the Library of Congress

ISBN 90-411-1585-4

Published by Kluwer Law International,
P.O. Box 85889, 2508 CN The Hague, The Netherlands.

Sold and distributed in North, Central and South America
by Kluwer Law International,
101 Philip Drive, Norwell, MA 02061, U.S.A.
kluwerlaw@wkap.com

In all other countries, sold and distributed
by Kluwer Law International, Distribution Centre,
P.O. Box 322, 3300 AH Dordrecht, The Netherlands.

Printed on acid-free paper

Printed in the Netherlands.

TABLE OF CONTENTS

PREFACE

Shortly after the Chemical Weapons Convention entered into force on 29 April 1997 the Department of International Law of Utrecht University's Faculty of Law, jointly with the *Werkgroep Wapenbeheersingsrecht van de Nederlandse Vereniging voor Internationaal Recht* (Committee on Arms Control Law of the Netherlands Branch of the International Law Association), and under the auspices of the International Law Association's International Committee on Arms Control and Disarmament Law, organized a seminar on some international law issues concerning the Chemical Weapons Convention and the newly established international organization under this treaty, namely the Organization for the Prohibition of Chemical Weapons (OPCW) with its seat in The Hague. This seminar was held on 2 July 1997 in the Senate Hall of Utrecht University under the chairmanship of the Dean of the Law Faculty, chairman of the *Nederlandse Vereniging voor Internationaal Recht* and Director of Studies of the International Law Association, Professor Alfred Soons. A distinguished and learned audience consisting of academics, diplomats and (international) civil servants all involved in either general international law or in the work of the OPCW debated two subjects.

The morning session was devoted to the obligations *inter se* of the signatories of the Chemical Weapons Convention, an international law issue with special relevance for arms control treaties given the security interests of States Parties to these treaties in maintaining at a minimum a *status quo* between all signatories. The case of the Chemical Weapons Convention, a treaty with carefully balanced commitments, is illustrative in this respect, for at the time of the First Conference (May 1997) 165 States had signed the Convention, whereas at that time only 88 had ratified it and it had entered into force for 87 States. Amongst the States that had only signed was at that time the Russian Federation, one of the two principal possessors of chemical weapons. At the time of publication this situation has changed substantially for as in September 2000 174 States had signed, with 139 States having ratified or acceded. This issue, however, also bears relevance for other arms control treaties like the Comprehensive Test Ban Treaty (CTBT), which has not entered into force yet.

The afternoon session, chaired by Dr. Julie Dahlitz (chairperson of the ILA Committee on Arms Control and Disarmament Law) dealt with the institutional aspects of the OPCW and with its supervisory functions. For this newly established international organization is the first of its kind completely devoted to supervision of arms control commitments. As such, this topic concerning the international arms control law also has relevance for the law of international organizations.

The papers presented by the rapporteurs Jan Klabbers and Eric Myjer led to in depth comments by the invited commentators Dieter Fleck, Thilo Marauhn, Johan Rautenbach, Jerzy Sztucki and Bert Vierdag and to a lively debate. Regretfully, some other commentators had not handed in their comments in written form. But as far as possible, given all the nuances and fine-tuning, this discussion has been summarized in the report by Tim Sneek.

The organizers are very grateful to Ige Dekker who both in the realization of the seminar and of this book played an active, stimulating and crucial role. Also Leontien de Bekker deserves praise for her unrelenting support and patience in the finalisation of the publication of this volume, a task which she embarked upon in a professional way. The Netherlands Ministry of Foreign Affairs' support for the seminar is gratefully acknowledged. As far as the actual organization of the seminar is concerned, Marieke Klap needs to be mentioned for her skills in this respect. Also the contribution of the research assistent Maaike de Langen is greatly appreciated. Last but not least, the editor is indebted to Annebeth Roosenboom of Kluwer Law International, who graciously gave sufficient breathing space to the editor when faced with a conglomerate of unexpected delays and guided it through to publication in the series *Nova et Vetera Iuris Gentium*. Both the organizers and the editor express the hope that the seminar and this resulting publication will contribute to the further study and development of the law of arms control.

This volume is dedicated to the memory of Dr. Koos Ooms (1925-1999), a Dutch biochemist of worldwide repute, who as a special advisor to the Netherlands Ministry of Foreign Affairs actively participated in the Geneva negotiations on chemical disarmament from the very early beginning in 1969 until the Chemical Weapons Convention was signed. In doing so he left his mark on the final results as he would do during the PrepCom phase in which he also took an active part. Not surprisingly, he was one of the very few with a detailed knowledge of the history of the negotiations and all the "ins and outs" inherent therein. Jokingly he once remarked that his year of birth, 1925, the year of the Geneva Protocol, had predestined him to work for so long on a chemical weapons ban. He remained active until the very last as a member of the United Nations Special Commission (UNSCOM) on the disarmament of Iraq. Koos Ooms, an *alumnus* of Utrecht University in the true sense, was a modest man, who to the great delight of the students in this Faculty was always willing to share his knowledge, thereby managing to bridge theory and practice.

Eric P.J. Myjer
Utrecht

LIST OF CONTRIBUTORS

Dieter Fleck	Director Department of International Agreements & Policy, Federal Ministry of Defence, Bonn, Germany and Rapporteur of the Committee on Arms Control and Disarmament Law of the International Law Asssociation
Jan Klabbers	Associate Professor of International Law at the University of Helsinki, Finland
Thilo Marauhn	Research Fellow at the Max Planck Institute for Comparative Public Law and International Law, Heidelberg, Germany
Eric P.J. Myjer	Associate Professor of Public International Law at the Europa Institute of Utrecht University, the Netherlands, member of the Committee on Arms Control and Disarmament Law of the International Law Asssociation and chairman of the Committee on Arms Control Law of the Netherlands Branch of the International Law Association
Johan Rautenbach	Acting Legal Advisor of the Organization for the Prohibition of Chemical Weapons, the Hague, the Netherlands
Tim Sneek	Directorate of Legal Affairs, Ministry of Defence, the Hague, the Netherlands
Jerzy Sztucki	Professor Emeritus of International Law at the University of Uppsala, Sweden
E.W. Vierdag	Professor Emeritus of Public International Law and International Relations, University of Amsterdam, the Netherlands

LIST OF ABBREVIATIONS

ACDA	United States Arms Control and Disarmament Agency
AJIL	American Journal of International Law
ASIL	American Society of International Law
BWC	Biological Weapons Convention
CD	Conference on Disarmament
CCD	Conference of the Committee on Disarmament
CTBT	Comprehensive Test Ban Treaty
CTBTO	Comprehensive Nuclear Test-Ban Treaty Organization
CWC	Chemical Weapons Convention
ENDC	Eighteen-Nation Disarmament Committee
FSCSP	First Session of the Conference of States Parties
GA	General Assembly
IAEA	International Atomic Energy Agency
ICJ	International Court of Justice
ILA	International Law Association
ILC	International Law Commission
ILM	International Legal Materials
IISS	International Institute for Strategic Studies
JCSL	Journal of Conflict & Security Law
LJIL	Leiden Journal of International Law
MBFR	Mutual and Balanced Force Reductions
NPT:	Non-Proliferation Treaty
NILR	Netherlands International Law Review
NTM's	National Technical Means
NVIR	Nederlandse Vereniging voor Internationaal Recht
OPCW	Organization for the Prohibition of Chemical Weapons
OPBW	Organization for the Prohibition of Biological Weapons
OSCE	Organization on Security and Co-operation in Europe
PCIJ	Permanent Court of International Justice
PrepCom	Preparatory Committee
PTS	Provisional Technical Secretariat
SALT	Strategic Arms Limitation Talks
SC	Security Council
SIPRI	Stockholm International Peace Research Institute
TS	Technical Secretariat
TTBT	Threshold Test Ban Treaty
UN	United Nations
UNIDER	United Nations Institute for Disarmament Research

UNSCOM	United Nations Special Commission
UNTS	United Nations Treaty Series
UK	United Kingdom
US	United States
VCLT	Vienna Convention on the Law of Treaties
WHO	World Health Organization
YILC	United Nations, Yearbook of the International Law Commission

THE LAW OF ARMS CONTROL, MILITARY SECURITY AND THE ISSUES: AN INTRODUCTION

Eric P.J. Myjer

1.The setting

As the title indicates this volume concerns *Issues of Arms Control Law and the Chemical Weapons Convention*, and in particular *Obligations* inter se and *Supervisory Mechanisms*. This of course might beg the question whether there exists such a separate area within international law that deserves to be distinguished as arms control law and also how this relates to other areas with regard to arms, force and its application, i.e. the law of collective security and the humanitarian law of armed conflict. This book, however, does not concern the niceties of such distinctions. For the purpose of this book it suffices to take the position that arms control law as a separate area of international law does indeed exist, even though it has only recently been recognized as such,[1] and that the Chemical Weapons Convention is a treaty belonging to it. There is one element in particular which is characteristic for this area of the law and that is the element of military security. This it shares with both the law of collective security and the humanitarian law of armed conflict. This element, therefore, at the same time demonstrates the interrelationship of the law of arms control with the law of collective security and the humanitarian law of armed conflict. On the basis of this distinguishing feature one could even distinguish a broader area of international law encompassing these three aforementioned areas, i.e. the law of military security. It is the concept of military security that thereby sets this broader area of international law apart from other areas of

[1] Compare Kolasa, who, referring to the disarmament and arms control agreements, remarks "they constitute an impressive collection which forms the basis for a nascent branch of international conventional law aimed at the regulation of disarmament and arms control issues." (at p. v) He then presents them as a system of treaties which, in his opinion, "gives birth to a new branch of international law -disarmament and arms control law". (at p. 1)
J. Kolasa, *Disarmament and Arms Control Agreements, A study on Procedural and Institutional Law* (1994). On the law of arms control in general see f.i. E.P.J. Myjer, The Law of Arms-control and International Supervision in 3*LJIL*3 (1990) pp.99-123/ M. Brus (et.al), *The United Nations Decade of International Law* (1991) at pp. 99-123; G. Lysén, *The International Regulation of Armaments: The Law of Disarmament* (1990); J. Dahlitz and D. Dicke (eds), *The International Law of Arms Control and Disarmament* (1991); J. Dahlitz (ed.), *Avoidance and Settlement of Arms Control Disputes* (1994). See also the -up till now- four reports of the Committee on Arms Control and Disarmament Law of the International Law Association: Report of the sixty-fifth Conference (pp. 389-403 (*first report* (1992); of the sixty-sixth (pp. 401-431), *Legal Restraints on Arms Proliferation* (1994); of the sixty-seventh (pp. 307-322), *Legal Remedies for Arms Control Impasse* (1996); of the sixty-eight (pp.164-178), *Further Constraints on Nuclear Weapons* (1998).

E.P.J. Myjer (ed.), Issues of Arms Control Law and the Chemical Weapons Convention, 1–10.

international law. In order to clarify this security context with regard to the Chemical Weapons Convention (CWC) in the following paragraphs the focus will first be on this element of security and on the ban on the use of force. Next these different areas of international law and in particular the law of arms control will be briefly discussed.

2. The concept of military security and the ban on the use of force

This concept may be taken either in the polemological[2] and military sense, or in the legal sense. In the former sense it points to the different notions of security[3] that States may entertain. From that point of view it could be held that in a general sense States need military power to contribute to the maintenance of international peace and security, a notion that can also be found as one of the purposes of the United Nations (Article 1 para. 1). It is not incidental that the notion of peace is linked to that of security, for peace[4] merely points to the absence of war or the threat of an imminent outbreak of war. In order to indicate that with peace in this sense there may still not exist a situation of (secure) independence, the notion of security is introduced. Security then points to the absence of the necessity to give in to foreign demands, be it via a direct military threat or via an indirect threat. It points to a state of national independence. This notion of security can be used in order to assess the function that a State attributes to its military power. In a general sense it can be held that there exists only a situation of optimal security if there is sufficient military power to withstand any possible form of foreign pressure, be it military, economic, political or diplomatic. However, it is possible to make a general distinction between *interest security* and *military security*. In case a State uses the notion of interest security it wants to be able to withstand ***any*** foreign pressure on its vital interests, be it via military means or otherwise, if need be by using military power or the projection of such power. If a State uses the notion of *military security in a broad sense* it intends to

---

[2] Polemology, conflict and peace research are closely related areas.

[3] Compare Jonathan Dean (*Ending Europe's Wars, the continuing search for peace and security*) (1994), (a former US ambassador and chief US negotiator at the MBFR arms control negotiations) who restricts himself to the concept of military security: "Security is the absence of fear and reasons for fear. It is a broad term covering many aspects: domestic public order, economic security, environmental security, and military security. This book (*Ending Europe's Wars*, author) focuses on military security, which involves conflict and systematic armed violence between states or within their borders. Although it does not make continual reference to the other wider dimensions of the concept of security, it has been written in vivid awareness of them", at xv.

[4] Peace in this sense is what polemology calls negative peace, in contradistincion to positive peace, or associative peace, which refers to a situation of justice acceptable to all parties involved. See on this B.V.A. Röling, *Volkenrecht en vrede (Public International Law and Peace)* (1985) at 18 et seq.

withstand any violation of its interests by military means, if need be by using military power or the projection of such power. *Military security* as used here is much more limited. It points to the notion that a State only intends to use its military power if it is actually being attacked by military means (or when it is ordered, or mandated, to do so by the Security Council).[5] In the area of arms control we find, for instance, reference to the notion of military security in the context of the OSCE in the document "A framework for arms control".[6] The context in which this document was adopted suggests that the reference is to the limited notion of military security. However, it is apparent that a number of (Western) States use the concept of security in a broader sense, which can be witnessed in the debate on "humanitarian intervention", whereby in undefined cases of "humanitarian emergencies" many Western policy-makers do not feel inhibited by the ban on the unilateral use of force, in cases other than self-defence, and profess the right to use unilateral force in case the Security Council cannot decide on the necessary action.[7] It is the notion of military security in the limited sense, however, that answers to the criteria of security in the legal sense, since under international law the use of military force contrary to the ban on the use of force is only allowed in case of self-defence or by or under the authority of the Security Council.[8] This central principle of law is derived from that area of international law that can be "characterized" as the *law of collective security*. It also appears as the core principle of the *law of military security*, for it is also central to the *law of arms control*. This is not surprising since the concept of *military security* applies with equal force to the area of arms control.

This has led us to the concept of security in the legal sense. As indicated above the primary purpose under the United Nations Charter is the maintenance of peace and security. The founders of the UN wanted to make

---

[5] Military security concerns the external structure in contradistinction to Laurence Lustgarten and Ian Leigh who look at the internal structure of national security and its relationship with parliamentary democracy. Laurence Lustgarten and Ian Leigh, *In from the cold, national security and parliamentary democracy* (1994).

[6] Lisbon Document 1996 (DOC.S/1/96, 3 December 1996), document issued by the government leaders and heads of state of the OSCE participating states at their Lisbon summit. In Part III, A framework for arms control (FSC.DEC/8 /96) under II "Challenges and risks" the following is stated:" 7. Challenges and risks in the field of military security still exist in the OSCE area and others may arise in the future. The framework will help to promote cooperative responses to challenges and risks that may be dealt with through arms control measures. In doing so, the following issues, inter alia should be addressed:- military imbalances that may contribute to instabilities; -inter-State tensions and conflicts, in particular in border areas, that affect military security;.."(Italics, author), reprinted in Helsinki Monitor, 1997, no 1 at 99.

[7] Compare for instance Nigel White, The legality of bombing in the name of humanity 5 *Journal of Conflict and Security Law* (2000), at pp. 27-43.

[8] Compare para. 105 2(c) of *The Legality of the Threat or Use of Nuclear Weapons*, Advisory Opinion, [1996] ICJ, 35 *ILM* (1996) at p. 831.

quite clear that peace alone was not sufficient. Goodrich and Hambro clarify that security should be understood in the military sense: "Peace must be accompanied by a feeling of security, security from war in particular".[9] In order to bring about this prime purpose, and its corollary the peaceful settlement of disputes, the system of collective security was established. Against the clearly stated background of a ban on the use of force in Article 2(4) Charter and the obligation to settle disputes peacefully in Article 2(3) the States Parties under this system granted the Security Council a monopoly on the use of force. The only exception to this monopoly is the case of self-defence in Article 51 of the UN Charter. Logically speaking, the notion of security in this limited sense should also determine a State's needs concerning armaments, both to be able to defend itself and to contribute to measures taken by the UN in the context of the system of collective security, be they peacekeeping or peace-enforcing. Practice, however, shows this not to be the case, which brings us to the dilemma of arms control.[10]

3. The law of military security and the interrelationship between the law of arms control, the law of collective security and the humanitarian law of armed conflict

The international law of military security concerns the military security of States and encompasses both the law of collective security,[11] the law of armed conflict, including humanitarian law, and the international law of arms control. Although each of these respective areas can be regarded as separate and distinct areas of international law, they are interrelated. Interestingly all three areas figure prominently in the advisory opinion of the International Court of Justice (ICJ) on the *Legality of the Threat or Use of Nuclear Weapons*[12] concerning the extent to which military force may be used in self-defence. In its analysis the ICJ deals with these areas respectively, which is already

---

[9] Goodrich and Hambro, *Charter of the United Nations, commentary and documents* (1946), at 56. Kelsen seems to find this distinction unnecessary. The word security does not expand the purpose of the UN: "Its is doubtful whether there is a difference between "peace" and "security". International security is guaranteed if international peace is maintained. It seems that the addition of the words "and security" is rather superfluous". H. Kelsen, *The Law of the United Nations* (1954), at 13. Obviously peace should then be read in the similar restrictive sense and not as something like "Positive peace". The founders were quite adamant that even a referral to international justice should not be added. See Goodrich and Hambro *ibid.* Also Kelsen p. 15 et seq. And Netherlands Ministry of Foreign Affairs, *Het ontstaan der Verenigde Naties* (1950), p. 19 et seq.

[10] Compare for instance the SIPRI Yearbooks.

[11] See E.P.J. Myjer, Some reflections on collective security and the use of force XLIV NILR (1997), 89-101 and in particular at 100.

[12] *The Legality of the Threat or Use of Nuclear Weapons*, Advisory Opinion, *supra* n. 8 at pp. 814-938.

apparent when it sets out to focus on the law "relating to the use of force enshrined in the United Nations Charter and the law applicable in armed conflict which regulates the conduct of hostilities, together with any specific treaties on nuclear weapons that the Court might determine to be relevant".[13] The Court (then) specifically deals with some of the core elements of the law of collective security.[14] In its *dictum*[15] the Court considers general international law with regard to the threat or use of nuclear weapons and stresses the scope of Articles 2 (4) and 51 of the UN Charter on the use of force and on self-defence. All this concerns the law of collective security. Looking at the question "whether there is any prohibition of recourse to nuclear weapons as such"[16] it focuses on conventional and customary law relating to arms control.[17] Next, in addressing "the question whether recourse to nuclear weapons must be considered as illegal in the light of the principles and rules of international humanitarian law applicable in armed conflict and of the law of neutrality"[18] the Court deals with the law of armed conflict.[19] It then draws the limits set by the law of armed conflict.[20] Furthermore, there are the mixed arguments[21] relating both to self-defence and the principles and rules of humanitarian law, which led to its ambivalent opinion not being able to conclude "definitively whether the threat or use of nuclear weapons would be lawful or unlawful in an extreme circumstance of self-defence, in which the very survival of a State would be at stake". [22] In focusing on the self-defence exception the Court underlines the core principle on the use of force, namely its ban under Article 2(4) UN Charter, which is central to the law of collective security. In its deliberations the Court not only takes into consideration the principles of proportionality and necessity in the application of military force in self-defence, but also the general principles of the humanitarian law of armed conflict. In other words "[...]the Opinion reaffirms that *jus ad bellum* and *ius in bello* are complementary and coexist in their application, not in conflict with one another".[23] Interestingly the Court in fact outlines in legal terms the breadth of the only acceptable security concept, i.e. military security

[13] Para.34, *ibid* at p. 821.
[14] Paras. 37-51, *ibid*, at pp. 822-823.
[15] Paras. 105(2)(A(B)(C), *ibid* at p. 831.
[16] Para.53, *ibid*, at p. 823.
[17] Paras. 53-77, *ibid* at pp. 823-827.
[18] Para. 74, *ibid*, at p. 827.
[19] Paras. 75-87, *ibid*. at pp. 827-828.
[20] In paras. 105(2)(D) and (E), *ibid* at 831.
[21] Paras. 90-97, *ibid*, at pp. 829-830.
[22] Para 105 (E), *ibid*. at p. 831. On the Court's ambivalence see I.F.Dekker and W.G. Werner, The Completeness of International Law and Hamlet's Dilemma, Non-Liquet, The Nuclear Weapons Case and Legal Theory, *Nordic Journal of International Law* 2000, p. 1-23, at pp. 21-22.
[23] Greenwood, *ibid*, at 265.

in the limited sense as discussed above in para. 2, by painting in stark terms not only when an exception from the central principle on the non-use of force is allowed for -the self-defence exception-, but even from the core principles of the humanitarian law of armed conflict by referring to "an extreme circumstance of self-defence, in which the very survival of a State would be at stake". And in conclusion as an *obiter dictum*, most interestingly, in this connection it formulates a central principle of the law of arms control, namely that "There exists an obligation to pursue in good faith and bring to a conclusion negotiations leading to nuclear disarmament in all its aspects under strict and effective international control".[24] Furthermore, the considerations on good faith are highly relevant for arms control treaties in general.

With regard to international law sub-distinctions concerning force and arms and the use thereof have been made earlier, for instance by Röling. He made a distinction concerning the character of rules of international law that control weapons ("weapons law"): 1) the rules of armed conflict, the *ius in bello*; 2) the rules of disarmament law; and 3) the rules that victors impose ("victors law").[25] Elsewhere he adds a fourth category, in fact one that forms part of the law of collective security, namely the *ius ad bellum.*[26] Reference to the relationship between the law of armed conflict and the law of arms control can also be found by Neuhold when he remarks: "The *international law of war and international humanitarian law* are related to the efforts in these three (arms control, disarmament and confidence and security-building measures, author) areas. Their norms restrict the means and methods which may be employed in armed conflicts and protect certain groups of persons and objects from hostilities. *It must be added that the lines between these four concepts are often blurred in practice* (Italics, author)."[27] Another example is Murphy, who

[24] Para 105 2(F), *ibid.* at p. 831.

[25] B.V.A.Röling, in: *Mededelingen van de Nederlandse Vereniging voor Internationaal Recht*, no.62 November 1970, p. 7-9.

[26] "Vier Arten von Bestimmungen also: hinsichtlich des Kriegverbotes (jus ad bellum), hinsichtlich des Kriegsrechtes (jus in bello), hinsichtlich des Abrüstungsrechtes und hinsichtlich des Rechtes der Sieger". In W.Schaumann, *Völkerrechtliches Gewaltverbot und Friedenssicherung* (1971).: at 94. He then expands on this in his introduction (pp.XIX -XXX, especially XXV-onwards) to E.P.J. Myjer, *Militaire Veiligheid door Afschrikking, verdediging en het geweldverbod in het Handvest van de Verenigde Naties (Military Security via Deterrence, Self-Defence and the Ban on the Use of Force in the Charter of the United Nations)* (1980) and in his contribution "the Law of Arms Control and Disarmament" in *Essays in international law in honour of Judge Manfred Lachs* (1984). On disarmament law and its distinction from other categories of international law concerning military force and warfare, see also J.H. Burgers, The Netherlands and Disarmament pp. 254-259 in: T.M.C. Asser Institute, *International Law in The Netherlands* (1979)

[27] H. Neuhold (Legal aspects of arms control agreements, in: *Festschrift für Ignaz Seidl-Hohenfeldern* (1988) p 428.

remarks "Arms control, disarmament, non-proliferation and its safeguards are closely related to regulation of the use of force".[28]

What has been discussed above may help to explain why these areas can be treated within a single conceptual framework. This is not to say that there is a merging of the law in these areas, for each separate area will continue to have its specific characteristics; take, for instance, the aspect of responsibility. A breach in the case of the law of armed conflict would more readily lead to individual responsibility than in the case of arms control law where it would, as a rule, lead to state responsibility. But there is more than a mere emerging inter-dependency. Given that each of these areas may have elements in common that are characteristic for any of the other respective areas, it can be held that there are points (areas) in which two or three of the areas interlock. To put it differently: within any of the areas similar norms and principles may be applied given that all three (may) have to do with elements like military force, weapons, fighting techniques -including targeting- and military security, both in the sense of secured from and secured against. The coincidence of norms and principles applied in relation to these specific -and distinguishing- elements in any of the respective areas forms the distinguishing characteristic of the international law of military security in relation to other areas of international law. Furthermore, it can be noted that these three areas appear to be operating more and more "on the same plane", whereby borders become blurred (disappear), or at least become semi-permeable. As such, the distinction between the law of collective security, the law of armed conflict and the law of arms control is different from that between the *ius in bello* and *ius ad bellum* -a distinction that has become blurred anyway.[29] Furthermore, it appears that there is a certain relationship between some of the notions that can be derived from the dictates of international relations and norms and principles applied within the international law of military security. This is the contrext in which the Chemical Weapons Convention, belonging to the law of arms control, should be viewed.

4.The law of arms control

Under international law only *use* of force by a state to preserve military security in the above limited sense is allowed, which includes the use of force ordered by or on behalf of the Security Council. In other words, use of force for different purposes is forbidden.[30] This, however, does not automatically lead to

---

[28] J. Murphy, Force and Arms, in: O. Schachter & C. Joyner (eds.), *United Nations Legal Order* (1995), p. 301.

[29] Compare Ch. Greenwood, Jus ad Bellum and Jus in Bello in the Nuclear Weapons Advisory Opinion, at 258, in: L.Boisson DeChazournes & Ph.Sands, *International law, the International Court of Justice and Nuclear Weapons*(1999).

[30] Compare Article 5 of the Definition of aggression, UN GA 3314/XXIX (14 Dec. 1974).

a restriction on the *possession* of weapons by states. Unless agreed otherwise, possession of weapons is still allowed, as stressed by the court

> "...[I])n international law there are no rules, other than such rules as may be accepted by the State concerned, by treaty or otherwise, whereby the level of armaments of a sovereign State can be limited...".[31]

In this "grey area" there appears to be a tendency by States to accumulate more weapons than actually necessary to answer the limited notion of military security, but instead to also allow for unilateral use of force to project (protect) broader security interests if they so decide.

The law of arms control aims exactly at the regulation of the possession of armaments. Although in general one finds simultaneous reference to arms control and disarmament and consequently to the law of arms control and disarmament, I will only refer to the law of arms control since disarmament can be seen as a form of arms control. Furthermore, already the definition of arms control law will reflect a coincidence with the law of collective security and the law of armed conflict. The international law of arms control can be defined as that part of international law that concerns the internationally agreed (recognized) limitations on the use of military force (in general) and on the use and/or possession of armaments (in particular), whether in respect of the level of armaments, their character or deployment, and with the applicable supervisory mechanisms.[32] The law of arms control therefore not only concerns the material norms agreed upon, but also the institutional law. This is not surprising for supervision is always regarded as an essential element of arms control as reflected in the well-known objective of "..general and complete disarmament under strict and effective international control".[33] The institutional law of arms control concerns first and foremost the laws relating to the different existing systems of supervision of the respective material norms.[34] It could be held that especially the further development of a body of institutional law of arms control that allows for effective supervision of arms control

---

[31] I.C.J. Report 1986 (Nicaragu v. United States of America), p. 135, para. 269), as confirmed in I.C.J. Report, 8 July 1996 (Advisory Opinion (1996); legality of the threat or use of nuclear weapons) under 21, *supra* n .

[32] This definition is partly based on Hedley Bull's definition of arms control, H. Bull, *The Control of the Arms Race* (1961), at ix.

[33] Compare: the Treaty on the Non-Proliferation of nuclear weapons (1968), preamubular and Article VI: the ICJ advisory opinion on *The Legality of the Threat or Use of Nuclear Weapons* [1996] 99-103 and 105 (2) (F) pp. 830-831; the Treaty on the Prohibition of the emplacement of nuclear weapons and other weapons of mass destruction on the seabed and the ocean floor and in the subsoil thereof (1971) preambule; Convention on the prohibition of the development, production and stockpiling of bacteriological (biological) and toxin weapons and on their destruction (1971), preamble; Comprehensive Test Ban Treaty (1996), preamble.

[34] Compare Myjer, *supra* n.1 at 104.

obligations is a prerequisite for the further development of material norms in this area.[35] For without effective supervision it will be extremely difficult to attain far-reaching arms control and disarmament measures, as is recognized- not without reason- in most arms control treaties as indicated above. We could already see this in the case of the NPT and its related safeguards agreements allowing for inspection by IAEA inspectors.[36] Furthermore, the elaborate supervisory system of the CWC and comparable ones, such as that of the CTBT and that proposed for the BWC, being a case in point. This may also explain, not taking into consideration the extensive annexes attached to the CWC, the fact that already with its, some rather lengthy, 24 Articles, it belongs to the most extensive arms control treaties.[37] The extensive annexes - the Verification and the Confidentiality Annex- are a further extension of supervisory rules, for they detail and support the supervisory mechanism respectively.

It is in this context that the different contributions to this book should be viewed. The first part of this volume then concerns the Obligations *inter se* of the signatories of the Chemical Weapons Convention, an international law issue with special relevance for arms control treaties like the Comprehensive Test Ban Treaty. Here the element of military security may help to explain why the general international law doctrine of obligations *inter se* is especially important. For, given their security interests, it is crucial for States that are either party or signatory to arms control treaties that at a minimum a *status quo* between all the signatories is maintained. Jan Klabbers' article on interim obligations solicted wide-ranging comments from Dieter Fleck, Thilo Marauhn, Johan Rautenbach, Jerzy Sztucki and Bert Vierdag.

The second part of this book deals with the specific issue of the supervisory mechanism of the Chemical Weapons Convention (CW) and more in particular with the institutional aspects of the Organization for the Prohibition

---

[35] A recent study in this field is Jan Kolasa, *Disarmament and Arms Control Agreements*, *supra* n. 1. He presents the arms control and disarmament treaties as a system of treaties; "Basic treaties are presented in their full, formal complexity, and the main emphasis is put on the interrelations and mutual interdependence between them. In fact, they are presented as a system of treaties which gives birth to a new branch of international law -disarmament and arms control law. This law is mostly composed of well developed various kinds of procedures", at 1. "And it is rather surprising that this important trend in the evolution of contemporary system of international law has not found a proper place in the general theory of present international law." at 14.

[36] Compare with regard to the IAEA Article XII Statute of the International Atomic Energy Agency. INFCIRC/66; INF/CIRC/Rev.1; INFCIRC/66/Rev.2. Article III of the Treaty on the Non-proliferation of Nuclear Weapons (1970). IAEA INF/CIRC/153 (Cor). Comp. Kolasa *ibid* at 13.

[37] Kolasa, *supra* n. at 7.

of Chemical Weapons (OPCW) and its supervisory functions. Eric Myjer's article on this issue led to detailed comments by Dieter Fleck, Johan Rautenbach and Thilo Marauhn.

At the close of each part of this volume a summary report of the discussion prepared by Tim Sneek can be found. The full text of the Convention (without annexes) is included in this volume.

STRANGE BEDFELLOWS: THE 'INTERIM OBLIGATION' AND THE 1993 CHEMICAL WEAPONS CONVENTION

Jan Klabbers

1. Introduction

On January 13, 1993, the Convention on the Prohibition of the Development, Production, Stockpiling and Use of Chemical Weapons and on their Destruction[1] (CWC) was opened for signature, the expectation being that it could enter into force in 1995. Since it took some time before the CWC attracted a sufficient number of ratifications to enter into force, the question arose whether or not some substantive[2] obligations contained in the CWC would nevertheless rest upon those states that had signed or ratified, prior to the CWC's entry into force.

Due to the recent entry into force of the CWC, that question has lost some, but not all of its importance. For one thing, there are still a number of states that have not yet expressed their final consent to be bound. Second, and arguably more important, the question is bound to surface in connection with similar regimes. Thus, foreign offices were recently contemplating the possible existence of similar obligations in relation to the comprehensive nuclear test ban treaty.

Such obligations prior to the CWC's entry into force cannot rest upon signatories or ratifying states by virtue of the CWC alone, as the CWC does not provide for provisional application.[3] If such obligations exist, they must exist by virtue of a rule of general international law.[4] The pertinent international legal rule is known as the rule on the "interim obligation"; it has been formulated in Article 18 of the Vienna Convention on the Law of Treaties, which reads:

---

[1] Text in 32 International Legal Materials (1993), 804-873.

[2] As opposed to certain formal obligations, such as the obligation to respect the provision on entry into force. This obligation derives from Article 24, paragraph 4, of the Vienna Convention on the Law of Treaties.

[3] Cf. Article 25 of the Vienna Convention on the Law of Treaties. See generally E.W. Vierdag, "Spanningen tussen recht en praktijk in het verdragenrecht", *Preadvies Nederlandse Vereniging voor Internationaal Recht* (1989), 3-87, esp. 7-35.

[4] As the International Law Association's Committee on Arms Control and Disarmament put it in its Third Report, presented to the 1996 Helsinki Conference of the ILA, impasse situations not only occur during negotiations but also after the finalization of agreements: "The discussion of legal remedies for arms control in this broader sense has to be based on traditional principles of international law." (at 5).

E.P.J. Myjer (ed.), Issues of Arms Control Law and the Chemical Weapons Convention, 11–29.

> "A State is obliged to refrain from acts which would defeat the object and purpose of a treaty when:
> (a) it has signed the treaty or has exchanged instruments constituting the treaty subject to ratification, acceptance or approval, until it shall have made its intention clear not to become a party to the treaty; or
> (b) it has expressed its consent to be bound to the treaty, pending the entry into force of the treaty and provided that such entry into force is not unduly delayed."

Article 18 is a rather puzzling provision, and has not unreasonably been called "an enigma".[5] In order to be applied, several complicated questions must be answered: What constitutes the object and purpose of a treaty? How do we identify the object and purpose? What acts would defeat a treaty's object and purpose? Those questions themselves give rise to several other, equally difficult questions: is there, for example, a distinction between the object on the one hand, and the purpose on the other? Does the phrase object and purpose have the same meaning in different circumstances, regardless of whether it concerns the interim obligation, the permissibility of reservations,[6] or the interpretation of treaties?[7]

As a preliminary matter, the present paper is written on the assumption that Article 18 of the Vienna Convention represents present-day customary international law, and is thus not merely opposable to parties to the Vienna Convention, but to other states as well. Whether Article 18 codified existing custom at the time the Vienna Convention was concluded is debatable; strictly speaking, it presumably did not.[8] McNair, for example, writing in 1961, formulated the rule as follows: "... one party to a treaty must not, pending ratification, do anything which will hamper any action that may be taken by the other party if

---

[5] Joni S. Charme, "The interim obligation of Article 18 of the Vienna Convention on the Law of Treaties: Making sense of an enigma", 25 *George Washington Journal of International Law and Economics* (1991), 71-114.

[6] Cf. Article 19 (c) of the Vienna Convention: "A State may ... formulate a reservation unless ... the reservation is incompatible with the object and purpose of the treaty."

[7] Cf. Article 31 of the Vienna Convention: "A treaty shall be interpreted ... in the light of its object and purpose". Other provisions of the Vienna Convention referring to the object and purpose of a treaty include Article 41 (on modification), Article 58 (on suspension between some treaty partners only) and Article 60 (on breach). For a general analysis, see Jan Klabbers, "Some problems regarding the object and purpose of treaties", 8 *Finnish Yearbook of International Law* (1997, 138-160).

[8] International judicial and arbitral practice was scarce, providing little authoritative guidance. In the 1910 *Iloilo claims* case, the tribunal reportedly found that obligations took effect upon ratification (3 *Annual Digest*, at 336); the 1928 decision in *Megalidis v. Turkey* specified the interim obligation as "the duty to do nothing which might impair the operation" of a treaty prior to its entry into force (4 *Annual Digest*, at 395). The PCIJ declined to deal with the issue in both the *Mavrommatis* case ([1925] Publ. PCIJ, Ser. A, no. 5, at 39) and the *German interests in Polish Upper Silesia* case ([1926] Publ. PCIJ, Ser. A, no. 7, at 40).

and when that treaty enters into force ..."[9] Arguably, such a rule is stricter than Article 18, in that it refers not just to acts defeating the object and purpose of a treaty, but refers to "anything which will hamper any action".[10]

Yet, to say that strictly speaking the pre-Vienna Convention customary rule differed from Article 18 is perhaps to overstate the point, as in practice the distinction between McNair's formula and Article 18 appears to have been negligible. Indeed, post-Vienna Convention practice suggests as much, with both types of formulas being invoked since 1969, the year the Vienna Convention was concluded.[11]

With respect to the Chemical Weapons Convention, one author has concluded that indeed certain obligations rest upon signatories and ratifying states pending the CWC's entry into force. According to Dinstein, pending entry into force both signatory states and ratifying states, while allowed to continue to produce and stockpile chemical weapons, are prohibited from *accelerating* the production and stockpiling of chemical weapons. Moreover, Dinstein suggests that there may be some borderline issues, for instance regarding the question whether mere testing of new weapons, without resorting to production, would be permissible.[12]

Dinstein's careful suggestions already indicate that the interim obligation does not, with respect to the CWC, limit states' freedom in intolerable ways. Put differently and rather bluntly, with respect to a treaty such as the CWC, Article 18 of the Vienna Convention is virtually meaningless, for reasons which will be discussed below. Thus, I respectfully disagree with Professor Dinstein,

---

[9] Cf. Lord McNair, *The law of treaties* (Oxford 1961), at 200; see also Philippe Cahier, "L'obligation de ne pas priver un traité de son object et son but avant son entrée en vigeur", in *Mélanges Fernand Dehousse* (Paris 1979), 31-37, arguing that at least the duty upon signatories constituted an innovation.

[10] Other writers contend that the rule as formulated in the Vienna Convention was declaratory of existing custom. See, for example, Mark E. Villiger, *Customary international law and treaties* (Dordrecht 1985), at 321.

[11] Thus the Dutch government, in 1975, prior to acceding to the Vienna Convention, used words reminiscent of McNair's formula, whereas the Swiss government, prior to acceding, invoked the Article 18 formula. See Paul V. McDade, "The interim obligation between signature and ratification of a treaty: issues raised by the recent action of signatories to the Law of the Sea Convention with respect to the mining of the deep seabed", 32 *Netherlands International Law Review* (1985), 5-47, at 13. The same instances are mentioned in Villiger, *supra* note 11, at 319-320. Villiger adds a 1979 statement of the US Dept. of State concerning an oral agreement, which appears closer to the Vienna Convention formula than to the McNair formula.

[12] Yoram Dinstein, "Ratification and universality", in Academie de Droit International, *Workshop 1994: The Convention on the Prohibition and Elimination of Chemical Weapons: a breakthrough in multilateral disarmament* (Dordrecht 1995), 151-165, esp. at 154. Applying the interim obligation to SALT II, Turner reached the conclusion that "a State would be prohibited from research and testing which would result in permanent and irreversible benefits prohibited by the terms of the treaty." Cf. Robert F. Turner, "Legal implications of deferring ratification of SALT II", 21 *Virginia Journal of International Law* (1981), 747-784, at 764.

and submit that, careful as he is, he still makes more of the interim obligation than is warranted.

As far as the scope of the present paper is concerned, I will discuss only those obligations possibly arising from the interim obligation as formulated in Article 18 of the Vienna Convention. An argument could be made, and quite cogently so, that at the very least the use of chemical weapons is prohibited under customary international law; if so, the obligation not to use chemical weapons prior to the entry into force of the CWC stems from international custom, not from the CWC itself. Whatever the answer may be, considerations of time and space do not allow me to address this matter. Similarly, I will refrain from discussing possible obligations based on other international instruments, be they bilateral or multilateral, except and insofar as they touch upon the interim obligation incurred by the signing or ratification of the CWC. Moreover, I will leave aside the possible effects (if any) that signing or ratifying may engender under domestic law.[13]

Nonetheless, I do feel that it is imperative to address the possibility of obligations having arisen, prior to the CWC's entry into force, through the operation of the principle of estoppel,[14] as both the principle of estoppel and Article 18 of the Vienna Convention seem to follow logically from the principle of good faith. The discussion of the estoppel principle as a possible source of obligations will take place in the last part of this paper. I will start by outlining the CWC, and discuss Article 18 of the Vienna Convention and its limits with respect to the CWC, while trying to place this in a somewhat broader perspective.

2. The Chemical Weapons Convention: an outline

Concluded in January 1993, the CWC is a highly complex legal instrument, consisting of a core document of XXIV articles and a number of annexes, which form an integral part of the CWC.[15] Although reservations to the annexes are tolerated to the extent that they are compatible with the CWC's object and purpose, the CWC itself will not tolerate reservations.[16] Nevertheless, the Convention is open for universal membership,[17] and is subject to ratification.[18]

---

[13] Domestic judges may sometimes apply a treaty prior to its entry into force, anticipating that entry into force will soon follow or, occasionally, upon the theory that the unratified treaty reflects customary international law. Several examples are listed in Jan Klabbers, *The concept of treaty in international law* (The Hague 1996).

[14] For a suggestion to that effect, see the Third Report of the ILA's Committee on Arms Control and Disarmament Law, *supra* note 4, at 6.

[15] Art. XVII CWC.

[16] Art. XXII.

[17] Art. XVIII.

[18] Art. XIX.

One of the priority concerns of the negotiators was the temporal factor.[19] Article XXI:1 provides clear evidence of the drafters' intention not to rush into things:

> "The Convention shall enter into force 180 days after the date of the deposit of the 65th instrument of ratification, but in no case earlier than two years after its opening for signature."

The number of 65 required ratifications, although perhaps somewhat high,[20] is by no means unusual.[21] What is somewhat unusual, however, is the provision that the Convention shall not enter into force for the first two years after being opened for signature.[22] The rationale will be obvious: it was thought wise to afford states the opportunity to seriously prepare themselves to take on far-reaching obligations, which involve or may involve the amendment of penal laws, the creation of facilities (perhaps even agencies) with respect to verification, the construction of destruction facilities, and an examination of those aspects related to chemical weapons upon which the CWC establishes a regime of declarations.[23]

Much of the declarations envisaged in the CWC are themselves activated only after the passage of a certain amount of time, always measured from the moment the Convention enters into force. Thus, under Article III, a State Party shall declare "not later than 30 days" after the CWC's entry into force in its case, whether it owns chemical weapons, where these are stored, how many there are, *et cetera*. Similarly, not later than 90 days after the Convention's entry into force, chemical weapon production facilities shall be closed.[24]

In a number of situations, the entry into force of the Convention thus sets off a "chain-reaction". As indicated, on-site inspection may only start after the declaration under Article III has been made, which is itself a provision 'triggered' by the entry into force of the Convention. Indeed, the CWC even

---

[19] See generally also Jozef Goldblat, "The 1993 Chemical Weapons Convention: a significant step in the process of multilateral disarmament", in Academie de Droit International, (*supra* n. 12 (Dordrecht 1995), 15-25.

[20] The 1978 Vienna Convention on Succession of States in Respect of Treaties required only 15 ratifications, to name just one example.

[21] Cf. UNCLOS III, which required 60 ratifications.

[22] 'Unusual' is perhaps too strong a term at least in the context of arms control agreements. There is, for example, a similar provision in the Comprehensive Test Ban Treaty.

[23] See, for example, Terence Taylor, "The Chemical Weapons Convention and prospects for implementation", 42 *International and Comparative Law Quarterly* (1993), 912-919; Panel, "Implementing the Chemical Weapons Convention: progress and challenges", in 88 *Proceedings of the American Society of International Law* (1994), 221-238.

[24] Art. V:7 CWC.

envisages an "order of destruction" of both chemical weapons and production facilities.[25]

Moreover, as the CWC also aims at establishing an international organization, a nexus exists between institutional and substantive provisions. It is the stated task of the OPCW to achieve the object and purpose of the CWC, to ensure implementation of its provisions, and to provide a forum for consultation and cooperation.[26] Yet, convening the plenary organ - the Conference - is also explicitly made dependent on the entry into force of the CWC.[27]

3. Outlining Article 18 of the Vienna Convention on the Law of Treaties

In its opinion on *Reservations to the Genocide Convention*, the International Court of Justice recognized that signatory states may have a rather special position with respect to a certain treaty regime. While not yet treaty partners, their signature does grant them some rights, such as the right to object to reservations. Based on this notion, it has been argued that Article 18 of the Vienna Convention establishes the corollary obligation incurred by signatory states.[28]

While this view may seem attractive for its intellectual orderliness, it is not entirely convincing, for two main reasons. One of them is that it would sponsor an inequitable parity between signatory states and ratifying states. If signatory states have made the first step on the road towards acceptance of a treaty, then ratifying states have clearly performed a second step as well. Yet, as will be shown, the obligation resting upon them by virtue of Article 18 is essentially the same as the one resting upon signatory states and, moreover, it is also doubtful whether their status as ratifying states affords them more rights than signatories are afforded. Second, if the thesis that the interim obligation is not suitable for certain types of treaties holds true, then it follows that there is little relevance in speaking of rights and corollary obligations. As I will attempt to demonstrate, with treaties such as the CWC the interim obligation is largely empty, so to regard it as a corollary of any rights resting upon signatories is not very productive.[29]

---

[25] Arts. IV:6 and V:8 CWC, respectively.

[26] Art. VIII:1 CWC.

[27] Art. VIII:10 CWC.

[28] Cf. E.W. Vierdag, "The ICJ and the law of treaties", in Vaughan Lowe & Malgosia Fitzmaurice (eds.), *Fifty years of the International Court of Justice: essays in honour of Sir Robert Jennings* (Cambridge 1996), 145-166, at 149.

[29] Moreover, the thesis that Article 18 is the corollary obligation of any rights signatories may possess finds little support in the works leading up to the Vienna Convention. There is no indication in the works of any of the Special Rapporteurs that such a thesis was considered. If anything, the theory underlying Article 18 would appear to derive from a contractual analogy, as does so much of the law of treaties. Compare, for example, Anthony Carty, *The decay of international law* (Manchester 1986).

Article 18 of the Vienna Convention makes a distinction between the legal position of states which have signed a treaty but not yet ratified it, and those which have both signed and ratified a treaty. Signatory states are bound not to defeat the object and purpose of a treaty unless and until they will have made clear their intention not to become parties; ratifying states, however, are so bound until either the treaty enters into force or such entry into force is unduly delayed.

While the entry into force of the CWC has been somewhat delayed, this delay has not been excessive by any standard. For instance, the Vienna Convention on the Law of Treaties itself entered into force some 11 years after its text was adopted; the Third United Nations Convention on the Law of the Sea took even longer, and required some creative legal work, to enter into force; and the 1978 Vienna Convention on the Succession of States in Respect of Treaties, whilst only requiring 15 ratifications, only entered into force very recently, i.e. almost 20 years after conclusion. With that in mind, the period of less than 4 ½ years between conclusion and entry into force of the CWC cannot be considered to amount to undue delay.[30]

While Article 18 of the Vienna Convention creates a situational difference between signatory states and ratifying states, this distinction leaves the obligation of Article 18 untouched. Both signatories and ratifying states are "obliged to refrain from acts which would defeat the object and purpose of a treaty". The distinction between signatories and ratifying states merely relates to the conditions under which the interim obligation comes to an end.

In this respect, an important point concerning signatories is the provision that for them the interim obligation comes to an end once they have made clear their intention not to become a party. It could be argued, and has in fact been argued, that an act defeating a treaty's object and purpose would provide a clear indication that a signatory state has little intention of becoming a party. The International Law Commission, in preparing what was to become Article 18 of the Vienna Convention, duly noted the point, but eventually left it unanswered. Nonetheless, legal logic dictates that the argument falters: if signatories could be released from a prohibition by doing precisely that which is prohibited, the prohibition would be rendered meaningless.[31]

---

[30] Indeed, in preparing the Vienna Convention, it was tentatively suggested by Sir Humphrey Waldock, in response to a question posed by the British government, that a period exceeding 10 years would possibly constitute undue delay. Cf. *Yearbook of the International Law Commission* (1965/II), at 45.

[31] Villiger, *supra* note 10, at 322, reaches the same conclusion in relation to Article 18, although via a different route. Somewhat awkwardly perhaps, he founds his argument on the purpose of Article 18.

4. Identifying the object and purpose of the Chemical Weapons Convention

Although the CWC refers to its object and purpose in several places,[32] it contains no definition thereof. Consequently, establishing the CWC's object and purpose becomes a matter of interpreting the Convention itself.[33] The question then presents itself which aspects of the Convention shed some light on its object and purpose.

The point of departure of the analysis must be that the Convention itself does not entirely coincide with its object and purpose. After all, if such were the case, the requirement of ratification would effectively become redundant. Put differently, not every departure from a provision of the CWC pending ratification or entry into force will automatically defeat the CWC's object and purpose,[34] for this would mean that the CWC would have effectively entered into force upon signature, which is clearly at odds with the language of Article XIX.[35]

But how, then, can the object and purpose of a treaty be found?[36] The most famous reference in international law to a treaty's object and purpose is undoubtedly contained in the ICJ's Advisory Opinion on *Reservations to the Genocide Convention*.[37] Faced with the question whether reservations to the Genocide Convention would be permissible, in the absence of a clause allowing for reservations, the Court concluded essentially that reservations which would not run counter to the Convention's object and purpose would be permissible.

Yet, the Court was not very clear as to what exactly constituted the object and purpose of the Genocide Convention, or on how the object and purpose could be identified. In the Court's opinion, the Convention "was manifestly adopted for a purely humanitarian and civilizing purpose." And it proceeded by stating that "its object on the one hand is to safeguard the very existence of certain human groups and on the other to confirm and endorse the most

---

[32] Cf. Article VIII (A):1; Article XXII.

[33] Here a peculiar circularity appears: identifying the CWC's object and purpose requires us to interpret the Convention in the light of, as Article 31 of the Vienna Convention puts it, its object and purpose.

[34] A similar opinion is demonstrated by the 1992 decision of the Judicial Division of the Dutch Council of State, in *S.E.B. v. State Secretary for Justice*. Reported in 25 *Netherlands Yearbook of International Law* (1994), 528-530.

[35] See generally also J. Mervyn Jones, *Full powers and ratification* (Cambridge 1947), at 81, noting that such a proposition "would make a signed but unratified treaty at least provisionally binding."

[36] Compare generally also Klabbers, *supra* note 7.

[37] [1951] ICJ Rep. 15.

elementary principles of morality."[38] From this it was implied "that as many States as possible should participate".[39]

The Court used the words "object" and "purpose" rather interchangeably, and even added the word "implication". Logically speaking, it would seem that the implication follows from the object and purpose. Thus, the fact that a Convention aims at universal adherence cannot be equated with its object and purpose, but must be implied from it.[40]

The Court appeared to rely primarily on two distinct phenomena in order to delimit the object and purpose: it referred to the preamble to the Convention, and to the preparatory documents adopted by the United Nations General Assembly, more particularly the 1946 Genocide resolution.[41]

The importance of a treaty's preamble for delimiting its object and purpose was reaffirmed by the ICJ in a curious passage in the 1986 *Nicaragua* case.[42] The Court here held that in violating certain provisions of a treaty which had been in force for some decades, the United States had also, and quite independently, violated the object and purpose of that particular treaty.[43] It identified the object and purpose by referring explicitly to one of the treaty's preambular provisions,[44] and added that the object and purpose of a friendship treaty is "the effective implementation of friendship in the specific fields provided for in the Treaty, not friendship in a vague general sense",[45] thus underlining the importance of the terms of the treaty in determining its object and purpose.[46]

Obviously, there are good grounds to consider that, up to a point, both the *Genocide* opinion and the *Nicaragua* case must be distinguished from the question of the object and purpose of the CWC. In the *Genocide* opinion, it concerned the question of the compatibility of reservations, which as a legal

---

[38] *Ibid.*, at 23.

[39] *Ibid.*, at 24.

[40] Compare, however, Jonathan I. Charney, "Entry into force of the 1982 Convention on the Law of the Sea", 35 *Virginia Journal of International Law* (1995), 381-404, esp. at 398-399, who holds that the object and purpose of the Law of the Sea Convention is to provide an effective or comprehensive legal regime ensuring the participation of all or most interested states.

[41] [1951] ICJ Rep. 15, at 23.

[42] [1986] ICJ Rep. 14.

[43] Judges Oda and Jennings, in their individual dissenting opinions, understandably found it difficult to accept this proposition. See Judge Oda's opinion, at 250, and Judge Jennings' opinion, at 542. Compare also Hugh Thirlway, "The law and procedure of the International Court of Justice 1960-1989 (part four), 63 *British Yearbook of International Law* (1992), 1-96, at 53, calling the Court's finding "an innovation of doubtful validity".

[44] [1986] ICJ Rep. 14, at 138, para. 275

[45] *Ibid.*, at 137, para. 273.

[46] This comes dangerously close to saying, as Manfred Lachs earlier put it with some sense of irony, that the object and purpose of a treaty is really *pacta sunt servanda*. Cf. Manfred Lachs, "The development and general trends of international law in our time" 169 *Recueil des Cours* (1980/IV), 9-377, at 190.

problem is quite different from the question concerning the interim obligation. In the *Nicaragua* case, at issue was not the existence of any interim obligation; instead, it concerned a treaty which had already been in force for some decades.

Nevertheless, both decisions provide some methodological guidance concerning the identification of the object and purpose of a treaty. As was the case with the Genocide Convention, the CWC was concluded under the auspices of the United Nations, and was preceded by several resolutions adopted by the General Assembly. Thus, Resolution 2827:A (XXVI) of 16 December 1971 confirms the desirability of "reaching early agreement on effective measures for the prohibition of the development, production and stockpiling of chemical weapons ..."[47] Moreover, paragraph 1 of the same resolution refers to Article IX of the 1972 Biological Weapons Convention, which "affirms the recognized objective of effective prohibition of chemical weapons".[48]

The desirability of reaching an early agreement on the eradication of chemical weapons was reaffirmed in Resolution 2827:B (XXVI), which, however, also went further in urging states:

> "to undertake, pending agreement on the complete prohibition of the development, production and stockpiling of chemical weapons and their destruction, to refrain from any further development, production or stockpiling of those chemical agents for weapons purposes which because of their degree of toxicity, have the highest lethal effects and are not usable for peaceful purposes."[49]

While this provision was controversial enough to compel 10 states, among which were France, Turkey, the UK and the US, to abstain, nonetheless it points in the same direction as the provisions contained in Resolution 2827:A (XXVI).

The preamble to the CWC consists of 10 considerations. Some of these, such as the rather gratuitous reference to the desire to contribute to the realization of the purposes and principles of the Charter of the United Nations,[50] are of little help when it comes to identifying the object and purpose of the CWC. They are simply too vague or general, or too factual.[51] Some of the remaining considerations, however, refer to other treaties concluded in the same field, suggesting that the CWC is somehow related to the 1972 Biological

---

[47] Text in 11 *International Legal Materials* (1972), 418. See paragraphs 2 and 4. This resolution was adopted by 110 votes in favour and none against, with only France abstaining.

[48] Convention on the Prohibition of the Development, Production and Stockpiling of Bacteriological (Biological) and Toxin Weapons and on their Destruction. Text in 11 *International Legal Materials* (1972), 309.

[49] Adopted on 16 December 1971, text in 11 *International Legal Materials* (1972), 420.

[50] Consideration no. 2.

[51] Cf. Consideration no. 7, in which the signatories recognize that the use of herbicides as a method of warfare is prohibited under international law.

Weapons Convention and, in particular, the Protocol for the Prohibition of the Use in War of Asphyxiating, Poisonous or Other Gases, and of Bacteriological Methods of Warfare (hereinafter: the Geneva Protocol). Indeed, the CWC is specifically directed at "complementing" the Geneva Protocol.[52]

Whereas some preambular considerations imply that the main object and purpose of the CWC is to eliminate chemical weapons and prohibit their use, several others underline other, quite distinct, aims. Thus, *desiderata* aims such as that achievements in the field of chemistry be used exclusively for the benefit of mankind,[53] or enhancing the economic and technological development of states parties through free trade in chemicals and exchange of information,[54] are not evidently related to eradication of chemical weapons.

This can lead to one of two conclusions: either the CWC possesses several objects and purposes, which are deemed to be of equal weight, or some objects and purposes are less important than others. Hypothetically, it is well possible that treaties possess several distinct objects and purposes.[55] It would be, for example, quite difficult to single out the overriding object and purpose of treaties such as the Versailles Treaty, the Treaty on European Union, or the 1982 Convention on the Law of the Sea. With treaties such as these, the selection of their object and purpose will either be more or less arbitrary, resulting in doing injustice to parts of the treaty concerned, or be so abstract as to be rendered meaningless.[56]

Nonetheless, as far as the CWC is concerned nothing hinders selecting eradication of chemical weapons and prohibition of their use as the object and purpose of the Convention. Most of the pertinent preambular provisions point in that direction, as do the previously adopted General Assembly resolutions; even the title of the CWC makes it clear that the CWC is not about trade in chemicals, or economic development, but about banning chemical weapons altogether.

It will be recalled that in the *Nicaragua* case, the International Court of Justice also looked at the text of the treaty concerned in order to determine its object and purpose. Obviously, with such an enterprise, some treaty provisions are more important than others. The object and purpose can hardly be derived from clauses on, for example, entry into force, or depository functions. As far as the CWC is concerned, surely the most important provisions are laid down in Article I, entitled "General Obligations".[57] In peremptory language, Article I

---

[52] Consideration no. 6.

[53] Consideration no. 8.

[54] Consideration no. 9.

[55] It has also been argued that a treaty's object is something different from its purpose. Compare Elizabeth Zoller, *La bonne foi en droit international public* (Paris 1977), esp. at 74.

[56] See generally D.W. Greig, "Reciprocity, proportionality, and the law of treaties", 34 *Virginia Journal of International Law* (1994), 295-403.

[57] Similarly, Walter Krutzsch & Ralf Trapp, *A commentary on the Chemical Weapons*

states explicitly that States Parties undertake "never under any circumstances" to acquire or use chemical weapons. Whether or not it is helpful to describe such an obligation as "totally binding"[58] is debatable; the points to note, however, are the strictness of the language as well as the pivotal place this obligation has been given in the scheme of the Convention.

In short, it follows from a cursory review of some antecedent documents, the preamble to the CWC, as well as its title and text, that the object and purpose of the CWC can be summarized as the elimination of chemical weapons and the prohibition of their use. Having thus identified the CWC's object and purpose, the next section will analyze how (if at all) this object and purpose can possibly be defeated.

5. Defeating the object and purpose

There exists a considerable degree of uncertainty as to the conditions under which acts can be said to actually defeat the object and purpose of a treaty pending ratification or entry into force. Several questions come to the fore. First of all, should such acts be intentional, or will accidental or incidental acts also qualify? Secondly, presuming that a certain type of act may potentially defeat the object and purpose of a treaty, are there any quantitative requirements?

Bearing in mind that a treaty pending ratification or entry into force has not yet become law, and mere signatories have not even expressed their consent to be bound, it is submitted that the starting point of the analysis still rests with the freedom of state behaviour. *Pacta sunt servanda* does not yet, as such, apply.[59]

The legislative history of Article 18 of the Vienna Convention indicates that the question as to whether or not acts defeating its object and purpose must have been intended to do so, defies simple answers.[60] Whereas the International Law Commission's first Special Rapporteur on the law of treaties, J.L. Brierly, was not convinced of the legal nature of the interim obligation to begin with, and thus devoted little attention to it, his successor Lauterpacht at one point advocated the necessity of criminal intent, so to speak. In his first report on the law of treaties, Lauterpacht proposed that states were to refrain "from any act intended substantially to impair the value of the undertaking as signed".[61]

Convention (Dordrecht 1994), at 12.

[58] *Ibid.*, at 12.

[59] As Article 26 of the Vienna Convention aptly recalls, the *pacta sunt servanda* rule applies only to treaties "in force". Morvay even went as far as proposing to delete, in what was to become Article 18 of the Vienna Convention, the interim obligation for signatories. See Werner Morvay, "The obligation of a state not to frustrate the object and purpose of a treaty prior to its entry into force: comments on art. 15 of the ILC's 1966 draft articles on the law of treaties", 27 *Zeitschrift für ausländisches öffentliches Recht und Völkerrecht* (1967), 451-462.

[60] But see Villiger, *supra* n. 10, at 323.

[61] Lauterpacht I, *Yearbook of the International Law Commission* (1953/II), draft Article 5 (2):b.

While such a statement, notwithstanding interpretative problems surrounding the notion of intent generally,[62] is clear enough in its own right, Lauterpacht's commentary obfuscated the matter in no small measure. Lauterpacht commented on his proposal that:

> "it only refers to acts intended, and not merely calculated, to impair the value of the obligation as signed. For the purpose of the rule is to prohibit action in bad faith deliberately aiming at depriving the other party of the benefits which it legitimately hoped to achieve from the treaty and for which it gave adequate consideration."[63]

As is apparent from this quotation, Lauterpacht posited a distinction between an act intended to have a certain effect, and an act calculated to have a certain effect. Unfortunately, he did not elaborate on this distinction, and neither did his successors as ILC Rapporteurs, Fitzmaurice and Waldock. Both claimed to be merely following Lauterpacht's lead, consistently using conjugations of the verb "to calculate".[64]

Later commentators have held, some more explicitly so than others, that to insist on a strict intent-requirement would render Article 18 at any rate unworkable. Thus, an insistence on intent, amounting to having to prove bad faith, has generally (albeit mostly implicitly) been rejected. Instead, it has been proposed to focus on a legitimate expectations test.[65]

Perhaps most explicit in this regard is Paul McDade, who proposed:

> "The emphasis should be on conduct a state can expect as a result of the obligation of good faith rather than defining which actions constitute bad faith. Examining the legitimate expectations which each state is entitled to expect regarding the treaty which has been signed and the conduct of other states in relation thereto is likely to be more fruitful than focussing on bad faith or attempting to prove subjective intent to abuse a set of rights."[66]

---

[62] See, for example, Klabbers, *supra* n. 13, esp. ch. 3.

[63] See Lauterpacht I, *supra* n. 61, at 110.

[64] Compare Fitzmaurice I, *Yearbook of the International Law Commission* (1956/II), proposed Articles 30 (1):c and 33 (c) (at 113-114); Waldock I, *Yearbook of the International Law Commission* (1962/II), proposed Articles 9 (2):c and 12 (3) (at 46 and 53, respectively). In the ILC's 1962 report to the General Assembly, draft Article 17 also spoke of "acts calculated". *Ibid.*, at 175.

[65] See, for example, Villiger, *supra* n. 10, at 321. A clear link with legitimate expectations was also created by the European Court of First Instance in its recent decision in case T-115/94, *Opel Austria GmbH v. Council* (decision of 22 January 1997, *European Court Reports* 1997, page II-0039). For an analysis, see Jan Klabbers, "Protection of legitimate expectations in EC law deriving from an international agreement prior to its entry into force: the *Opel Austria* decision of the Court of First Instance", 95 *Lakimies* (1997, 732-742).

[66] McDade, *supra* n. 11, at 21.

McDade derives his proposal from what is, in his view, the rationale of the interim obligation, which is "to ensure that a state does not negotiate and conclude a treaty with another or others, gain rights under the treaty and then act in such a way as to reduce the benefits agreed upon."[67] Indeed, unwittingly perhaps, Lauterpacht endorsed a similar conception, focussing as he did on "consideration" and referring to the "value" of an obligation.[68]

The logical consequence of concentrating on consideration or legitimate expectations is that the scope of Article 18 will be rendered rather limited. Consideration, the existence of which in international law is not universally accepted,[69] clearly has some material or tangible overtones. Likewise, for a state to have legitimate expectations under a treaty prior to its entry into force, somehow connotes a bargain of sorts, which can be translated into measurable units, such as money, tariffs, or arms.

In other words: the scope of Article 18's application would, if the focus rests on consideration or legitimate expectations, largely be limited to those treaties which somehow involve an exchange. Indeed, most if not all judicial decisions in which the interim obligation has been mentioned revolved around property rights.[70] Obviously, property rights lend themselves easily to bargains: X will cede a piece of territory in exchange for something else, usually either a sum of money or another piece of territory. Similarly, anything which can be reduced to an exchange of measurable units can be subject to the interim obligation: several authors have, not without reason, given the hypothetical example of a treaty providing for a relative decrease in tariffs.[71] Clearly, a rise in tariffs pending entry into force of a treaty providing for a relative reduction would run counter to the object and purpose of the treaty, as it would seriously upset the bargain.[72] Notably, however, the same cannot be said where the treaty establishes an absolute tariff level: the object and purpose of a treaty providing for, for example, a zero-tariff on product Y will not, normally speaking, be defeated if, pending entry into force, one of the parties raises its tariff on product Y.[73]

If it is agreed that a bad faith test would render Article 18 completely unworkable, and it is agreed that a legitimate expectations test would be more apt, what, if any, are the legitimate expectations raised by the CWC prior to its

---

[67] *Ibid.*, at 20.

[68] See the quotation accompanying *supra* n. 63.

[69] Cf. Klabbers, *supra* n. 13, esp. at 86.

[70] Compare the decisions discussed above, *supra* n. 8.

[71] See, for example, Morvay, *supra* n. 59.

[72] Provided, of course, that decreasing tariffs is part of the object and purpose of the particular treaty concerned, and probably also provided the increase is substantial.

[73] It would be different if raising this tariff would result in diminishing the other party's industry to such an extent that product Y can no longer viably be produced and therewith competition would effectively be abolished.

entry into force?[74] The CWC, as noted earlier, establishes an absolute obligation: States Parties will be under a duty to dispose of all their chemical weapons and close all their production facilities, according to certain time-schedules, from the moment the Convention enters into force. These duties are triggered by the CWC's entry into force, and operate regardless of the number of weapons or facilities presently operating.

That implies, obviously, that States Parties may legitimately expect, after the CWC's entry into force, that these duties will be met. However, prior to the CWC's entry into force, it would seem that no obligations in this respect can derive from the interim obligation. Whether a signatory or ratifying state doubles, triples, or even quadruples its stock of weapons prior to the CWC's entry into force is, for purposes of the interim obligation, largely irrelevant.

Of course, a state which quadruples its existing weapons supplies might run into serious financial and practical problems, leaving it unable to meet its obligations once the Convention enters into force. If so, it can clearly be held to be in breach of the Convention and be confronted with compliance-inducing measures under the CWC's regime[75] and, presumably, general international law. Moreover, it will not be allowed to invoke its own behaviour as a mitigating circumstance. In short: raising the number of existing weapons would make little sense in the face of the future obligation to eradicate them, but it could hardly be argued that it results in defeating the Convention's object and purpose, not even under a lenient legitimate expectations test. After all, allowing the other prospective parties to legitimately expect that a state does not increase its stock prior to ratification or entry into force would amount to making a mockery of both the requirement of ratification and the entry into force of the Convention.

It could be argued that while the above may hold true with respect to raising the level of weaponry, it would not be so with respect to the use of chemical weapons. The CWC's object and purpose, as noted above, was after all not just to get rid of existing weapons, but also to prohibit the use of chemical weapons. And clearly, so the argument could go, using chemical weapons pending the CWC's entry into force would defeat the CWC's object and purpose.

Yet, even this argument, taken on its own, is bound to falter. Whereas the object and purpose of the CWC is clearly to prohibit the use of chemical weapons, under the Convention such use will only be prohibited as from the date of the Convention's entry into force. To hold otherwise would, again, amount to neglecting the Convention's provisions on ratification and entry into force. Moreover, had the states which concluded the Convention intended to outlaw the use of chemical weapons with immediate effect, they could have done so explicitly by either agreeing to apply the Convention's regime

[74] Additionally, whose legitimate expectations are at issue? Those of the contracting states, or rather those of entities within those contracting states? Compare Klabbers, *supra* n. 65.

[75] Cf. Article XII.

immediately, or to apply it from an early date onwards regardless of the number of instruments of ratification deposited at that time, or to apply it provisionally. In the absence of such provisions, and as long as state sovereignty remains the single most important ordering mechanism in international relations, restrictions on the freedom of states cannot lightly be presumed.[76]

That is not to say, of course, that states are presently at liberty to use chemical weapons as they see fit. A good number of states are bound, as a matter of treaty law, by the provisions of the 1925 Geneva Protocol, and there are also good grounds to suppose that the prohibition of the use of chemical weapons forms part and parcel of customary international law, and must perhaps even be regarded as a rule of *jus cogens*. In other words: states will be prohibited from using chemical weapons, but not by virtue of the interim obligation, since strictly speaking the use of chemical weapons prior to the CWC's entry into force cannot be considered to defeat the CWC's object and purpose: using such weapons now will in no way diminish the desired aim of protecting people from their scourge once the CWC enters into force.[77]

All this leads to the inevitable conclusion that the interim obligation as contained in Article 18 of the Vienna Convention will be appropriate with respect to certain types of treaties only. Roughly speaking, it will be of use in respect of treaties of a more or less contractual nature, where the agreement reflects a bargain between the parties, but its utility is limited to prohibiting only the most outrageous behaviour when it comes to more or less law-making treaties. There is simply very little possibility to actually defeat the object and purpose of law-making treaties prior to their entry into force.

We may well postulate that the inapplicability of the interim obligation when it comes to treaties of a predominantly law-making character finds its cause in the largely contractual origins of the law of treaties. An obligation that makes perfect sense when it comes to agreed exchanges makes a lot less sense with respect to documents purporting to lay down objective and universal rules of behaviour.[78]

6. A brief word on estoppel

It may be asked whether the principle of estoppel may apply in such a way as to create substantive obligations for states which have signed or ratified the CWC

---

[76] To paraphrase the *Lotus* case, [1927] Publ. PCIJ, Series A, no. 10.

[77] Again, the one exception would appear to operate in very extreme cases, in which there would be no people left to protect due to the use of chemical weapons.

[78] As the political scientist would say, the diffuse reciprocity underlying, for example, arms control regimes, makes it difficult to apply mechanisms which have been devised in response to situations based on specific reciprocity. For a conceptual analysis of reciprocity, see Robert O. Keohane, "Reciprocity in international relations", in his *International institutions and state power: essays in international relations theory* (Boulder Colo., 1989), 132-157.

pending its entry into force. It should be pointed out at the outset that there is, in the present context, an important distinction between the principle of estoppel and the interim obligation; the two are distinct legal phenomena. Put differently: the interim obligation cannot itself be based on the principle of estoppel, and the work of the International Law Commission in preparing Article 18 in no way indicates that the interim obligation was so based.

It follows that the mere act of signing a treaty, or ratifying it, cannot as such give rise to an estoppel. Hence, an estoppel-based argument must rely on different acts, as is indeed suggested in the Third Report of the Committee on Arms Control and Disarmament Law of the International Law Association. Thus, the report states that "political declarations could create a degree of confidence which, where the other side relies on that confidence, may lead to a legal obligation on the basis of estoppel."[79]

Generally speaking, for an estoppel to arise several conditions must have been met: a state must have made certain representations inducing another state or other states to rely on those representations, either to their detriment or to the advantage of the state making the representations.[80] As Sir Ian Sinclair has recently pointed out, the International Court of Justice has been remarkably reluctant in identifying situations of estoppel in international law.[81]

On the assumption that, in the context of the elimination of chemical weapons, states have indeed made the sort of political declarations as alluded to by the ILA's Rapporteur on Arms Control and Disarmament, the question remains whether these can properly be construed as giving rise to an estoppel leading to a legal obligation. Several considerations might be seen to militate against this proposition.

First of all, it is difficult to see how such declarations could possibly induce reliance on the part of other states, given the circumstances. Perhaps the most relevant of these circumstances is the conclusion of the Chemical Weapons Convention itself: where it is open to states to express their consent to be bound by the Convention, incurring obligations by other methods is not lightly to be presumed. Indeed, as the ICJ held in the *North Sea Continental Shelf* cases, even Germany's declared intention to proceed to ratification of the treaty at issue in those cases did not satisfy the Court.[82] And as the Chamber deciding

---

[79] *Supra* n. 4, at 6.

[80] See, for example, Sir Gerald Fitzmaurice's separate opinion in the *Temple of Preah Vihear* case, [1962] ICJ Rep. 6, at 63, stressing that "what it really means is that these statements, or this conduct, must have brought about a change in the *relative* positions of the parties, worsening that of the one, or improving that of the other, or both" (emphasis in original - JK).

[81] Sir Ian Sinclair, "Estoppel and acquiescence", in Vaughan Lowe and Malgosia Fitzmaurice (eds.), *supra* n. 28) 104-120.

[82] *North Sea Continental Shelf* cases, [1969] ICJ Rep. 3, at 26, para. 31.

the *Gulf of Maine* case held, even dispensing with the element of detriment or prejudice, estoppel "presupposes clear and consistent acceptance".[83]

Secondly, there is precisely that matter of detriment or prejudice: to what extent can claims be made that representations made by some states have caused a shift in the relative positions of those states vis-à-vis other states? While answering this question would require a detailed analysis of the statements made and the responses of others thereto, which is beyond the scope of the present paper, in all generality it is submitted that such would either imply that the states making such declarations have continued to acquire (or facilitate the acquisition, perhaps) of chemical weapons, or other states have purposefully abstained from such efforts. While theoretically this possibility cannot be excluded, it would seem that especially the second of these circumstances implies a great deal of *naiveté* on the part of those states: to halt one's own armaments programmes simply because other states have made ostensibly non-legal statements to do so is not something a responsible political leader will want on his or her record.

But of more principled importance is another point: statements which are clearly not intended to give rise to legal rights and obligations will simply not be regarded as doing so, and that is something that the process of estoppel is unable to change. It will be recalled that in the *Nuclear tests*[84] cases the ICJ referred, far from convincingly in many an observer's view,[85] to the relevance of intent. In the later *Frontier Dispute*[86] case, the Chamber of the Court clarified this to mean that where a state has little choice other than to express itself unilaterally, such unilateral statements may acquire the character of legally binding undertakings.[87] But, where such choice does exist (as in the *Frontier Dispute* case itself), unilateral statements cannot too easily be converted into legally binding undertakings.

When it comes to the CWC states have, of course, ample opportunity to express themselves without having to resort to unilateral declarations. Indeed, there is an impressive treaty waiting to enter into force: all that is required is a signature and the deposit of an instrument of ratification. Given the existence of the CWC, it cannot easily be presumed that states had any intentions other than purely political ones when praising the qualities of the CWC and the desirability of all that it stands for. Following the World Court's standing case

[83] [1984] ICJ Rep. 246, at 309, para. 145.

[84] [1974] ICJ Rep. 253, 457.

[85] Compare, for example, Alfred P. Rubin, "The international legal effect of unilateral declarations", 71 *American Journal of International Law* (1977), 1-30; Martti Koskenniemi, *From Apology to Utopia: the structure of international legal argument* (Helsinki 1989), esp. at 307.

[86] [1986] ICJ Rep. 554.

[87] Cf. Jan Klabbers, "Informal agreements in international law: towards a theoretical framework", 5 *Finnish Yearbook of International Law* (1994), 267-387, esp. 341-346.

law, such declarations cannot, given the circumstances, give rise to binding rights and obligations.

A related argument, albeit a hypothetical one, could hold that if states declare that they will apply the terms of the CWC from now on, they would be estopped from later denying this. Surely, there is some truth in the argument, but equally surely, that truth does not go by the name of estoppel. There is quite simply no legal problem if a group of states decide to apply a certain treaty prior to its entry into force: the group concerned will do so, however, by virtue of a collateral agreement.

7. Concluding remarks

Treaties are, generally, only binding upon those states which have expressed their consent to be bound. There is no doubt that international law is utterly flexible in this respect: as Article 11 of the Vienna Convention has it, consent to be bound can be expressed in various ways, including the open-ended "any other means if so agreed". The key-words will be clear: any means may be used to enter into undertakings, provided they rest on agreement. In the absence thereof, trying to hold states bound through the backdoor of either the interim obligation or estoppel may even prove counter-productive: a state bound against its will may not be overly inclined to respect its obligations thus incurred.

More importantly, it is not even necessary to resort to either the interim obligation or to estoppel. As noted before, many states are already bound by the 1925 Convention; in the absence of any persistent objectors, all states are bound by the customary prohibition on at least the use of chemical weapons. In such circumstances, there is little to be gained, and a lot to be lost, by insisting that states have become bound by virtue of either the interim obligation or estoppel.

COMMENTS

E. W. Vierdag

Let me say first of all, that I think Dr. Klabbers' paper is a lucid and learned analysis of the problems posed by the rules laid down in Article 18 of the Vienna Convention on the Law of Treaties, a provision qualified by some observers as an 'enigma'. Well, it is now my turn to present a few 'enigma variations' of my own; but I am afraid they will not be as entertaining, let alone as musical, as those composed by Edward Elgar.

On a number of points made by Klabbers I agree with him; especially the legal significance of ratification - to mention just one example - must not be played down. With the admonition of the Court in the North Sea Continental Shelf cases in mind, to which Klabbers aptly refers, that significance must be fully acknowledged. All the more so, as ratification is in many democratic states for the parliamentary organ the act which engages parliament in the process of treaty making. It is typically the act for which parliamentary approval is required by national constitutions. So to engage in any form of commitment short of ratification raises the question of what remains of parliamentary powers, and this should accordingly be done with appropriate caution.

Also, I agree with him on the customary law character of the principle embodied in Art. 18. But that does not solve the problems of the article's exact purport, as the meaning of rules of customary international law is very seldom clear and precise. I also agree with his position that 4 ½ years between the adoption of the text and entry into force is not 'undue delay' in the sense of Art. 18 for states that have ratified.

However, a colleague of mine in Amsterdam, who is a most stimulating lecturer, often exclaims in order to encourage his students to engage in discussion: '*laten we het niet onnodig met elkaar eens zijn*!' - meaning something like: 'let us not agree with each other unnecessarily'. So I shall place a few question marks in the margin of the paper, intended to further the discussion on the *inter se* obligations of signatories to multilateral treaties, such as the Chemical Weapons Convention (CWC).

I disagree with Dr. Klabbers' view that Art. 18 is - I quote - 'virtually meaningless' 'with respect to a treaty such as the CWC' (as is said in his Introduction). Of course, for states that have ratified the CWC and in that way have contributed to its relatively early entry into force, Art. 18 has lost its significance. After entry into force, only signatory states have to comply with

E.P.J. Myjer (ed.), Issues of Arms Control Law and the Chemical Weapons Convention, 31–34.

whatever it is that Art. 18 stipulates. The concept 'signatory state' has been given a clear interpretation by the Court in the Genocide Opinion: it is a state that definitively has entered into a certain relationship with the treaty, and it cannot ignore the treaty and act as if it had nothing to do with it.

As regards the temporal aspect of Art. 18, especially the one in sub-paragraph a, Dr. Klabbers has rightly observed that an act by a signatory state that defeats the object and purpose of a treaty, and is therefore by itself also a violation of Art.18, cannot as such be regarded as an indication that this state has made its intention clear that it will not become a party to that treaty. Indeed, the contrary view would result in the - at least from the legal point of view - absurd conclusion that the violation of an obligation could simply terminate its validity.

Still, the very fact that such views have - according to Dr. Klabbers (at p. 17) - in fact been put forward demonstrates how easily the meaning of Art. 18 can be misunderstood by ignoring its background. The preparatory work of Art. 18 shows that - beginning with the Lauterpacht Report - a variety of formulae and conceptions have been put forward. Nonetheless it does disclose some of this background; but Art. 18 is one of the provisions of the Vienna Convention where the differences between the ILC draft and the text ultimately adopted by the UN Conference in 1969 are the most striking. This not only automatically reduces the authority of the ILC's commentary on Art. 18 considerably, but also and, moreover, the text as adopted no longer really reflects much of its background. But I should nevertheless like to quote one key sentence from the ILC commentary on Art. 18: 'That an obligation of good faith to refrain from acts calculated to frustrate the object of the treaty attaches to a State which has signed a treaty subject to ratification appears to be generally accepted' (Yb. 1966, 202).

For an understanding of interim obligations it is useful to look back especially to the interbellum, the time between World War I and II, when very serious attention was paid to the ideas that are now contained in Art. 18: first of all, one must mention the Judgment of the Permanent Court of Int. Justice in the case concerning certain German Interests in Upper Silesia of 1926; but also the work done by such authorities as, for example, Paul Fauchille (1925), Dionisio Anzilotti (1929), who explicitly relied on that judgment, and Harvard Research on the law of treaties (1935) - to mention just some of the more influential of observers. They all point at the one crucial element that really forms the background of those ideas: the principle of good faith in the conclusion of treaties, whether that particular term is expressly mentioned or not. Let me give just one example: Art. 9 of the Harvard Research draft, to which, by the way, a very richly documented and useful commentary is added. It is stated as follows:

> "Unless otherwise provided in the treaty itself, a State on behalf of which a treaty has been signed is under no duty to perform the obligations stipulated, prior to the coming into force of the treaty with respect to that State; under some circumstances, however, good faith may require that pending the coming into force of the treaty the State shall, for a reasonable time after signature, refrain from taking action which would render performance by any party of the obligations stipulated impossible or more difficult."[1]

If one understands what the principle of Art. 18 stands for, one would never venture to suggest that the violation of the principle terminates its validity. If Art. 18 is looked at in this light, one is tempted to question seriously whether, and if so, why Art. 18 would be 'virtually meaningless' as regards the CWC. Having said that, I realise that I shall presumably not be able to offer ready-made answers to the questions raised by Dr. Klabbers. The concept of good faith is a volatile one, and lawyers will have to use all their skills to apply it properly. As Judge Higgins sternly reminds us in her recent monograph on international law[2] 'It is not enough to be familiar with the current "buzz-words" of international law. There is a contemporary trend of mindless invocation of the fashionable concepts - self-determination, rights *erga omnes, uti possidetis*, etc. But these are not *mantras*, the mere chanting of which is sufficient in itself' [...]. So we will have to see what good faith exactly means in the context of the CWC.

Before I attempt to address that problem itself I should like to comment first on the distinction made by Dr. Klabbers in respect of the effect of Art. 18 between so-called contractual treaties and legislative treaties, and on his view that Art.18 can be useful in cases of contractual treaties, but not so much in cases of legislative ones. Apart from my deep distrust as regards the validity of making these categories, I have serious doubts whether this view is correct. Almost all comprehensive multilateral treaties appear to contain elements of both categories, making the distinction difficult to maintain. If Art. 18 is about good faith in treaty-making, multilateral treaties are of course not to be excluded from its operation. Even if a multilateral treaty is predominantly 'legislative', it embodies a consensus *ad idem* among a number of states, and signatory states can, pending ratification, damage the interests of the other states participating in the treaty by their behaviour in the sense of Art. 18. And, of course, the CWC is a multilateral treaty.

It is time to attempt to see what Art. 18 as a principle of good faith means in the concrete case of the CWC. I must confess that at this point I am entering what

---

[1] Harvard Law School: Research in International law III, Law of Treaties, 29 *American Journal of International Law* (1935), Suppl., p. 635 et seq., Art. 9, Comment, at p. 778.

[2] Rosalyn Higgins, *Problems & Progress, International Law and How We Use it* (1994), at p. 267.

to me is largely *terra incognita*. Well, there is, of course, first of all the most remarkable stipulation contained in Art. XXI sub-paragraph one, that there shall be no entry into force of the Convention earlier than two years after its opening for signature. In my view a provision such as this surely enhances the importance of the question of the obligations *inter se* of signatory states pending ratification. Further, if I were to qualify the Convention as a whole, I think it might be best characterized as a comprehensive 'stand-still' régime. Whatever it may demand of parties, it demands of states related to it by signature pending ratification an abstention from further producing, let alone using chemical weapons. It is at this point where I cannot agree with Dr. Klabbers' view (pp. 25,26), that signatory states are still completely free - in the light of Art. 18 - to double or triple their stocks of such weapons, up until ratification. If the matter is approached from the principle of good faith, such a position seems to me hardly tenable.

If the minimal effect of Art. 18 is indeed that the signature of the CWC turns the Convention into a stand-still régime, then no full applicability of the Convention may be expected; but to me, at least, one of the effects of good faith in treaty-making resulting from Art. 18 is very clear as regards the CWC: no stockpiling after signature. As Dr. Klabbers has said: 'Let us get rid of chemical weapons!' So I think it is right to insist again: no stockpiling after signature!

COMMENTS

Thilo Marauhn

1. Introduction

Jan Klabbers argues that Article 18 of the Vienna Convention on the Law of Treaties (VCLT) is "virtually meaningless"[1] with regard to the Chemical Weapons Convention (CWC). His argument flows from a thoughtful and elaborated discussion of the rights and duties of the CWC signatories. However, his approach suffers from being limited to what may be called the perspective of "traditional principles of international law".[2] The following remarks will demonstrate that it is possible to define the rights and duties of signatories of a multilateral regime-building treaty[3] (such as the CWC) in a more meaningful way if the above-mentioned traditional principles are applied and developed so as to cope with the particular needs of arms control.

To begin with, I want to underline the relevance of defining the rights and duties of signatories to a multilateral arms control or disarmament agreement. As has been argued in the Third Report on Legal Remedies for Arms Control Impasse of the International Law Association's (ILA's) Committee on Arms Control and Disarmament Law, it is possible that, after the finalisation of an agreement, a situation of impasse occurs before the treaty enters into force as such or for an individual signatory.[4] When looking at the weeks and months before the entry into force of the CWC, in particular at the position of very important states such as the United States and Russia, it is beyond doubt that - although there was no impasse *stricto sensu* - there was some danger of not achieving even the first step towards what the Convention was designed to achieve. This shows that the occurrence of an impasse situation is not a problem restricted to whether or not agreement on a multilateral treaty has been reached. It also touches upon the question of who actually participates

---

[1] J. Klabbers, Strange bedfellows: the 'interim obligation' and the 1993 Chemical Weapons Convention at p. 13.

[2] These principles have been identified by the International Law Association's Committee on Arms Control and Disarmament Law as the basis for a discussion of legal remedies for arms control impasse; see The International Law Association, Report of the Sixty-Seventh Conference held at Helsinki (1996), 307 (311), para. 7.

[3] On the concept of regime formation in the context of chemical disarmament see P. Herby, Building the Chemical Disarmament Regime, *Arms Control Today* 23 (1993), issue no. 7, pp. 14 et seq.; and, in particular, T. Bernauer, *The Chemistry of Regime Formation: Explaining International Cooperation for a Comprehensive Ban on Chemical Weapons* (1993), passim.

[4] The International Law Association (*supra* n. 2), 311, para. 7.

E.P.J. Myjer (ed.), Issues of Arms Control Law and the Chemical Weapons Convention, 35–45.

and implements such a convention. Moving a step further, impasse may also be related to perceived or actual implementation deficits. The conditions which the U.S. Senate linked to its Resolution of Ratification of the CWC may suffice as an illustration.[5]

In view of these problems and lacking any particular treaty clause as to provisional application, the starting point of a discussion on how to overcome such impasse situations outlined above must be Article 18 of the VCLT.[6] While there is no disagreement in this respect, the question arises how to interpret Article 18. To put my position into perspective, I want to quote Julie Dahlitz's article on Security Council powers and possibilities in the context of avoiding and settling arms control disputes. She argues with regard to the Security Council that "it would be distorting and unproductive to consider only a hermetically sealed legalistic segment of the composite problem, ignoring the climate in which it is to operate. Useful and practical consequences are what international law was designed to serve. The law has to be further developed and applied in that spirit if it is to continue to benefit the international community."[7] The already mentioned Third Report of the ILA's Committee on Arms Control and Disarmament Law in its paragraph 7 argues that "lawyers have to use and develop specific rules, procedures and institutions to cope with particular needs of arms control", and the Report stresses that "the law of arms control and disarmament may be seen as part of an evolutionary process developing rights and obligations in the interest of mankind as a whole."[8] This underlines the need for a dynamic and evolutionary interpretation. On the other hand, it is equally important to bear in mind what Jan Klabbers has pointed out, namely that there is a need to be careful not to develop interpretations or arguments that are counterproductive: "a state bound against its will may not be overly inclined to respect its obligations thus incurred".[9]

---

[5] For a summary of the Senate Resolution of Ratification see *Arms Control Today* 27 (1997), issue no. 4, pp. 29 et seq. The complete text of the resolution can be found on the homepage of the Arms Control Association at http://www.armscontrol.org.

[6] On the relevance of the law of treaties with regard to arms control and disarmament agreements see generally N. Ronzitti, Problems of Arms Control Treaty Interpretation, in: J. Dahlitz and D. Dicke (eds.), *The International Law of Arms Control and Disarmament* (1991), 115 et seq. and G. Lysén, The Adequacy of the Law of Treaties Regarding Arms Control Agreements, in: J. Dahlitz (ed.), *Avoidance and Settlement of Arms Control Disputes* (1994), 123 et seq. As to Article 18 of the VCLT in this particular context see H. Neuhold, Legal Aspects of Arms Control Agreements, in: K.-H. Böckstiegel et al. (eds.), *Völkerrecht, Recht der Internationalen Organisationen, Weltwirtschaftsrecht: Festschrift für Ignaz Seidl-Hohenveldern* (1988), 427 (433).

[7] J. Dahlitz, Security Council Powers and Possibilities, in: Dahlitz (*supra* n. 6), 57 (59).

[8] The International Law Association (*supra* n. 2), 311, para. 7.

[9] Klabbers p. 29.

2. Methodology

The first question to be addressed as to the interpretation of Article 18 of the VCLT is how to provide a constructive understanding of this provision. The primary focus must be on discerning the object and purpose[10] of Article 18, a provision which I consider to be a codification of the (pre-)existing customary international law interim obligation.[11] Jan Klabbers bases his discussion of the *ratio legis* of Article 18 on a review of the *travaux préparatoires*, on literature dealing with Article 18 and on jurisprudence. While the *travaux préparatoires* are an accepted supplementary means of interpretation,[12] literature and judicial decisions play a somewhat different role. They are not referred to at all in Articles 31 to 33 of the Vienna Convention. However, Article 38, paragraph 1(d), of the Statute of the International Court of Justice qualifies them as "subsidiary means for the determination of rules of law". This provision only gives them a limited role in defining the law. It is admitted, nevertheless, that their "persuasive power ... may sometimes give them greater significance than they enjoy formally".[13] This notwithstanding, international tribunals and learned writers are only persuasive in so far as they respect the provisions of the VCLT or their customary international law equivalent. As to the problem under consideration, the ICJ's Advisory Opinion on *Reservations to the Genocide Convention*[14] and the 1986 *Nicaragua Case*[15] may only provide - as Klabbers himself argues - "some methodological guidance concerning the identification of the object and purpose of a treaty".[16] Neither of the two amounts to an interpretation of Article 18.

What I want to suggest here is that one may arrive at a more meaningful interpretation of Article 18 with regard to the CWC by giving more weight to the dynamic elements of *ratio legis*, the context and State practice than to

---

[10] Reference may be made to Article 31 of the VCLT which, inter alia, stipulates: "1. A treaty shall be interpreted in good faith in accordance with the ordinary meaning to be given to the terms of the treaty in their context and in the light of its object and purpose.".

[11] It is not disputed that the status of Art. 18 is the subject of controversy. Nevertheless, there are good reasons to consider Art. 18 as a codification of existing customary international law. See J.S. Charme, The Interim Obligation of Article 18 of the Vienna Convention on the Law of Treaties: Making Sense of an Enigma, *George Washington Journal of International Law and Economics* 25 (1991), 71 (77 et seq.).

[12] Article 32 of the VCLT provides that: "Recourse may be had to supplementary means of interpretation, including the preparatory work of the treaty and the circumstances of its conclusion, in order to confirm the meaning resulting from the application of article 31, or to determine the meaning when the interpretation according to article 31 (a) Leaves the meaning ambiguous or obscure; or (b) Leads to a result which is manifestly absurd or unreasonable."

[13] A. Watts and R. Jennings, *Oppenheim's International Law*, Vol. I (9th ed. 1992), 41 in respect of decisions of international tribunals.

[14] ICJ Rep. 1951, 15, 23 et seq.

[15] ICJ Rep. 1986, 14, 137 et seq.

[16] Klabbers, p. 20.

legislative history, *travaux préparatoires* and the conceptual ideas of learned writers. What is even more important is that such an approach gives more room to the primary actors in the process of interpreting a treaty, namely States Parties. While international courts and tribunals have a role to play in treaty interpretation it is important to remember that treaties have to be interpreted and applied primarily by the parties to the treaty.[17]

It is admitted that an analysis of the *rationales* of the drafters of Article 18 and of the examples provided in their works "fail to adequately inform the meaning of article 18", thus leaving a signatory State "unsure of the *precise* nature of its interim obligation".[18] On the other hand, it is quite clear that Article 18 was and is intended to give legal significance to the signing of a treaty, irrespective of whether this is a bilateral or a multilateral, a contractual or a regime-building agreement. This means that an argument considering Article 18 as inappropriate with regard to regime-building treaties such as the CWC is not convincing. Jan Klabbers argues that:

> "the interim obligation as contained in Article 18 of the Vienna Convention will be appropriate with respect to certain types of treaties only. Roughly speaking, it will be of use in respect of treaties of a more or less contractual nature, where the agreement reflects a bargain between the parties, but its utility is limited to prohibiting only the most outrageous behaviour when it comes to more or less law-making treaties. There is simply very little possibility to actually defeat the object and purpose of law-making treaties prior to their entry into force."[19]

Notwithstanding whether or not the distinction between contractual and law-making treaties is a meaningful one,[20] I think that this interpretaion is too restrictive and too static. Interpreting a treaty provision must always seek to make the provision useful and the treaty effective.[21] I want to argue that if one comes to the conclusion that a particular interpretation of Article 18 limits its applicability to only a certain segment of the field of application of the VCLT as a whole and if it is possible to find another interpretation that makes more of Article 18, then the interpreter has to choose the latter in order to render Article 18 effective.

---

[17] Cf. R. Bernhardt, Interpretation in International Law, in: R. Bernhardt (ed.), *Encyclopedia of Public International Law*, Vol. II (1995), 1416 (1417).

[18] Charme (*supra* n. 11), 104; italics in the original.

[19] Klabbers, p. 26.

[20] For a discussion of the notion of law-making treaties see Jennings and Watts (*supra* n. 13), p. 1203 et seq. They consider this notion as "controversial and theoretically faulty" but "nevertheless of some practical importance" (p. 1204).

[21] This means to apply the maxim *ut res magis valeat quam pereat*; cf. Jennings and Watts (*supra* n. 13), p. 1280 et seq. The ICJ in the *Anglo-Iranian Oil Co. Case* admitted in principle that a treaty should be interpreted so as to attribute a reason and meaning to every word in the text (ICJ Rep. 1952, 93 (105)).

3. The Interim Obligation

In the following I want to develop a few ideas on the interpretation of Article 18 of the VCLT with regard to multilateral arms control and disarmament agreements before finally addressing a few particularities of the obligations of signatory States of the CWC.

First, Article 18 attaches a particular significance to a State's signature, pending the entry into force of the treaty. The legal consequences flowing from signature in this particular case extend beyond the adoption or authentication of the text of the treaty as referred to in Article 9 of the VCLT. On the other hand, signing a multilateral arms control or disarmament agreement does not amount to an expression of a State's consent to be bound as referred to in Article 12 of the VCLT. Further, signature under Article 18 gives rise to a particular obligation but it does not lead to provisional application which is governed by Article 25 of the VCLT. In other words, Article 18 entails an obligation, though a limited one. The fact that signature is not irrelevant may prevent states from signing whatsoever without considering the legal consequences. However, the obligation assumed under Article 18 can only be specified with regard to a particular treaty which means that the obligation is a flexible one. This fits together with the flexibility of the international legal system as such. Taking up a perspective offered by Thomas Franck[22] and applied to Article 18 by Joni Charme[23] a rule "carrying a great degree of uncertainty" may be "capable of constructively regulating State behaviour" if States perceive "the rule as sound or just".[24] This seems to be exactly the case with Article 18. States seem to regard the interim obligation as sound and just.[25]

In order to illustrate this, I want to briefly address the Threshold Test Ban Treaty (TTBT)[26] as well as SALT I and II.[27] The TTBT, signed in July 1974, only entered into force after a new protocol providing on-site verification for some tests had been signed in 1990.[28] In the early 1980s, however, both the USSR and the United States, declared that they intended to abide by the provisions of the Treaty as long as the other party would also do so. It is

---

[22] T.M. Franck, *The Power of Legitimacy among Nations* (1990), 76 et seq.

[23] Charme (*supra* n. 11), 104 et seq.

[24] *Ibid.*, 105.

[25] See the conclusions presented by Charme (*supra* n. 11), 107.

[26] Treaty between the USA and the USSR on the Limitation of Underground Nuclear Weapon Tests and Protocol, 13 *ILM* (1974), 906 et seq.

[27] Interim Agreement between the USA and the USSR on Certain Measures with Respect to the Limitation of Strategic Offensive Arms and Protocol, 11 *ILM* (1972), 791 et seq.; Treaty between the USA and the USSR on the Limitation of Strategic Offensive Arms (SALT II), Protocol, Agreed Statements, Common Understandings and Memorandum of Understanding, 18 *ILM* (1979), 1112 et seq.

[28] Protocol to the Treaty between the USA and the USSR on the Limitation of Underground Nuclear Weapon Tests, 29 *ILM* (1990), 971 et seq.

interesting to note that the United States Government referred to the interim obligation. The U.S. President in 1987 declared that "... neither Party has indicated an intention not to ratify. Therefore, both Parties are subject to the obligation under customary international law to refrain from acts that would defeat the object and purpose of the TTBT".[29] Numerous references to non-compliance on the part of the other side, however, suggest that the two states considered themselves to be bound not only as far as the object and purpose of the Treaty were concerned. Thus, it is possible to argue that they were legally bound not to defeat the object and purpose of the Treaty and politically bound to respect the Treaty as a whole.[30] The legal situation is more complicated as far as SALT I and II are concerned. In this case the interim obligation was relevant until, in 1981, the United States announced it would not ratify the SALT II agreement, which left both parties under only a political obligation to abide by the treaty limits until, in 1986, U.S. President *Reagan* declared that the United States would no longer respect the SALT II limitations.[31] Irrespective of how these developments are qualified in detail, they underline the fact that Article 18 and its customary law equivalent are of relevance for arms control agreements and that states consider such agreements to have legal implications prior to their entry into force.[32] As far as the CWC is concerned, reference may be made to the following Message of the President of the Russian Federation to the First Session of the Conference of the Parties to the CWC:

> "... Pending the ratification of the Convention Russia intends to refrain from any action that would deprive the Convention of its object and purpose. After we signed the Convention we have been honouring and will continue to honour the commitments regarding the non-development and non-production of chemical weapons; their non-transfer, directly or indirectly, to anyone; the non-use of chemical weapons; the renunciation of engaging in any military preparations to use them, of providing assistance, encouraging or inducing, in any way, anyone to engage in any activity prohibited by the Convention; the non-use of riot control agents as a method of warfare. We have taken measures ensuring that toxic chemicals and their precursors are developed, produced and acquired, stored, transferred and used only for purposes that are not prohibited by the Convention.

---

[29] *U.S. Department of State Bulletin*, June 1987, 37 (41).

[30] Cf. M. Bothe, Rechtsfragen der Rüstungskontrolle im Vertragsvölkerrecht der Gegenwart, in: M. Bothe and W. Graf Vitzthum, Rechtsfragen der Rüstungskontrolle im Vertragsvölkerrecht der Gegenwart (Legal Questions of Arms Control in Contemporary International Treaty Law). *Berichte der Deutschen Gesellschaft für Völkerrecht*, Heft 30 (1990), 31 (74).

[31] For details see G. Lysén, *The International Regulation of Armaments: the Law of Disarmament* (1990), 103 et seq.

[32] Cf. Bothe (*supra* n. 30), 77 and Lysén (*supra* n. 31), 103 footnote 38.

> Russia has also been engaged in preparations for actual destruction of chemical weapons. A federal law on the destruction of these weapons has been passed ...".[33]

Second, in this particular context Article 18 has to be interpreted against the background that arms control and disarmament law is a process.[34] International law is a means to influence state behaviour, albeit not the only one. Politically and legally binding norms are closely interrelated. Often international law norms emerge out of political norms. A constructive interpretation of Article 18 has to take into account that multilateral treaty making is a long and protracted process,[35] beginning with, first, contacts at the diplomatic level, followed by a political commitment to negotiate. Subsequently, states sometimes agree upon a "soft law" instrument[36] which can temporarily take the place of a not yet agreed treaty. Then, after signature, an often long and complicated process begins whereby the domestic authorities, on the basis of the domestic constitution, determine how and whether the state will consent to be bound by the treaty. Once the treaty has entered into force, this process continues with implementation at the national and the international level, nowadays usually including a treaty review at certain intervals.[37] All this illustrates that signature within the meaning of Article 18 is no more but also no less than a particular step within the process of influencing state behaviour. It may be considered as the first step in relations between states from the political into the legal realm. As Gloria Duffy puts it with regard to the further steps to be undertaken by the parties to an agreement, "... the end of the negotiations is, in fact, only the beginning of the arms control process. The test of arms control's success is whether the parties to an agreement abide by its terms over time, and whether each side recognises and credits the other side's compliance ...".[38] It is important to note that the Chemical Weapons Convention is one of the best examples to

---

[33] This Message formed part of a statement issued by the delegation of the Russian Federation at the First Session of the Conference of the States Parties to the Convention on the Prohibition of Chemical Weapons on 6 May 1997. The author wishes to thank the Media and Public Affairs Branch of the External Relations Division of the Technical Secretariat of the OPCW for providing the unofficial translation of the text.

[34] E.P.J. Myjer, Supervisory Mechanisms and Dispute Settlement, in: Dahlitz (*supra* n. 6), 149 (149).

[35] See, inter alia, W. Lang, Negotiation as diplomatic Rule-Making, *International Negotiation* 1 (1996), 67 et seq.

[36] For a discussion of the concept of soft law in international relations cf. W.M. Reisman, The concept and functions of Soft Law in international politics, in: *Essays in honour of Judge Talim Olawale Elias* (1992), 135 et seq.

[37] Cf. K. Ipsen, Explicit Methods of Arms Control Treaty Evolution, in: Dahlitz and Dicke (*supra* n. 6), 75 et seq.

[38] G. Duffy, *Compliance and the future of arms control: report of a project sponsored by the Center for International Security and Arms Control* (Stanford University 1988), 1, as quoted by Myjer (*supra* n. 34), 149 footnote 3.

underline this "cautious process of treaty making ... (that) may encourage the acceptability of implementing agreements even prior to their formal entry into force".[39]

Third, turning to the "object and purpose" as included in Article 18 of the VCLT it is noteworthy that more recent arms control and disarmament agreements do not only consist of substantive but also procedural norms. There are not only norms limiting or prohibiting certain activities but there is also a set of rules designed to ensure compliance with these norms. This is particularly true for the Chemical Weapons Convention. The CWC is aimed at and designed to ban chemical weapons *effectively*.[40] The negotiators were careful not to draft an international instrument which - though legally binding - would have little impact and remain pure paperwork. Making the CWC effective required a treaty structure ensuring that there is a degree of compliance without resorting to the traditional means of law enforcement. States had to be provided with incentives to comply with the ban on chemical weapons. Prominent among these incentives is the building of confidence between the parties.[41] In particular, it is important that states can trust in another party's adherence to the obligations assumed under the treaty. This requires means to clarify misconceptions as well as techniques to avoid and settle disputes.[42] As to Article 18 of the VCLT, this means that the object and purpose of the CWC cannot be limited to a ban of chemical weapons[43] but must include the effectiveness of such a ban. Thus, at least the rationale of the procedural obligations included in the CWC must form part of its object and purpose.

A parallel reasoning applies to the interpretation of the term "defeat". While it is true that defeat amounts to more than the mere violation of a

---

[39] The International Law Association (*supra* n. 3), 312, para. 9.

[40] See T. Marauhn, Towards an Effective CWC Regime, in: American Society of International Law and Netherlands International Law Association, Contemporary international law issues: new forms, new applications. Proceedings of the *Fourth Hague Joint Conference*, The Netherlands, July 1997 (1998) pp. 95 et seq.

[41] On the confidence-building function of procedures of verification see W. Lang, Compliance with Disarmament Obligations, *Zeitschrift für ausländisches öffentliches Recht und Völkerrecht* 55 (1995), 69 (72). As Thomas Bernauer puts it: "Monitoring and verification are ... substitutes for trust. If states trusted each other totally, monitoring of compliance with a treaty would be redundant." (*supra* n. 4), 222. See also J.P. Perry Robinson, The Verification System for the Chemical Weapons Convention, in: D. Bardonnet (ed.), *The Convention on the Prohibition and Elimination of Chemical Weapons: A Breakthrough in Multilateral Disarmament* (1995), 489 et seq.

[42] Cf. Myjer (*supra* n. 34), passim. See also J. Dahlitz, Introduction, in: Dahlitz (*supra* n. 6), 1 (4): "The avoidance of arms control disputes, and the settlement of such disputes should they arise, depends on the creation of accepted norms and their observance within the framework of international law."

[43] Klabbers, however, argues that the "object and purpose of the CWC can be summarised as the elimination of chemical weapons and the prohibition of their use" (*supra* n. 1), p. 22.

particular treaty provision, defeat must not necessarily be a single act.[44] It can also be a process of undermining the treaty regime, in particular the effectiveness of the treaty. While abiding by the most essential substantive obligations a signatory state may well undermine the treaty's effectiveness in devaluating the supervisory mechanisms established by the treaty.

4. Concluding Remarks on the Chemical Weapons Convention

In his paper Jan Klabbers underlines that the substantive obligations "are triggered by the CWC's entry into force, and operate regardless of the number of weapons or facilities presently operating. [...] a State which quadruples its existing weapons supplies might run into serious financial and practical problems, leaving it unable to meet its obligations once the Convention enters into force. If so, it can clearly be held to be in breach of the Convention [...]" He continues that "raising the number of existing weapons would make little sense in the face of the future obligation to eradicate them, but it could hardly be argued that it results in defeating the Convention's object and purpose [...]".[45] This argument is not convincing since it draws an unnecessarily sharp line between the pre-"entry into force" behaviour of a State and the legal situation after the CWC's entry into force. Article 18 of the VCLT is designed to exactly bridge this "gap". It is important to bear in mind the following statement of François Rigaux: "For the lawyer, fact and law do not belong to two different worlds, as if fact occupied the earthly space of crude factuality and law was accommodated in a celestial universe of pure normativity."[46] It is "[u]seful and practical consequences [...] what international law was designed to serve".[47] The interpretation presented by Jan Klabbers, however, would allow signatory states to systematically undermine the CWC even before its entry into force, thus not only providing an incentive for other states not to ratify the Convention and eventually preventing the Convention from entering into force at all.

Underlying this restrictive interpretation seems to be a misinterpretation of the time-frames included in the Convention, not only for its entry into force (Article XXI of the CWC) but also for the beginning of various verification measures. All the time-frames have been set so narrowly that a signatory state that is ill-prepared for implementing the Convention may easily run into severe difficulties once the Convention has entered into force. The period of 180 days after the date of the deposit of the 65th instrument of ratification and the CWC's entry into force serves to give the parties sufficient time to prepare

---

[44] But see Klabbers, *ibid*, p. 25.

[45] Klabbers *ibid*, p. 25.

[46] F. Rigaux, The Concept of Fact in Legal Science, in: P. Nerhot (ed.), *Law, Interpretation and Reality* (1990), 38 (48).

[47] Dahlitz (*supra* n. 7), 59.

for implementing the CWC. These time-frames were not intended to give other states more time to consider whether or not to ratify the Convention. Also, universality was to be achieved from the very beginning.[48] This was the reason for including restrictive provisions on trade in chemicals with non-parties.[49] Finally, with the exception of Article XXI, paragraph 1, of the CWC time-frames are always phrased "not later than" and not "not earlier than".[50] All this underlines the fact that the Convention itself has been drafted in a way that signatory states have to prepare as far as possible for the time when the Convention enters into force for them.

This is not only true for individual states but also for the treaty regime as such. The Organization for the Prohibition of Chemical Weapons (OPCW) is not meaningful in itself, but only as a means of supervision. As Eric P.J. Myjer underlines, the OPCW has "as its sole purpose the supervision of compliance with the core ("general") obligations of States Parties under Article I".[51] The CWC is based on the understanding that the OPCW must be functioning at the time of entry into force of the Convention which means that states were under an obligation to prepare for this moment in time. They had to develop a preparatory structure which has been built up in the form of the Preparatory Commission and the Provisional Technical Secretariat.[52] This, in my view, is another strong indication that after signing the treaty, states were under an obligation to begin preparing for the implementation of the treaty which may be considered to be even more than the limited obligation included in Article 18 of the VCLT.

To conclude, the CWC is a convention which does not begin to work from the moment of entry into force but before that date. Awaiting the entry into force of the Convention but not participating in the preparations for this date could amount to a violation of Article 18 of the VCLT by a signatory state. Also, pending entry into force, both signatory states and ratifying states are at least prohibited from accelerating production and stockpiling of chemical weapons. One may even arrive at the conclusion that the testing of new

---

[48] See generally Y. Dinstein, Ratification and Universality, in: Bardonnet (*supra* n. 41), 151.

[49] See CD/CW/WP.357; see also CWC, Verification Annex, Part VII, paras. C.31 and 32, and Part VIII, paras. C.26 and 27. For a discussion of these provisions cf. T. Marauhn, *Der deutsche Chemiewaffen-Verzicht. Rechtsentwicklungen seit 1945* (1994), 343 et seq. and W. Krutzsch and R. Trapp, *A Commentary on the Chemical Weapons Convention* (1994), 444 et seq. and 452.

[50] To give just one example, Art. III, para. 1of the Convention stipulates that "Each State Party shall submit to the Organization, not later than 30 days after this Convention enters into force for it, the following declarations, [...]".

[51] E.P.J. Myjer, The Organization for the Prohibition of Chemical Weapons: closer towards an international arms control organization. A quantum leap in the institutional law of arms control, pp. 62-63.

[52] For an analysis of the legal basis of the establishment of the Preparatory Commission and its powers see F.C. Calderón, The Preparatory Commission for the Organization for the Prohibition of Chemical Weapons, in: Bardonnet (*supra* n. 41), 27 et seq.

weapons is not permissible.[53] Whether the actions of a particular signatory state amount to a violation of its obligations under Article 18 of the VCLT with regard to the CWC is a matter to be decided in each particular case. This comment was designed to show that Article 18 of the VCLT is meaningful with regard to the CWC, not only as far as the substantive obligations are concerned but also in respect of the implementation of a supervisory mechanism intended to make the CW ban effective.

[53] For a discussion of these matters see Dinstein (*supra* n. 48), 154.

COMMENTS

Jerzy Sztucki

First of all, I apologize for my loose and unstructured remarks. I received the invitation to this Seminar at rather short notice, and the paper by Dr. Klabbers only 45 hours ago. But I have read it carefully and was much impressed by his all-sided, refined and stringent analysis of the phrase, or concept, of 'object and purpose of a treaty' and of the so-called 'interim obligation' under Article 18 of the Vienna Convention on the Law of Treaties, especially its relationship to the Chemical Weapons Convention (CWC).

The question arises, however, whether the phrase in question and the 'interim obligation' deserve such a sophisticated legal analysis; and I shall try to explain the reasons behind my reflection.

You will recall that when the International Court of Justice (ICJ), in its advisory opinion on *Reservations to the Genocide Convention,*[1] used - indeed, to the best of my knowledge, *introduced* - the phrase 'object and purpose of a treaty', it did so in a relatively simple context. The reservations at issue were related to Article IX of the Genocide Convention, providing for obligatory jurisdiction of the Court in disputes concerning the interpretation or application of the Convention;[2] thus, not to any of its substantive clauses. For the purpose of our discussion we can leave aside the general humanitarian and political motives behind the Court's recognition of the admissibility of the reservations at issue and behind its 'flexible' approach to the question of reservations in general.

Formally, the Court explicitly related its pronouncement to the Genocide Convention only. But at the same time the advisory opinion reflects the awareness of the Court that what it was going to say would anyway have broader impact and meaning, the more so since the questions put before it were formulated in general and abstract terms.[3] Had it been possible, *in reality,* to limit strictly the impact of the Court's opinion to specific reservations to the specific convention, then the Court could probably have simply said that the reservations were admissible because they did not affect any *substantive obligations under the Convention.* But the general implication of such a statement would have been totally wrong, since a reservation may be admissible even if it does affect a substantive obligation under a treaty. The criterion of admissibility or inadmissibility of a reservation had thus to be

[1] Cf. ICJ, Reports 1951, p. 24. The advisory opinion was rendered by a majority of 7 to 5.

[2] For the text of the Convention cf. UNTS, vol 78 (No. 1021), p. 277, at 282.

[3] Cf. *supra* in n. 1, at 16-17, 20-21, and 31.

E.P.J. Myjer (ed.), Issues of Arms Control Law and the Chemical Weapons Convention, 47–55.

sought 'somewhere deeper', closer to the very core and essence of a treaty and with reference to its more basic and fundamental features than just one substantive clause or another. The phrase 'object and purpose of a treaty' apparently, in the understanding of the majority of the Bench, adequately reflected the criterion sought.

As Dr. Klabbers observed, the Court has not revealed the exact meaning of that phrase. Neither can it, for that matter, be found in the preparatory works of the Vienna Convention. True enough, the Court in a way explained the object and purpose of the Genocide Convention, but the dissenting Judges had several alternatives at hand.[4] Parenthetically, it can be added that the definition of 'Object of statute' in such an authoritative reference publication as 'Black's Law Dictionary' sounds like a simple paraphrase: 'Aim, intent or purpose of its enactment. End or design which it is meant to accomplish...',[5] and another law dictionary offers the following inspiring explanation of the term 'Object': 'The term includes whatever may be presented to the mind as well as to the senses [...]; it may be used as having the sense of effect'.[6] In '*Words and Phrases Legally Defined*' the entry 'Object' - in the context of company law only - contains a quotation from a judgement rendered in 1958 and reading, *inter alia*: "The expression 'main objects' is nowhere defined" (the term 'object' alone is not commented upon).[7] It would therefore be perhaps too much to expect the Court to give a stringent and generally valid definition of the 'object and purpose of a treaty' which apparently can be the subject of varying interpretations, as demonstrated by the dissenting opinions I mentioned earlier.

But the Court did not even indicate any specific method or methods by which to establish the 'object and purpose of a treaty'. Moreover, the Court clearly indicated that the admissibility of a reservation is subject to individual appreciation by States against the criterion of the 'object and purpose of a treaty',[8] which, in its turn, as already mentioned, can also be individually interpreted.

Thus, the Court itself deprived the 'object and purpose of a treaty' of an objective and unambiguous legal meaning. The results are reflected in State practice. For instance, a glance at the reservations to the Convention on Privileges and Immunities of the Specialized Agencies or to the Convention on Diplomatic Relations, and at the objections to those reservations will reveal that the same reservation has been objected to by some States with reference to

---

[4] Cf. *ibid.*, p. 44.

[5] *Black's Law Dictionary*, 6th ed., West Publ. Co., St. Paul, Minn., 1990, p. 1073.

[6] *Bouvier's Law Dictionary and Concise Encyclopedia*, 3rd revision being 8th ed. (Rawle ed.), West Publ. Co, St. Paul, Minn. 1914 (repr. 1984). vol. 2, p. 2390.

[7] *Words and Phrases Legally Defined*, 2nd ed. (Saunders ed.), vol. 4, Butterworth London 1969, p.2. The supplements do not contain any relevant entries.

[8] Cf. *supra* in n. 1, at p. 26

its alleged incompatibility with the object and purpose of the Convention, and by some others without such a reference. Moreover, sometimes *the same State* objected to a reservation with reference to its 'incompatibility... etc.', and later on objected to *the same reservation* made by another State without that reference. And finally, there is an example of a State which found a reservation made by another State 'incompatible...', but still explicitly declared that it was not objecting to it.[9] Many more instances of this kind could be quoted.

In my opinion, the phrase 'object and purpose of a treaty' is, by its very nature, too general to be susceptible of strict legal definition. It is not the most felicitous one from the legal point of view. But a handy capsule formula has been coined; it has been endowed with the authority of the Court; it has been, moreover - because of its flexibility - convenient as not constraining States too much; and so, it has made a brilliant career in the Law of Treaties.

I have devoted perhaps too much attention to reservations, while our discussion is focussed on 'interim obligations' under Article 18 of the Vienna Convention on the Law of Treaties, more specifically in the context of the Chemical Weapons Convention. But I wanted to recall the origin of the phrase 'object and purpose of a treaty' and the circumstances in which it was born, the more so since the ambiguity of that phrase in the context of reservations is the same in the context of 'interim obligation', apart from the other ambiguities of Article 18 of the Vienna Convention. Dr. Klabbers has noted that the phrase appears in three provisions of the Vienna Convention on the Law of Treaties - in Articles 18, 19 and 31 - and has raised the question of whether the meaning of that phrase is the same in all the three contexts. Now, on the premise that the meaning of the phrase is flexible (and I cannot see any other premise which would adequately reflect the reality) and is open to a variety of interpretations, it appears that the same flexibility and the same possibility of varying interpretations equally characterizes all the three cases and, consequently, they may well coincide. In this sense the meaning of the phrase in question can be regarded as the same in all the three articles.

One notes, however, a difference in the language used in Articles 18 and 19, respectively, to describe possible conflicts with the 'object and purpose of a treaty'. Article 19 speaks of "incompatibility" with that object and purpose, while the language of Article 18 is much more 'dramatic'. It speaks of "acts which would defeat the object and purpose of a treaty". That phrase has a flavour of mortal finality. A treaty the object of which has been 'defeated' becomes by simple logic 'objectless', i.e. meaningless. And it is perhaps arguable that all parties are then relieved of their obligations under such a treaty; and I fully share the opinion of Dr. Klabbers that it is difficult to see

---

[9] Cf. *Multilateral Treaties Deposited with the Secretay-General*, Status at 31 December 1995, United Nations, New York 1996, at pp. 52 and 59 resp.

how it may be possible for a State "to defeat the object and purpose of a treaty", if this phrase is to be taken literally. It may be appropriate here to recall that the corresponding Article 15 in the final draft of the International Law Commission speaks of "acts tending to frustrate the object of a ... treaty".[10] This sounds perhaps somewhat more sensible. But the Drafting Committee at the Vienna Conference changed the language to the present one, with a rather curious motivation: "in the interest of clarity".[11] In my opinion, the change, on the contrary, has made the provision in question even more obscure. But I am inclined to admit, at least theoretically and generally, that the conduct of signatory States - and in some situations perhaps even of a single State - can render a treaty wholly or partly ineffective in practice. And it is in this meaning that I am speaking of 'interim obligation'.

However it might be, it seems to be clear that any attempt to establish the contents of 'interim obligation' under Article 18 of the Vienna Convention must take as a point of departure a specific treaty - in our case the Chemical Weapons Convention - rather than the meaning of the words used in that article. For, 'object and purpose of a treaty' is always related to a particular instrument. That does not mean, however, that this method will lead us any farther.

But, to start with: what is the object and purpose of the CWC? It is arguable that it is the *elimination of the use* of chemical weapons, and that all the other obligations relating to the development, production, stockpiling and destruction of those weapons are of only subsidiary character, as *means* to ensure that the object and purpose of the Convention will be achieved. But it is also arguable that the object and purpose of the CWC is the *elimination of the possibility to use* chemical weapons. It can even be claimed that this is the better interpretation since the development, production, stockpiling, use and destruction are enumerated in the title of the Convention in one breath, as if being of equal standing. But this, in turn, can be countered by the argument that the title indicates the 'subject' of the Convention rather than its 'object' ("Convention on..." - not "Convention for...", as titles sometimes read). This, in turn, can be countered by an opinion that "for all practical purposes the words subject and object are synonymous".[12] Thus, even the question of the object of the CWC may be, and no wonder, open to discussion, let alone the question of what can 'defeat' that object and what is meant by 'defeat'.

Now that the CWC is already in force, only para. (a) of Article 18 of the Vienna Convention is of practical relevance. But what have the signatory

---

[10] YILC 1966, vol. II, p. 202.

[11] UN Conf. on the Law of Treaties, Off. Rec., 1st sess., p. 361 (62nd meeting of the Committee of the Whole).

[12] *Loc. cit.* in n. 6, *supra* (one exception is given). Cf. also Bridge. *The Council of Europe French-English Legal Dictionary*, Council of Europe Press 1994, p. 217.

States to do or not to do in order to be in compliance with that provision, the applicability of which has a transitory character?

The general and basic obligations specified in Article 1 of the CWC are binding upon *parties*. What is the impact of those obligations upon the conduct of *signatories*, if it has to be in conformity with Article 18(a) of the Vienna Convention?

There is, probably, no doubt that in our case a signatory State has, for instance, no 'interim obligation' to commence the destruction of chemical weapons, to stop their production or to embark upon preparations for these measures for which the CWC has established a time-table which is applicable *after* its entry into force for a given State. The same would *mutatis mutandis* most probably be true in many cases even without such a time-table.

But what if a signatory State, pending its 'provisional status' - to use the words of the Court[13] - continues or intensifies the development of *new types* of chemical weapons, accelerates their production (an example mentioned by Dr. Klabbers), or, for that matter, *uses* chemical weapons - to give some tentative examples of conduct which may be questionable from the point of view of its consistency with the 'interim obligation'?

Is such a conduct at variance with that obligation, or is it a manifestation of a clear intention not to become party to the Convention? For, the former excludes the latter and *vice versa*. As Dr. Klabbers noted, the question of whether such conduct can be an expression of a State's intention arose in the International Law Commission during the course of preparing the present Article 18, but was left without an answer; and Dr. Klabbers does have a point in saying that if a State could be relieved of a prohibition by doing exactly what is prohibited, then that prohibition would be meaningless. Now, it is very possible that just the latter is true; and Dr. Klabbers himself seems to be not very far from reaching that conclusion. I am wondering, however, whether the argument is equally applicable to *parties* to a treaty in force and to *signatory* States.

A party to a treaty in force can relieve itself from a prohibition under that treaty only by denouncing it in due course - in some situations perhaps also by making a reservation. If a party to a treaty in force does what is prohibited, it *violates* a treaty – which is different from relieving itself from the prohibition. A signatory State cannot 'violate' a treaty which is not in force for that State. It is true that - in the words of the ICJ - "signature constitutes the first step to participation in the Convention",[14] but that first step does not obligate a signatory to take the next step and expressly consent to be bound. Nor does it prevent a signatory from taking a retrograde step, by making it 'clear', in one way or another, that it is not going to become a party to a treaty. This is a

---

[13] Cf. *supra* in n. 1, at p. 28

[14] *Ibid.*

lawful unilateral act; and nothing prohibits the manifestation of this intention *per facta concludentia*. The question of when an intention is 'clear' is another question which is subject to interpretation. But it seems that a delayed, even a much delayed ratification, is *per se* no 'clear' expression of intention, bearing in mind that the time factor ("undue delay") in para. (b) of Article 18 is not mentioned in para. (a).

Anyway, in my opinion, the question of what is inconsistent with the 'interim obligation' and when this will occur, as well as what is a clear expression (and also when it will occur) of an intention not to become a party to a treaty - in our case the CWC - cannot be answered unequivocally, in a manner which is applicable to all situations. Challenging conduct by a State pending its 'provisional status' is not necessarily conclusive evidence that it does not intend to become a party to a treaty, or that it will not as a party scrupulously fulfil all the treaty obligations. Its challenging conduct may be caused by a variety of circumstances - perhaps of a more or less transitory character. Moreover, a signatory State is free to reconsider its intentions - *both ways* - without any formal act. The assessment will inevitably depend on a number of circumstantial factors and - again - may vary between individual States.

There is, of course, no complete analogy between the question of prohibition of chemical and of nuclear weapons, but there are indeed similarities. And if one reflects on the implications of the recent advisory opinion of the ICJ in which it was unable to take a definite position on the question of the legality of the use of the latter in extreme circumstances of self-defence when the very survival of a State is at stake,[15] then perhaps not even such drastic conduct as the *use* of chemical weapons by a *signatory* of the CWC must always necessarily be regarded as being in conflict with the 'interim obligation' or as a manifestation of a clear intention not to become a party to the CWC. And, if so, then less drastic, though still questionable, conduct will perhaps deserve a still more tolerant attitude.

To put it succinctly, we are here moving in an area where everything is ambiguous, uncertain, open to argument, flexible and relative - indeed, in no less then three respects: (1) what is exactly 'the object and purpose' of a given treaty?; (2) what specific conduct 'would defeat' that object and purpose?; and (3) when is the intention of a signatory 'clear'?

I therefore share Dr. Klabbers' opinion that, from the strictly legal point of view, Article 18 of the Vienna Convention is rather meaningless when an attempt is made to apply it to the CWC; and that the same is true, in general, with respect to multilateral treaties aimed at establishing objective regimes. But I am afraid that when he suggests that Article 18 of the Vienna

[15] Cf. ICJ Reports 1996, p. 36. The relevant paragraph was adopted by a casting vote of the President, the Judges having been equally divided.

Convention may be of use with respect to agreements reflecting a bargain between the parties - a give-and-take deal - he is still too lenient with respect to that Article.

Let us take, for instance, a convention on mutual legal assistance, which can probably be regarded as a bargain. Let us assume that under that convention a party will accept requests by another party to hear witnesses and will transmit to the requesting party the protocols of hearings translated to the language of that party. Let us further assume that State A has signed the convention but the convention is not yet in force (or not in force *for* State A). The question then arises: would signatory State A 'defeat the object and purpose' of that convention if it declines a request of another State? If not, what other conduct would have that effect? Is State A, as a signatory, expected to comply with the request? If so, what is then the difference between 'interim obligation' and provisional application (which may be decided unilaterally)? Or should it perhaps comply with the request on a 'fifty-fifty' basis – e.g. to arrange for a hearing but to transmit the protocol without translation?

I am unable, of course, to maintain safely that it is impossible to find a specific meaning of Article 18 in relation to *any* treaty or category of treaties. But I venture to submit that such a specific meaning can be established only more or less exceptionally - also in relation to treaties having the character of a bargain.

It may be recalled that, at the Vienna Conference, the British delegation formally proposed the deletion of the present Article 18, as being "virtually impossible to apply in practice".[16] But the proposal was rejected by an overwhelming majority, including the United States (otherwise critical) and the Soviet Union (France, also critical, abstaining),[17] mainly as a general expression of the fundamental principle of good faith; but perhaps also as an attempt to embody in the Vienna Convention an analogous opinion formulated in the past – albeit in a somewhat vague and not exactly the same terms - by the authorities quoted by Professor Vierdag and, for that matter, also by Dr. Klabbers.

It is in this very general sense, and in the light of the general motives underlying the vote at the Vienna Conference that the meaning of Article 18 must be seen. For it is one of the rules of interpretation that treaty provisions must not be interpreted so as to render them totally meaningless. In my opinion, Article 18 is to be regarded as a reminder for signatory States that they are no longer completely free in their conduct in matters regulated by a given treaty (until and unless they have made clear their intention not to become parties to that treaty). They must give a thought to possible steps likely to provoke undesirable adverse reaction on the part of other States

---

[16] *Supra* in n. 10, *supra*, p. 97 (19th meeting of the Committee of the Whole).

[17] Cf. *ibid.*, p. 105 (20th meeting of the Committee of the Whole).

(signatories or parties). And the other States are free to react, individually or collectively, in a negative fashion when faced with conduct by signatory States of which they disapprove. On both sides it will be a matter of appreciation. And it may be the subject of discussion, whether such a negative response must be kept within the limits of acts of retortion, since no provision of the treaty in question has as such, been violated; or whether it may take the form of reprisals, as a reaction to the violation of an 'interim obligation' with unclear specific contents.

I am fully aware that my position can be objectionable on the ground that this is not a legal position. This may very well be so, but it was the International Court of Justice which, as I tried to demonstrate earlier, deprived the concept 'object and purpose of a treaty' of its strict legal meaning, by having admitted its subjective interpretation. And it was the drafters of Article 18 of the Vienna Convention who redoubled the effects of the Court's position, by introducing the indefinable concept of 'defeat' of that object and purpose.

As a somewhat tentative guidance - by no means conclusive or watertight - it can perhaps be said that when a treaty provides for positive action, like for instance - in the case of the CWC - the destruction of chemical weapons, a signatory State may, pending the entry into force of the Convention regulating it, remain totally inactive, without running the risk of charges of non-compliance with an 'interim obligation'. Conversely, when a treaty provides for the prohibition or discontinuance of an action, such as - in the case of the CWC - non-use of chemical weapons or halting their production, an action flagrantly contrary to such provisions, such as the use of those weapons or an acceleration of their production, can - although not necessarily must - provoke charges of non-compliance with an 'interim obligation'.

Finally, I would like to add that the circumstantial factors which may influence the meaning of Article 18 of the Vienna Convention for a specific form of conduct must also include the question of *who* is the signatory State in question. I here have in mind certain experiences relating to the Treaty on Non-Proliferation of Nuclear Weapons (NPT). As is known, every non-nuclear State Party to the NPT is obliged, within 180 days from the entry into force of the Treaty for that State, to start negotiations with the International Atomic Energy Agency (IAEA) with a view to concluding a safeguard agreement providing for inspection; and the agreement must be concluded within 18 months from the start of negotiations.[18] Now, out of the 175 non-nuclear States Parties to the NPT (as per 31 December 1995) 65 have no safeguard agreement with the IAEA in force; and of these, 17 are in an 'interim position' (some of them since a quarter of century) as signatories of such agreements or as having their agreements approved by the IAEA but not

[18] For the text of the Treaty cf. UNTS, vol. 729 (no. 10485), p. 161, at 177.

by themselves.[19] And, in fact, nobody really cares, since all the States in question carry out no, or very insignificant, nuclear activities; and have manifestly no ambitions to acquire nuclear weapons. That some States for which safeguard agreements *are in force* do not comply with them is, of course, quite a different question.

The same question arises with respect to the CWC, although the situation is of course different. True enough, also in this case the States Parties to the CWC are very preoccupied with the fact that some 70 signatories have not yet ratified the Convention. But concern is being expressed over the fact that a permanent member of the Security Council, possessing considerable chemical weapons capability, is among them.[20] It is said that this is due to the need to secure financial assistance in order to destroy chemical weapons prior to assuming definite obligations under the CWC. However, the State in question did participate in the First Session of the Conference of the States Parties to the CWC (together with 33 other signatories); and, indeed, some offers of assistance had already been made.[21] Regardless of this particular case, the fact remains that delayed ratification, even by a State of particular importance in a given context, need not necessarily *per se*, as mentioned earlier, be an ominous sign. It may be caused by a variety of considerations other than an intention to retain freedom of conduct which "would defeat the object and purpose of the treaty".

Of course, I do not have a global command of treaty relations under multilateral treaties. But I still venture to submit that the main threat to 'objects and purposes' of treaties and to their effectiveness in practice does not emanate from signatories which have not become parties, but rather from States which, because of their negative attitude towards a treaty, have not even signed it; and from those which violate their obligations under treaties to which they are parties. This may be of little comfort but can perhaps mitigate excessive excitement as regards Article 18 of the Vienna Convention.

---

[19] Cf. IAEA, *The Annual Report for 1995*, (doc. GC(40)/8), pp.64-69.

[20] Note by the editor: This was the situation at the time of writing. As of September 2000, there are 139 States Parties and 35 Signatory States.

[21] Cf. OPCW Synthesis, Issue 17, April 1997, p. 1; also OPCW Press Release No. 154, 24 May 1997, p. 3.

SUMMARY OF DISCUSSION

(Strange Bedfellows: The 'Interim Obligation' and the 1993 Chemical weapons Convention)

Mr Kisselev[1]

Mr Chairman, as you may know, the Russian Federation is a Signatory State to the Chemical Weapons Convention. I have no objections to the thesis that arms control agreements have different regimes than "conventional" multilateral treaties.

One could say that during the negotiations on the CWC there were two groups of "negotiating parties". The first group consisted of States participating in the Conference on Disarmament, the second group encompassed States not participating in the Conference. One could also say that there were, in fact, three groups of States: States that would be affected by the Convention, admitting as much in public statements; States that would be affected by the Convention but would refrain from public statements; and States that would not be affected at all. This choice of distinction obviously influences the negotiating positions of States.

The history of the negotiations shows that States aimed at agreement on intent rather than agreement on the actual text of provisions. This, in turn, should be taken into account when explaining the discrepancy or relationship between Article 18 of the Vienna Convention on the Law of Treaties and the Chemical Weapons Convention. I am therefore a proponent of the narrow or "unwide" interpretation of Article 18. In this case, the intent of the States was twofold: first, they aimed at a ban on chemical weapons. The CWC would serve the purpose of declaring the illegality of chemical weapons. Second, the Convention would apply to international trade in chemicals, especially in view of dual-purpose goods.

I do not share the notion of defeat which emanates from the comments by Dr Marauhn. For example, I would like to refer to Article VII of the CWC. In the opinion of the Russian Federation this obligation applies to Signatory States and obliges a Signatory State to implement Treaty obligations in national legislation.

---

[1] At the time Counsellor and Deputy Head of Delegation of the Russian Federation to the OPCW.

E.P.J. Myjer (ed.), Issues of Arms Control Law and the Chemical Weapons Convention, 57–59.

Prof Sztucki

Mr Chairman, let me remind you of the Genocide Convention Case which was submitted to the International Court of Justice. The reservations in this case related to the compromissory clause and not to the substance of the Convention. Yet, the Court used a more general interpretation of the "object and purpose" of the Convention. It looked at the whole of the Convention, rather than focusing solely on the substantive part. In the "communis opinio" the signature of a State is a reminder of conduct in good faith. It is nothing more than a "signal" that the freedom of action for that State is not unlimited.

The Vienna Convention on the Law of Treaties does not specify who is to decide on the "defeat of the object and purpose" of a Treaty. What can then be tolerated, and what cannot? Should this decision rest with all States or International Organizations themselves? Should a decision depend on the circumstances? I would suggest that defining the "object and purpose" of a Treaty is a highly individualized matter. Moreover, a distinction between contractual treaties and other treaties is not relevant. In the end, for the CWC "defeat of the object and purpose" emanates from the States that have not signed up to the Convention, and States that do not exclude the possibility of the use of chemical weapons.

Dr Fleck

Mr Chairman, with regard to the interpretation of "object and purpose" of a Treaty, one should look at State practice. An excellent case can be derived from the Open Skies Agreement under the CFE provisions. Also, I agree with Dr Klabbers that there is no obligation for a State to ratify a Treaty once it has signed. This relates to the fact that the signing of a Treaty should also be regarded as an element of confidence building.

Dr Dahlitz[2]

Mr Chairman, as much as we may talk about the legality in agreements, I would like to suggest that the "morality" in arms control agreements cannot be ignored. The interim obligation of a signature is related to the environment for ratification. In other words, States should not create an adverse environment for ratification. States can then be confident that wishes or intentions are complied with and this is exactly the purpose of the law. In addition, the signature of a State is a message to the "ratifying organs" of that State and ensures that States do not subterfuge.

---

[2] Chairperson of the Committee on Arms Control and Disarmament Law of the International Law Association.

Dr Klabbers
Mr Chairman, I notice that there is a reliance on the comments on law as much as on other elements such as good faith, morality and political declarations. The term of art which is frequently used is "process". But what does it mean in legal terms? Law has a problem with the so-called process character; examples of this position can be found in the practice of State succession.

Prof Vierdag
Mr Chairman, I would like to submit that the approach from the Law of Treaties to the Law of Arms Control is weaker than vice versa. This is related to the essence of confidence building which is encompassed in arms control agreements and the principle of estoppel.

Dr Marauhn
Mr Chairman, law is not a state, law is a process. What do courts do? They define law and apply law. Interpretation is, in fact, applying the law. Law is also aimed at being respected by individuals and States alike. Therefore, I am not convinced by the arguments of Prof. Koskenniemi, from which Dr Klabbers derives some of his arguments.

States should not be forced into signing what they do not want to sign. Vice versa, an interpretation of the interim obligation should take this argument into account. Indeed, I would think that the sovereignty of States remains a predominant element in the discussions over interim obligations.

Utrecht, 2 July 1997
Reporter : Tim Sneek

THE ORGANIZATION FOR THE PROHIBITION OF CHEMICAL WEAPONS: MOVING CLOSER TOWARDS AN INTERNATIONAL ARMS CONTROL ORGANIZATION? A QUANTUM LEAP IN THE INSTITUTIONAL LAW OF ARMS CONTROL

Eric P.J. Myjer*

I. Introduction

Someone had stuck a piece of paper on the wall of the *Congresgebouw* in The Hague where the PrepCom working groups of the Organization for the Prohibition of Chemical Weapons (OPCW) were meeting on a daily basis in order to fill in the basic structure of the Chemical Weapons Convention (CWC)[1] to be presented to the First Conference of States Parties for approval. The paper indicated how far one still had to come in order to attain the necessary 65 ratifications before the entry into force of the Convention. After that point was finally reached on 31 October 1996 by the deposit of the Hungarian instrument of ratification[2] the paper was replaced by a calender "which ticked away" the days up to the required 180 days after the deposit of this 65th instrument of ratification when "EIF" (entry into force) of the Convention would be attained on 29th of April 1997. In the meantime at the Catsheuvel, an open spot almost opposite the *Congresgebouw*, builders were -finally- busily laying their concrete foundations for the OPCW building.

Since that time the building has been completed, and, after more than four years of PrepCom work, the First Conference of States Parties has been held,[3] the initial declarations have been submitted and the inspection teams have started their work.

After the many years of negotiations it somehow seems a miracle that this point finally has finally been reached, for the international community has been rather reticent about achieving quick results in this area. It took 20 years after the Biological Weapons Convention was concluded as well as the end of the Cold War before the negotiations in the Conference on Disarmament led to the

* This is an updated version from the seminar.
This contribution is tributed to Bert Vierdag, Professor Emeritus of Public International Law and International Relations at the University of Amsterdam, for his stimulating role in the advance of research into and teaching of arms control law.

[1] Convention on the Prohibition of the Development, Production, Stockpiling and the Use of Chemical Weapons and on Their Destruction, 32, *ILM*, pp. 800-873.

[2] *Ibid*, Art. XXI.

[3] From 6 May - 23 May 1997.

E.P.J. Myjer (ed.), Issues of Arms Control Law and the Chemical Weapons Convention, 61–139.

Chemical Weapons Convention (CWC) as signed in January 1993.[4] "The significance of this achievement lies in the fact that it is the first multilaterally negotiated treaty which provides for the ban of an entire category of weapons of mass destruction under strict and universally applied international control".[5] The total ban on chemical weapons, in other words on a complete category of weapons of mass destruction, is to be realized by prohibiting the development, production or retention of chemical weapons. The scope of the CWC is much wider than that of the BWC for biological weapons for it also includes a commitment *never under any circumstances to use* chemical weapons. A complete disarmament of this category of weapons is foreseen as States which possess such weapons will have to destroy all the existing chemical weapons as well as the production facilities. The use and production of certain chemicals will be restricted because they might be used as precursors in the development of chemical weapons. Control of these restrictions will of necessity involve civilian chemical industries. This first comprehensive ban on both the possession as well as the use of a complete category of weapons therefore not only involves the military establishment, but also large sections of States Parties' civilian chemical industries. This raises the problem of the protection of confidential business information.[6]

No such expansive agreement, however, would have been possible without agreement on an effective mechanism to control compliance with these undertakings. For that purpose this Convention at the same time establishes the Organization for the Prohibition of Chemical Weapons (OPCW), a specialised international organization, within the UN family, with as its sole[7] purpose the supervision of compliance with the core ("general") obligations of States

---

[4] For a comprehensive compilation of documents and decisions on the Convention see L. Woollomes Tabassi (ed.), *OPCW, The Legal Texts* (1999). For general commentaries see for instance: D. Bardonnet (ed.), Hague Academy of International Law, *The Convention on the Prohibition and Elimination of Chemical Weapons: A Breakthrough in Multilateral Disarmament* (1995); W. Krutzsch and R. Trapp, *A Commentary on the Chemical Weapons Convention* (1994); B. Kellman and E.A. Tanzman, *Manual for National Implementation of the Chemical Weapons Convention* (1998) (2nd); M. Bothe, N. Ronzitti and A. Rosas (eds), *The New Chemical Weapons Convention- Implementation and Prospects* (1998).

[5] A.J.J. Ooms, History of the Negotiations of the Chemical Weapons Convention, unpublished paper, at 1.

[6] To which element also the US Senate attaches great importance. See Condition 16 (Protection of Confidential Information), Ratification Resolution, *Senate Congressional Record*, April 24, 1997, at S 3655.

[7] Notwithstanding the role of the OPCW under Article X regarding the provision of assistance and protection against chemical weapons. The formulation in Article VIII A (1) suggests an autonomous task for the OPCW beyond supervision of compliance of the core commitments under Article I, by the provision of a forum "for consultation and cooperation among States Parties". This, however, should be viewed as functional in the context of supervision of compliance.

Parties under Article I.[8] Thereto this international organization -the OPCW- has wide powers for verifying compliance locally, on a Member State's territory, not only routinely on-site (routine inspections) at predetermined places, but also at the request of States Parties via challenge inspections to be undertaken by the standing international inspectorate of the OPCW.

It is remarkable that States Parties were willing for the common good (the ban on chemical weapons) or because of their interdependence[9] to allow for these inroads into their territorial sovereignty. Features like these give the CWC compliance-control mechanism its unique character.

Another outstanding feature, and for political purposes highly necessary, is the universal character of this treaty which is reflected in the high number of required ratifications (65) before the treaty enters into force and in the high number of States Parties (139[10] at the time of writing) and Signatory States (35), which may lead to an almost universal membership. This aspect of universality is also reflected in the fact that the organization will be part of the UN system as reflected in the special agreement between the United Nations (UN) and the OPCW.[11] It is, however, an independent, autonomous international organization.

---

[8] It appears to be an international organization of which, in the words of I. Seidl-Hohenveldern, the *raison d'être* is the control of member states' compliance with a certain purpose. For him this is even the *raison d'être* of any international organization for "These entities were established to grant their member states a better control of each other's activities towards the fulfilment of a given purpose". Another example would be the Commission for the Navigation of the Rhine. In: N. Blokker & S. Muller, *Towards More Effective Supervision by International Organizations* (essays in honour of H.G. Schermers) (1994) at 255. I agree with Blokker/Muller (at 275) that this function, supervision of rule compliance by the member states, is a "classical function of International organizations". But I differ, however, with Seidl-Hohenveldern that this is always the *raison d'être,* for an important function of a general international organization also lies in its ability for decision-making and acting as a forum.

[9] Writing about supervision by International Organizations in general :"Interdependence has forced states to accept encroachments of sovereignty; not only by the formulation of international obligations, but also by some degree of surveillance over their observance of these obligations and even, to a limited extent, the possibility of sanctions being imposed in case of non-compliance. Thus, interdependence is the bridge between supervision and sovereignty. It is the magic word which reconciles these two seemingly irreconcilable concepts."Blokker/Muller, *supra* n. 8, at 310.

[10] As of September 2000.

[11] "The United Nations recognises that the OPCW, by virtue of the Convention, shall function as an idependent, autonomous international organization in the working relationship with the United Nations established by this Agreement." (Article I, para. 2), *Agreement Concerning the Relationship between the United Nations and the Organization for the Prohibition of Chemical Weapons*, signed 17 October 2000. In view of an earlier decision by the Conference (C-IV/DEC.4, 2 July 1999), the Executive Council recommended the Conference to approve the draft of this agreement and authorized the Director to sign it for provisional application pending approval by the UN General Asssembly and by the

Aspects like these led to the OPCW being appraised from many sides as a unique international organization both from a political point of view as well as from a legal point of view.[12] This in itself is sufficient reason to take a closer look at this organization. Another reason being that this CWC mode of supervision has already been applied in the case of the Comprehensive Test Ban Treaty (CTBT) with its Comprehensive Nuclear Test-Ban Treaty Organization[13] and that attempts are made to foresee a comparable supervisory mechanism for the Biological Weapons Convention (BWC) that does not yet have any supervisory mechanism,[14] since at the time of concluding the BWC the military usefulness of these weapons was anyhow considered to be low. Furthermore, the International Atomic Energy Agency (IAEA) in considering strategies to strengthen the effectiveness of NPT safeguards had an independent expert group (SAGSI) appointed that came up with the recommendation "that the CWC offers approaches for verification and investigation that may be adaptable to the NPT".[15] Developments like these make necessary an analysis of the OPCW as a model for future international organizations with a supervisory role in the sphere of arms control. Such an analysis is the main purpose of this contribution. I will thereby (also) look into the question whether the OPCW as an international organization in the area of arms control with its specific supervisory purpose is as unique as it appears.

For analytical purposes I will make use of the concept of supervision as used with regard to international economic organizations with its three separate functions. These functions are the *review function* (evaluating State behaviour for its conformity with an agreed rule of international law); the *correction*

Conference (EC-MXI/DEC.1.,1 September 2000).

[12] Compare Krutzsch et al., n. 4 at 125; Also Bernauer, *The Chemistry of Regime Formation: Explaining International Cooperation for a Comprehensive Ban on Chemical Weapons* (1993): The International Institute for Strategic Studies (London) called CWC "the most ambitious disarmament agreement ever negotiated", International Institute for Strategic Studies (IISS), *Strategic Survey 1992-1993*, at 214.

[13] Compare Article II (the Organization) of the Comprehensive Test Ban Treaty and its extensive Protocol with annexes that are integral to the treaty, opened up for signature September 24, 1996, 35 *ILM* 1439-1478. See G. den Dekker, *Internationale controle en handhaving van het verbod op kernproeven*, Utrecht University (1997) (ISBN 90-5213-095-7).

[14] Compare the "mechanism" contained in Article V of the BWC on consultation and cooperation between States Parties "in solving any problems which may arise in relation to the objectives of, or in the application of the provisions" and in Article VI that foresees the lodging of a complaint with the Security Council by a State Party "which finds that another State Party is acting in breach of obligations deriving from the Provisions of the Convention".

[15] See for an extensive comparative analysis: D.S. Gualtieri, B. Kellman, K.E. Apt and E.A. Tanzman, Advancing the law of weapons control - comparative approaches to strengthen nuclear non-proliferation, 16 *Michigan Journal of International Law*, (1995) at 1029-1111.

function (the correction of State behaviour, when it is established that a state has violated an international obligation); and the *creative function* (interpretation or clarification of the rules). For the sake of clarity, however, I will, add a fourth function, namely the *collection function*, which leads me to the following distinction: (1) collection function; (2) review function; (3) creative function; (4) correction function.

Chapter II will provide a historical description of the stages involved in the control of chemical weapons; *Chapter III* describes the general structure of the Convention and *Chapter IV* that of the OPCW in particular. *Chapter V* contains an analysis of the OPCW as an organization established to supervise compliance with the core obligations under the CWC. Thereby the focus will be on the four separate functions of the concept of supervision, respectively: the *collection function* (para. 2); the *review function* (para. 3); the *correction function* (para. 4) and the *creative function* (sources) (para. 5). Chapter VII will draw some general conclusions with regard to the CWC model of supervision. In so doing a comparison will be made with the "management model" of Chayes and Chayes. And what, in particular, can be concluded with regard to the international law of arms control? Chapter VIII ends with some concluding remarks.

II.The control of chemical weapons: historical development

1. The 1925 Geneva Protocol

The 1925 Geneva Protocol,[16] which is generally regarded as a landmark agreement in the prevention of the use of poisonous gases and bacteriological weapons, came into being as a reaction to the extensive use of poison gas in World War I, resulting in over a million casualties and over 100,000 deaths.[17] This protocol is a typical example of an arrangement which is generally regarded as belonging to the law of armed conflict,[18] for it is an agreement that

---

[16] The Protocol for the Prohibition of the Use in War of Asphyxiating, Poisonous or Other Gases, and of Bacteriological Methods of Warfare was signed on June 1925 and entered into force on 8 February 1928. It was originally a Protocol to the 1925 Convention for the Supervision of the International Trade in Arms and Ammunition and in Implements of War, Jozef Goldblat, *Arms Control, A Guide to Negotiations and Agreements* (1994) at 91. The United States only ratified in 1976 and deposited its instrument of ratification two weeks after it deposited its ratification of the Biological Weapons Convention respectively March 26 and April 10, 1975.

[17] T. Bernauer, *The Projected Chemical Weapons Convention: A Guide to the Negotiations in the Conference on Disarmament*, UNIDER (1990) at 11; Arms Control and Disarmament Agreements, texts and histories of the negotiations, United States Arms Control and Disarmament Agency (1996), further ACDA, at 95.

[18] L.C.Green, *The Contemporary Law of Armed Conflict* (1993), at 37. *Humanitarian Law in Armed Conflicts*- manual- Federal Ministry of Defence of the German Federal Republic (1992), at 17, 43.

restricts the use of a certain type of weapon as a means of combat.[19] However, it is also considered under arms control,[20] for at the same time it controls a (whole) category of weapons of a State Party. It is, in other words, the archetypal example of a treaty belonging to the international law of military security.

Whereas under The Brussels Declaration of 1874 and The Hague Conventions of 1899 and 1907[21] the use in war of toxic substances was already prohibited,[22] and under the 1899 Hague Declaration 2 the use of projectiles the sole object of which is the diffusion of asphyxiating or deleterious gases,[23] the use of both chemical and biological weapons are banned under the 1925 Geneva Protocol.[24] Emphasizing the demands made by humanity in justly condemning the use in war of these already prohibited substances[25] and "[..]that this prohibition shall be universally accepted as a part of International Law",[26] the Protocol also extends this prohibition to the use of bacteriological methods of warfare.[27] Given that the Protocol's terms leave considerable room for diverse interpretations,[28] there have been attempts to clarify the scope of the prohibition obligations under it.[29] The Protocol, however, is limited to a

---

[19] On the restriction of the right of parties to an armed conflict to choose means (and methods) of warfare, compare: Article 22 Hague Regulations, annex to Hague Convention IV of 18 October 1907 respecting the Laws and Customs of War on Land, in A. Roberts and R. Guelff, *Documents on the Laws of War* (1989), at 52; Article 35 para. 1 1977 Geneva Protocol I Additional to the Geneva Conventions (1949), in Roberts (et al.), at 409.

[20] Compare arms control handbook / manuals like J. Goldblat, Arms Control Agreements (1983) at 124; Goldblat, Arms Control, *supra* n. 17, for instance at 91-92, ACDA *supra* at 5.

[21] See Article 23(a) forbidding the employment of poison or poisoned weapons and Article (e) the employment of arms, projectiles and materials calculated to cause unnecessary suffering, in: Roberts (et al.) *supra* n. 19 at 39. Both the 1899 Hague Convention II and the 1907 Hague Convention contained general principles of customary international law prohibiting the use of poison and materials causing unnecessary suffering. *Ibid*, at 35.

[22] Bernauer, *supra* n. 17 at 11.

[23] A. Roberts et al., *supra* n. 19, at 35.

[24] See also B.V.A. Röling and O. Sukovic, *The Law of War and Dubious Weapons*, SIPRI (1976), in particular 11 et seq.

[25] "Whereas the use in war of asphyxiating, poisonous or other gases, and of all analogous liquids, materials or devices, has been justly condemned by the general opinion of the civilized world; [...] [W]hereas the prohibition of such use has been declared in Treaties to which the majority of Powers of the World are Parties;..", 1925 Geneva Protocol, preambular.

[26] "[..]To the end that this prohibition shall be universally accepted as a part of International Law, *binding alike the conscience and the practice of nations*". [emphasis added], 1925 Geneva Preambular Protocol; Röling, *supra* n. 24 at 11.

[27] "Declare:[..] agree to extend this prohibition to the use of bacteriological methods of warfare and agree to be bound as between themselves according to the terms of this declaration", 1925 Geneva Protocol.

[28] Roberts, et al, *supra* n. 19, at 137.

[29] Compare the 1969 Resolution 2603 A (XXIV) adopted by majority in the General Assembly. See also Roberts, et al., *ibid*, at 138 and Goldblat, *supra* n. 16 at 91.

situation of war and between the parties to it. The non-universal character of the Protocol therefore weakens its force. Furthermore, numerous States have made the reservation that it is binding only in relation to other States bound by it and ceases to be binding if the enemy or its allies fail to respect the prohibitions of the Protocol.[30] In other words they reserved the right to a "second strike" (a retaliatory strike). The dominant view, however, is that the ban under the Geneva Protocol evolved into a customary rule.[31] Furthermore, there are no mechanisms to verify compliance. Since the 1980s, however, this gap has been filled by the UN resolutions empowering the UN Secretary-General to investigate reports on possible violations of the Geneva Protocol.[32] In a joint statement on the Non-proliferation of Chemical Weapons the United States and the Soviet Union confirmed their intention to provide active support to the UN Secretary-General in conducting investigations into reported violations of the Protocol. They affirmed their intention to consider the imposition of sanctions against the violators of the Protocol, including, interestingly, those under Chapter VII of the UN Charter.[33]

---

[30] Compare reservations of the kind made by Parties to the Protocol like the UK ("The protocol is only binding on the United Kingdom as regards the powers which have signed and ratified or who have acceded to it and it ceases to bind the United Kingdom towards any Power whose armed forces or the armed forces of whose allies fail to respect the prohibitions", *Manual of Military Law* (1958) at 216). In other words, use in second strike would remain possible. Similar ones were made by countries like Canada, Belgium, France, the Netherlands or the USSR. The Protocol was "regarded by such states as containing not an absolute prohibition on the use of such weapons, but only as an agreement not to use such weapons first", Roberts et al., *supra* n. 19, at 138.

[31] Compare Roberts et al., *ibid.* at 138. No controversy regarding the ban on any use, also in second strike, is possible in the case of the CWC with its ban on use under any circumstances and exclusion of reservations. In the case of the BWC the question regarding the reservations was not solved as it does not contain a ban on its use, but concerns non-possession and production. However, notwithstanding the fact that there are 131 States Parties to the 1925 Convention (as of 1 July 1988 according to the US Department of State (and 114 according to the depositary) (Roberts et al., *supra* n. 19 at 21 and 144), whereas there are 91 States Parties to the BWC (ACDA *supra* n. 16 at 104) there does not appear to be much controversy nowadays about a ban on its use, either conventionally, or customary. According to F. Kalshoven (Arms, Armaments and International Law, *Recueil des Cours*, 1985-II, at 267) "(T)hese restrictions on application of the prohibition, and in particular the condition of reciprocity, have largely lost their significance with the entry of the prohibition into the body of customary international law". Compare also L. C. Green, *The Contemporary Law of Armed Conflict* (1993) at 131, or Röling, *supra* n. 24 at 7. See also the Final Declaration of the Conference of States Parties to the 1925 Geneva Protocol and Other Interested States and on the Prohibition of Chemical Weapons of 11 January 1989, 28 *ILM* (1989) pp. 1020-1022 as well as UN Doc. SIRES (1991) p. 1687, preambular.

[32] Goldblat, *supra* n. 16, at 92. This points to another coincidence of the law of collective security and the law of armed conflict.

[33] Soviet Union-United States joint statement on non-proliferation, issued June 4, 1990, 29 *ILM* 932-933.

The Protocol was reconfirmed once more in 1989, when in an attempt to speed up the process of negotiating a chemical weapons convention France, the depositary of the 1925 Geneva Protocol, convened a conference of States Parties to the Protocol and other interested States on the prohibition of chemical weapons. Besides giving an impetus to a prospective CWC the States Parties reaffirmed in their Final Declaration[34] the prohibition as established in the Protocol. Furthermore, they "reaffirm their full support for the Secretary-General for carrying out his responsibilities for investigations in the event of alleged violations of the Geneva Protocol".[35]

This development strengthens the majority view that the prohibitions contained in the Protocol have become part of customary law.[36] According to Roberts, however, some are of the opinion that the controversy over its interpretation and its reservations "have reduced the Protocol's usefulness as a guide under customary international law".[37] However, it retains the ban on first use.

2. The Biological Weapons Convention

Under the 1925 Protocol, prohibiting the *use* of both chemical and bacteriological weapons, States were still allowed to *possess* chemical and bacteriological weapons and to develop and stockpile them. After the adoption of the Protocol, the prevalent opinion has been that also the *possession* of chemical and bacteriological (biological) weapons should be prohibited simultaneously.[38] For there was the fear "that if one of them were to become the object of a prohibition it might look like a legitimisation of the other.[39] Since many States had reserved the right to use chemical and/or bacteriological agents in reply, and because, unlike biological weapons, chemical weapons had actually been used in war, many States maintained chemical weapons in their arsenal to deter the use of this type of weapons against them, and to provide a retaliatory capacity if deterrence failed. The aim of a simultaneous prohibition of both chemical and biological weapons therefore blocked progress, because many States were reluctant to give up their capability of chemical weapons "without reliable assurance that other nations were not developing, producing, and stockpiling chemical weapons".[40] In the 1960s, however, the conviction

[34] Final Declaration of the Conference of States Parties to the 1925 Geneva Protocol and other interested States on the prohibition of chemical weapons, Paris 7-11 January 1989, *ILM.* 1020-1022 (1989).
[35] *Ibid*, at 1022.
[36] See for instance Goldblat, *supra* n. 16, at 92. Bernauer, *supra* n. 17, at 12.
[37] Roberts et al., *supra* n. 19, at 139.
[38] J. Goldblat, The 1993 Chemical Weapons Convention: A Significant Step in the Process of Multilateral Disarmament, in Bardonet, *supra* n. 4, at 16.
[39] Ooms, *supra* n. 5, at 5.
[40] ACDA, *supra* n. 5, at 95.

grew that this deadlock should be broken and to opt for separate instruments for the control of biological weapons and chemical weapons respectively, for it was assumed that since a ban on biological weapons did not require intrusive verification it could therefore be concluded quickly.[41]

In 1969 the UK submitted to the Eighteen-Nation Disarmament Committee (ENDC) a draft convention concentrating solely on biological weapons. There was, however, no general acceptance of this approach, especially amongst the East Europeans. In the same year, however, the US renounced all biological weapons[42] and this was followed subsequently by countries like the UK.[43] Finally, in 1971 the Soviet Union and its allies agreed to concentrate first on a convention on biological weapons. This considerably speeded up the process, for shortly thereafter - after having worked out an agreed draft - the US and the USSR submitted separate but identical texts for a possible convention[44] to the Conference of the Committee on Disarmament (CCD[45]). This led to the Biological Weapons Convention,[46] which was the first international agreement since World War II to provide for the elimination of an entire class of weapons.[47] The Convention was opened for signature in 1972 and entered into force on 26 March 1975. In the BWC parties undertake not to develop, produce, stockpile, or acquire biological agents or toxins of types and in quantities that have no justification for prophylactic, protective, and other peaceful purposes, as well as weapons and means of delivery.[48]All such *matériel* is to be destroyed within nine months of the Convention's entry into force.[49] Interestingly, the Convention does not forbid the use of these weapons. It reconfirms, however, the prohibition of the 1925 Protocol on the use in war of chemical and bacteriolocial (biological) weapons, whereby *first use* was already forbidden; a prohibition that can now be regarded as one of customary

---

[41] Goldblat, *supra* n 16, at 93. According to Ooms, (*supra* n. 5, at 3) a role played whereby although these weapons had not been used on the battlefield during the Second World War there appeared "a renewed attention to this manner of warfare due to the use of riot control agents and herbicides by the United States in Vietnam and of the use of presumably mustard gas by Egypt in the Yemen".

[42] In November 1969 the President declared that the United States unilaterally renounced the first use of lethal or incapacitating chemical agents and weapons and unconditionally renounced all methods of biological warfare. "Henceforth the U.S. biological program would be confined to research on strictly defined measures of defense, such as immunization". ACDA, *supra* n. 17, at 95.

[43] ACDA, *ibid*, at 95.

[44] ACDA, *ibid*, at 96.

[45] The Eighteen-Nation Disarmament Commission was renamed after its enlargement to 26 members in August 1969. (ACDA, *ibid*. at 96). See also n. 60.

[46] Convention on the prohibition of the development, production and stockpiling of bacteriological (biological) and toxin weapons and on their destruction, of 10 April 1972.

[47] Goldblat, *supra* n. 16, at 96.

[48] Article I, BWC.

[49] Article II, BWC.

law.[50] But after States Parties would have destroyed their weapons in accordance with Article II, and not being allowed to acquire biological agents or toxins as agreed under Article I, both first and second strike use would in practice be excluded. Effective verification of the ban on the possession of biological (bateriological) weapons under the BWC, however, is lacking, for the BWC does not have any supervisory mechanism. Although within nine months after entry into force the States Parties will under Article II either have to destroy substances or "to divert to peaceful purposes", there is no duty to declare possession, nor is there any mechanism to control compliance. For that States Parties are dependent on their National Technical Means (NTMs). Especially this lack of a supervisory mechanism has been the subject of discussion, both at Review Conferences and by *ad hoc* groups.[51] The Second Review Conference of September 1986 led to a meeting of scientific and technical experts[52] with the task to develop procedures for implementing annual data exchanges.[53] The Third Review Conference of 1991 in its turn led to an *ad hoc* group of governmental experts "to identify, examine and evaluate from a scientific and technical standpoint potential verification measures with respect to the prohibitions of the convention": the VEREX group. The *ad hoc* group met four times in 1992 and 1993 and submitted a consensus report.[54] In September 1994 a special conference was convened to discuss this report and the Conference agreed to establish an *ad hoc* group to consider appropriate measures and draft proposals to strengthen the Convention and to be included in a legally binding instrument.[55] This led to two substantive meetings in 1995 with additional meetings in 1996. Interestingly it is the supervisory system of the CWC that acts as the model.

---

[50] See above at pp. 66-67 and in particular nn. 30 and 31.

[51] See for instance Winfried Lang, Verhinderung von Erfüllungsdefiziten im Völkerrecht, in Festschrift für Herbert Schambeck, *Verhinderung von Erfüllungsdefiziten im Völkerrecht Beispiele aus Abrüstungs und Umweltschutz* (1994), at 825-827.

[52] 31 March-15 April 1987.

[53] This led to the exchange of data as a Confidence Building Measure, in other words a voluntary system. The participation of states is low. See T. Stock et al. in *SIPRI Yearbook 1995*: Armaments, Disarmament and International security at 743-744.

[54] *Ad Hoc* Group of Governmental experts to Identity and Examine Potential Verification Measures from a Scientific and Technical Standpoint, Report, BWC/CONF.III/VEREX/9, Geneva 1993.

[55] This Ad Hoc Group should, inter alia, consider a system of measures to promote compliance with the Convention. "[M]easures should apply to all relevant facilities and activities. They should be reliable, cost effective, non-discriminatory and as non-intrusive as possible, consistent with the effective implementation of the system and should not lead to abuse; [..]", Special Conference of States Parties to the Convention on the Prohibition of the Development, Production and Stockpiling of Bacteriological (Biological) and Toxin Weapons and on Their Destruction, Geneva 19-30 1994, Final Report, BWC/SPCONF/1 at 9-10. In: *SIPRI Yearbook 1994*, at 746.

Interesting from the perspective of chemical weapons control, is the fact that the Biological Weapons Convention repeats the previously mentioned purpose of controlling both chemical weapons and biological weapons jointly,[56] as well as States Parties' explicit undertaking to conclude an early agreement on a chemical weapons convention.[57] In spite of this commitment certain great powers remained rather reluctant to divest themselves of chemical weapons[58] which were regarded as militarily useful, in contrast to biological weapons. It would take another 20 years and the end of the Cold War before the negotiations in the Conference on Disarmament finally led to the CWC as signed in January 1993.

3. Towards a ban on chemical weapons

Ever since 1969[59] at the Conference on Disarmament (CD), the Geneva-based multilateral forum for arms control negotiations, and its successors,[60] negotiations had taken place to reach an early agreement on the control of chemical weapons. Discussions only took place in plenary meetings of the CD and during informal consultations. However, when in 1980 a special subsidiary body of the CD (*ad hoc Working Group on Chemical Weapons*) was established the negotiations began to speed up, especially when in 1984 agreement was reached on the structure of a joint preliminary draft text.[61] In

---

[56] Compare the preambular Paragraph of the BWC that expresses States Parties' conviction "[..] that the prohibition of the development, production and stockpiling of *chemical and bacteriological (biological)* weapons and their elimination, through effective measures, will facilitate the achievement of general and complete disarmament under strict and effective international control, [...] (Emphasis added.)" Striking is also the para. that refers to "an agreement on the prohibition of *bacteriological (biological)* and toxin weapons "as" (emphasis added) a first possible step towards the achievement of agreement on effective measures also for the prohibition of the development, production and stockpiling of chemical weapons", which also expresses the determination to continue negotiations to that end.

[57] "Each State Party to this Convention affirms the recognized objective of effective prohibition of chemical weapons and, to this end, undertakes to continue negotiations in good faith with a view to reaching early agreement on effective measures for the prohibition of their development, production and stockpiling and for their destruction, and on appropriate measures concerning equipment and means of delivery specifically designed for the production or use of chemical agents for weapons purposes", Article IX, BWC.

[58] Goldblat, *supra* n. 38, at 16.

[59] Bernauer, *supra* n. 12, at 25 and "After the conclusion of the NPT in 1968, the Eighteen-Nation Disarmament Committee placed the question of chemical and biological weapons on its agenda under the heading "non-nuclear measures", at 24.

[60] Goldblat, *supra* n. 16, at 8. The Conference on Disarmament is the successor to the Ten-Nation Committee on Disarmament (1959-1960), the Eighteen-Nation Committee (1962-1969), the Conference of the Committee on Disarmament (1969-1978), and the Committee on Disarmament (1979-1983).

[61] Bernauer, *supra* n. 17, at 1.

1984 the name of the Working Group was changed to *Ad Hoc Committee on Chemical Weapons*. Its new mandate was "to start the full and complete process of negotiations, to develop and work out the Convention, except for its final drafting".[62]

In the meantime the US and the USSR, the possessors of the most expansive stocks, held several bilateral talks to see on what issues they were in agreement. In the end two issues stood out. First, there was substantial disagreement on the degree of intrusiveness of the verification of compliance, for instance via mandatory on-site inspection. Second, these countries wanted to maintain a residual stock of chemical weapons, until all chemical weapon-capable states had joined the projected multilateral convention.[63] Especially this latter aspect was not acceptable to the negotiating states, for the projected chemical weapons treaty had to be of a non-discriminatory nature unlike the Non-Proliferation Treaty. At the 1989 Paris Conference of the Parties to the 1925 Protocol specially convened by France to speed up the negotiating process the parameters for a universally acceptable convention were outlined. The participating states stressed:

> "[..] the necessity of concluding, at an early date, a Convention on the prohibition of the development, production, stockpiling and use of all chemical weapons, and on their destruction. This Convention shall be global and comprehensive and effectively verifiable. It should be of unlimited duration. [..]"[64]

In 1990 the US and the USSR signed a bilateral agreement.[65] The obvious aim of this agreement was to set -as done before with regard to many multilateral arms control agreements- the preconditions (minimum requirements) pertaining to a multilateral treaty. This treaty thereby contained measures to facilitate the early conclusion of a multilateral chemical weapons convention.[66] The principal obligations assumed by the US and the USSR in their bilateral agreement were to halt the production of chemical weapons; to reduce chemical weapon stockpiles to equal, low levels; and to accept measures necessary to

---

[62] Bernauer, *ibid*. at 6.

[63] See Goldblat, *supra* n. 16, at 99-101.

[64] Final declaration of the Conference of States Parties to the 1925 Geneva Protocol and other Interested States on the Prohibition of Chemical Weapons, January 11, 1989 sub. 3, 28 *ILM* (1989), at 1022. See also Goldblat, *ibid*, at 102.

[65] Agreement between the United States of America and the Union of Soviet Socialist Republics on Destruction and Non-production of Chemical Weapons and on Measures to Facilitate the Multilateral Convention on Banning Chemical Weapons, 1 June 1990, 29 *ILM* 934 (1990).

[66] Goldblat, *supra* n. 16, at 97.

verify compliance.[67] In spite of the fact that there was substantial agreement on reduction, each side wanted to keep 5,000 metric tons of chemicals. Furthermore, the technical capacity to manufacture chemical weapons was not restricted. Both parties were at the time not willing to give up the option under the 1925 Geneva Protocol to use weapons in retaliation. With regard to the prospective multilateral convention they appeared unwilling to unconditionally destroy all of their chemical weapons and production facilities. Both States went as far as to agree to reduce their stockpiles to 500 tons within eight years after the entry into force of the multilateral convention, but wanted to maintain a veto on a decision on the elimination of the remaining stock.[68] After the US abandoned this position in 1991 the multilateral negotiations speeded up and in September 1992 there was agreement on a draft Convention.

The scope of this Convention is much wider than the BWC and also includes the commitment never under any circumstances to use chemical weapons, thereby restricting the more limited non-use commitment of the 1925 Protocol (with its reservations). It foresees furthermore a ban on the production of a complete category of weapons, i.e. chemical weapons, the complete disarmament of States possessing such weapons via the destruction of the actual weapons and their production facilities within a period of 10 years, as well as the control of certain chemical substances (mainly) in the civilian industry that might be used as precursors in the development of chemical weapons. This is the first comprehensive ban not only to "disarm" a complete category of weapons, but also forbidding their use. It will, furthermore, not only involve the military establishment, but also large sections of State Parties' civilian chemical industry, which raises the touchy problem of the protection of confidential business information.

---

67 " ..(a) to cooperate regarding methods and technologies for the safe and efficient destruction of chemical weapons; (b) not to produce chemical weapons; (c) to reduce their chemical weapons stockpiles to equal, low levels; (d) to cooperate in developing, testing, and carrying out appropriate inspection procedures; and (e) to adopt practical measures to encourage all chemical weapons-capable states to become parties to the multilateral convention" (Article I, Agreement between the United States of America and the Union of Soviet Socialist Republics on Destruction and Non-production of Chemical Weapons and on Measures to Facilitate the Multilateral Convention on Banning Chemical Weapons, 1 June 1990, 29 *ILM* 934 (1990). Goldblat, *supra* n. 16, at 97.

68 Goldblat, *ibid.*, at 99. In an agreed statement attached to the 1 June 1990 agreement this was carefully worded.

III. The CWC: its substantive law

1.General

The system of the Convention is relatively straightforward. First of all, it contains the primary obligations, which deal with the central disarmament and non-proliferation obligations, including the "carrot and stick" obligations of Articles X (assistance and protection against chemical weapons) and XI (economic and technical development). The second category of obligations, the supporting or procedural obligations, support the operation of these central obligations and provide for the necessary elements to allow for the supervision of compliance with the core provision. It is, however, this very intricate system of supervision that lends the Convention its special character. On the one hand, there is a constant stream of -declared- information. On the other hand, this information is constantly being assessed, thereby providing actual information as to the state of compliance with the Convention. This substantially raises confidence[69] in the actual implementation of the treaty which is a prerequisite for obtaining universal membership. This is essential if chemical weapons are to be banned completely. A further element contributing to this end by raising confidence in the system of supervision is that it is recognized that the confidentiality of certain information obtained needs to be guaranteed. This not only concerns information that is provided by States Parties themselves, but also information collected by inspectors during the course of their inspection duties, be it in the civil chemical industry or not. The importance attached thereto follows not only from the fact that one of the Annexes to the Convention relates to confidentiality but also that one of the first subsidiary organs to be appointed is the Confidentiality Commission. To allow for an effective system of supervision the Convention foresees the creation of two types of institutions, namely at the national level in a National Authority and at the international level in the OPCW. Pivotal, in this respect, is the position of the OPCW. Furthermore, States Parties have to adopt national implementation measures.

The Convention itself is concise, counting only 24 Articles. There are, however, three annexes, the Annex on Chemicals, the Annex on Implementation and Verification (Verification Annex) and the Annex on the Protection of Confidential Information (Confidentiality Annex). The reason to opt for such a combination can be explained by the different amendment

---

[69] According to Chayes transparency 'may operate to promote treaty compliance'. In particular it provides reassurance that Parties will not be taken advantage of when complying and it deters actors from contemplating non-compliance. Abraham Chayes & Antonia Handler Chayes, *The New Sovereignty, Compliance with International Regulatory Agreements* (1995) at 135. See *infra*.

procedures to be applied to the Convention and to the Annexes respectively. For in the annexes we find the regulations with regard to the more technical and administrative details, which need to be able to be changed relatively easily. The Convention and annexes, however, only provide for the essential framework (structure) while the Preparatory Commission for the OPCW (PrepCom), which was established by the Paris resolution[70] at the signing ceremony of the CWC, was tasked with a mandate for the further elaboration of rules and policies for approval by the First Conference of States Parties,[71] such as the further development of inspection procedures,[72] or a confidentiality policy. The PrepCom, during the more than four years of its work, held 16 plenary meetings. It met for the first time from 8-12 February 1993 and held its final meeting from 9-15 April 1997. The actual work of the PrepCom was, however, carried out in between the sessions in its different "thematic" working groups. It did not succeed, however, in completely fulfilling its mandate and a number of unresolved issues were left for the consideration of the First Conference.[73] For a complete understanding of the system of the Convention it may therefore be necessary to consult both the reports of the 16 PrepCom plenary sessions as well as the decisions taken by both the First and the consecutive Conferences, both on the resolved and the unresolved issues, since some of the issues were not resolved at the First Conference and were either decided upon at one of the consecutive conferences or are still unresolved.

From a systematic point of view, within the Convention four main areas can be distinguished, namely *States Parties' obligations*; *States Parties' rights* (including protection and benifits); *supervision* or compliance control (including the establishment of the OPCW); and *treaty-related technicalities*.

---

[70] Resolution establishing the Preparatory Commission for the Organization for the Prohibition of Chemical Weapons, adopted in Paris during the signing ceremony of the Convention on the Prohibition of the Development, Production, Stockpiling and use of Chemical Weapons and on their Destruction 13-15 January 1993, *Legal Series PC-OPCW 1, 1994*.

[71] "..for the purpose of carrying out the necessary preparations for the effective implementation of the Convention[..] and for preparing for the first session of the Conference of the States Parties to that Convention", Paragraph 1, Paris Resolution, *ibid.*

[72] "The Commission shall develop, *inter alia*, the following draft agreements, provisions and guidelines for consideration and approval by the Conference of the States Parties....(a) Guidelines on detailed procedures for verification and for the conduct of inspections, in accordance with, *inter alia*, Part II, Paragraph 42, of the Verification Annex;[..] Recommendations for procedures to be followed in case of breaches or alleged breaches of confidentiality, in accordance with paragraph 18 of the Confidentiality Annex.", Paragraph 12 Paris Resolution, *ibid.*

[73] See Final Report of the Preparatory Commission for the Organization for the Prohibition of Chemical Weapons to the First Session of the States Parties of the Organization for the Prohibition of Chemical Weapons and to the First Meeting of the Executive Council of the Organization for the Prohibition of Chemical Weapons, *PC-XVI/37*, 15 April 1997. at 47-54.

Summarily one could therefore group the articles of the Convention in the following way:

Obligations: Articles I, III, IV, V and VI and also the Annex on Chemicals and the Verification Annex, provide and elaborate the central obligations.

Rights: These cannot only be found in Article X (the assistance and protection against chemical weapons) and Article XI (economic and technological development) (protection and benefits), but also in Article VI (activities not prohibited under this convention).

Supervision: Articles VIII (the organization), IX and XII (measures to redress a situation and to ensure compliance) and the two annexes, the one on verification, and the one on confidentiality, concern the machinery by which to ensure compliance with the Convention.

Final clauses and treaty-related technicalities; This category concerns, as such, the technical aspects of the treaty.[74] Article II provides definitions and criteria, Articles XIII (relation of the CWC to other agreements), XIV (settlement of disputes), XV (amendments), XVI (duration and withdrawal), XVII (status of the annexes), XVIII (signature), XIX (ratification), XX (accession), XXI (entry into force), XXII (reservations), XXIII (depositary) and XXIV (authentic texts).

This sub-division is introduced in order to clarify the general outline of the Convention and to systematize its different aspects. It cannot, however, be applied too rigorously since, for instance, States Parties' obligations not only concern their obligations relating to chemical weapons and related substances, but also those in relation to verification and compliance. The focus will therefore be on States Parties' obigations (paragraph 2), States Parties' rights (paragraph 3) concerning the central role of supervision (paragraph 4) and on the final clauses (paragraph 5), albeit summarily. Supervision in the above broad sense will be the issue of Chapter IV on the central role of the OPCW and on its institutional aspects and Chapter V in which the different functions of the OPCW in relation to compliance control (supervisory functions) will be analyzed.

2. Obligations of the States Parties

Article I contains the central obligation not to have, develop or in any other way obtain, chemical weapons and never to use them. Furthermore, it obliges States Parties never to assist in the transfer of such weapons. A noteworthy

---

[74] Articles XIII through XXIV are known as "housekeeping articles", D. Mahley, The Chemical Weapons Convention: an Overview, at 4: in: A.E. Smithson, The Chemical Weapons Convention Handbook, The Henry L. Stimson Center (1993).

exception to the general ban is the States Parties' undertaking not to use "riot control agents" as a method of warfare, meaning that they can be used for internal purposes, a purpose not prohibited under the Convention.[75] Each State Party furthermore undertakes to destroy the chemical weapons it owns or that it has abandoned on other states' territories, as well as any chemical weapons production facility. With regard to old and abandoned chemical weapons a special regime exists, as detailed in Annex Part IV (B). This general obligation falls into two parts. The first of these is the destruction of the existing chemical weapons and of the production facilities. The second obligation concerns the ban on future production of chemical weapons and their precursors. The former obligation is finite and will cease to exist under the Convention after a period of 10 years;[76] the latter obligation is infinite, and will involve the civilian chemical industry on a continuous basis, since that is the place where "listed" chemicals may be produced and consequently it is there that the continuing verification of compliance with regard to the non-production of chemical weapons and their precursors will take place.

One further obligation needs to be specifically mentioned, namely that of Article VII concerning the national implementation measures. To start with, each State Party will have to implement its core obligations and prohibit natural and legal persons anywhere on its territory or in any place under its jurisdiction from undertaking any activity prohibited for that State Party under the CWC,[77] and not to permit such activity in any place under its control.[78] Violators will have to be penalized, even if it concerns nationals that are outside its territorial jurisdiction.[79]

Furthermore, States Parties will have to establish a National Authority "to serve as the national focal point for effective liaison with the Organization".[80]
As the main (principal) obligations of the States Parties to the CWC the following can be distinguished:

primary obligations:

* non-development, non-production, non-stockpiling (I para. 1(a);

---

[75] "Purposes not prohibited under this convention" means: ..(d) Law enforcement including domestic riot control purposes". Article II, para. 9 (d).

[76] A State Party may submit a request for the extension of the deadline up to a maximum of 15 years. See Verification Annex, Part IV (A), paragraphs 24-28.

[77] Article VII, (1)(a).

[78] Article VII, (1)(b).

[79] Article VII, (1)(c).

[80] Article VII, (4). See also *Handelingen Tweede Kamer der Staten Generaal*, vergaderjaar 1994-1995, 23 910 (R 1515), nrs.1-2. In the Netherlands the Ministry of Economic Affairs is the appointed National Authority.

* non-use, both first use and retaliatory use (I para. 1(b); no transfer, directly or indirectly, to anyone (I para. 1(a); not to engage in any military preparation to use them (I para. 1 (c);
* not to assist, encourage or induce anyone to do anything prohibited for States Parties (I para. 1(d);
* destruction of existing stocks which it owns or possesses, or that are located in any place under its jurisdiction or control (I para. 2);
* destruction of abandoned stocks on the territory of another party (I para. 3);
* destruction of production facilities it owns or possesses, or that are located in any place under its jurisdiction or control (I para. 4);
* no restrictions impeding trade, development and promotion of scientific and technological knowledge in the field of chemistry for industrial, agricultural, research, medical, pharmaceutical or other peaceful purposes (XI, para 2(c));[81]
* facilitate the exchange of chemicals, equipment and scientific and technical information for non-prohibited purposes (XI);
* facilitate the exchange of equipment, material and scientific and technological information concerning means of protection against chemical weapons (X);
* provide information on programmes for protective purposes (X);
* provide assistance through the OPCW (X);

supporting or procedural (secondary) obligations such as:

* declaring possession of inventories of chemical weapons and production facilities (III paras. 1 (a),(b),(c);
* declaring any transfer of chemical weapons out of or into its territory (III para. 1 (a)(iv));
* drawing up of plans for the destruction and the execution thereof of weapons and destruction facilities (III paras. 1 (a)(v) and (c)(v));
* with regard to activities not prohibited, declaring relevant chemicals and facilities (development, production etc.) (VI);[82]
* allow for on-site inspections and/or monitoring with on-site instruments (IV paras. 4,5; V paras. 6, 7(b), 15; VI paras. 3,4,6; IX para. 10);

---

[81] "Developing states note that access to commercially valuable chemical technology is an important part of a larger effort to facilitate industrial development.[..] Nevertheless, it does not rule out the continuation of collective efforts to control the export of high-risk chemicals and technologies. (Author: Australia Group)."(Mahley, *supra* n. 74, at 4).

[82] See Mahley, *ibid*, at 1.

* institute national implementation measures, insuring compliance by natural and legal persons within its territory and under its jurisdiction (VII);
* establishing confidentiality standards for information received (VII);
* reviewing existing national regulations in the field of trade in chemicals for consistency with the object and purpose of CWC (XI);
* controlling the production of chemicals in the civilian industry (VI, para. 2);

3. Rights of the States Parties

Although it can be held that the obligations in the Convention are central, there would never have been a Convention if it did not also contain certain rights which are reciprocal to the obligations mentioned. They concern rights like the right to receive information or to have a situation clarified,[83] or indeed the right to a challenge inspection.[84] These are crucial rights with regard to the compliance control of other States Parties' obligations and are therefore instrumental in obtaining States Parties' compliance with the Convention. Furthermore, there are rights that are either exceptions to the duty not to produce chemical substances suitable for chemical weapons production, like the right to a controlled use or production of Schedule 1, 2 or 3 chemicals, or rights that were included in the Convention in order to stimulate technically less advanced states to join. This is what has been referred to as the "carrot and stick" provisions.

In the former case States Parties are allowed to make use of toxic chemicals and their precursors for purposes not prohibited by the Convention.[85] These include industrial, agricultural, research, medical, and pharmaceutical purposes, protective purposes, military purposes,[86] or law enforcement purposes.[87]

The latter case concerns Articles X and XI, as the debates, both in the context of the PrepCom as well as in the US Senate,[88] concerning the "rights

---

[83] Article IX, paras. 2-6.

[84] Article IX, para. 8.

[85] "To develop, produce, otherwise acquire, retain, transfer and use"(VI para. 1).

[86] Not connected with the use of chemical weapons and not dependent on the use of the toxic properties of chemicals as a method of warfare (Article II, para. 9 (c)).

[87] Including domestic riot control purposes, Article II, 9 (d).

[88] See for instance Senator Ashcroft: "There are the requirements, particularly in Articles X and XI of the treaty, which require us to share technology, to share information, and to share, in particular, the defensive technology of chemical weaponry. There is an anomaly in chemical weaponry which is challenging. It is that when you provide the defensive technology for chemical weapons, you are providing one of the essential components of delivering chemical weapons.[..] If a rogue state wants to deliver chemical weapons, one of the things they need to do is to acquire the defensive technology to defend against them and to protect their soldiers in delivery. That seems to me one of the substantial problems contained

issue" and the possible negative consequences thereof have shown. Article XI (Economic and Technological Development) is about the right to access to commercially valuable chemical technology and chemicals, whereas Article X concerns assistance and protection against chemical weapons. In particular, it concerns the right to participate in "the fullest possible exchange of equipment, material and scientific and technological information concerning means of protection against chemical weapons"[89] in case of being threatened with a chemical weapons attack or having suffered an attack.[90] A commentator notes that this provision "enables the treaty to nullify any potential political or military advantage of either a non-party developing chemical weapons or a party clandestinely developing chemical weapons". And that it is "one of the reasons why states should not waste their time, money, or effort trying to solve real or perceived national security problems by developing chemical weapons".[91] Especially these measures are intended as an incentive for the industrially less developed states. It is therefore curious to note that during the PrepCom a number of these countries blocked progress because they were of the opinion that Article XI was being interpreted too narrowly, thereby not offering enough (too little). In contrast, those opposed to the Convention in the American Senate, which almost led to non-ratification, based their opposition almost exclusively on Articles X and XI as offering too much. Furthermore, it is striking that in the preparatory phase most of the problems did not concern the actual issue of disarmament obligations, but rather the incentive issue: the rights.

Article X deals with protection against chemical weapons if ever they would be used against a State Party. For this purpose States Parties are allowed to conduct research. Central are Article X, paragraph 5 obliging the Technical Secretariat (TS) to provide a State Party with expert advice and assistance; and Article X, paragraph 6 concerning the right of States Parties to request and provide assistance bilaterally. Article X, paragraph 7, obligates States Parties "to provide assistance" through the OPCW. The measure of assistance, however, is voluntary ("and to this end elect one or more of the following measures"). This may amount to a financial contribution ("contribute to the voluntary fund for assistance)", or to declare within 180 days after the entry into force the kind of assistance it might provide.[92] It is therefore completely up to States Parties to decide for themselves, as the Convention does not oblige

in Articles X and XI. The risks far exceed the benefits." *Congressional Record, Senate,* April 24, 1974, at S3651. The resolution of ratification of April 24, 1997, therefore also contains expansive conditions relating to these Articles X and XI like under 7 (Continuing vitality of the Australia Group and national export controls) and 15 (assistance under Article X).

[89] Article X (3).

[90] See Smithson, *supra* n. 74, at 20.

[91] Mahley, *supra* n. 74, at 4.

[92] Article X, para. 7(c).

them to provide specifically described chemical assistance. The U.S. Senate did so by stipulating that the U.S. would not contribute to the voluntary fund for assistance under Article X, paragraph 7(a) and that for States Parties ineligible for certain assistance under the Foreign Assistance Act only limited assistance would be available.[93]

With regard to Article XI there exists the controversy surrounding the ending of the export controls of the Australia Group, since these would be contrary to the supposed lifting of trade restrictions under Article XI of the CWC.[94] (This "rights"issue therefore clearly constitutes an "obligation" issue for certain States Parties). To explain this issue a few words are necessary about the Australia Group. The Australia Group came into existence when it appeared in the eighties that in the Iraq-Iran War commercial trade in dual-use chemicals by Western countries was fuelling programs to develop and produce chemical weapons.[95] The original Australia Group of 15 members, that met informally for the first time in 1985, in 1986 adopted a 35-chemical warning list and in 1987 a core-list of 8 chemicals. All participants would formally control the core list of chemicals, whereas the warning list would be issued to the chemical industry for voluntary action.[96] Decisions by the Australia Group are not legally binding, they are taken by majority and there is no formal charter or constitution.[97] New members, however, need to have unanimous approval. By 1996 15 more members were admitted and the two previously mentioned lists were merged and by 1992 there were 54 chemicals listed. Furthermore, a list was drawn up for the control of dual-use chemical equipment.[98] The scope of its controls was furthermore extended by drawing up a list to also control the proliferation of biological weapons.

With the Australia Group regime still in force many developing countries regard the CWC as discriminatory. Why is it necessary, they claim, that States

---

[93] [..] for any State Party the government of which is not eligible for assistance under chapter 2 of part II (relating to military assistance) or chapter 4 of part II (relating to economic support assistance) of the Foreign Assistance Act of 1961- (i) no assistance under paragraph 7 (b) of Article X will be provided[..]; and (ii) no assistance under paragraph 7(c) of Article X other than medical antidotes and treatment will be provided[..]. Ratification Resolution, of April 24 1997, under 15, *Congressional Record Senate*, at S3655.

[94] "[T]he use of export controls, the Australia Group and the CWC have become mirred in controversy" , A.E. Smithson, *Separating Fact from Fiction: The Australia Group and the Chemical Weapons Convention* (The Henry L. Stimson Center (1997) at 6).

[95] Smithson, *ibid*, at 7 and "[..] companies and individuals from West Germany, Great Britain, Japan, Austria, Belgium, the Netherlands, Italy, Switzerland, France, and the United States, among other countries, had sold Iraq and Libya products that facilitated their proliferation aim" at 7-8, referring to Australia Group Document AG/Dec92/Press/Chair/9 (Paris: 22 December 1992).

[96] Smithson, *ibid*, at 8-9.

[97] Smithson, *ibid*, at 10, referring to different sources.

[98] See for the Australia Group Control List of Dual-use Chemical Manufacturing Facilities and Equipment and Related Technology, Smithson, *ibid*, annex 2, pp. 36-43.

that have agreed to chemical weapons disarmament would still be subject to an export control system aimed at exactly the same end? Illustrative in this respect is the clear position Brazil took in the following statement:

> "The second category of commitments - that is those related to free trade and cooperation among States Parties - is clearly defined in Article XI. These commitments have a logical ground, because many States, especially those that do not possess chemical weapons, would not be willing to give all the assurances of compliance with their disarmament and non-proliferation commitments under the Convention - by means of declarations and inspections - if, at the same time, they would be subject to trade restrictions as if they were not abiding by the Convention. Article XI is even more explicit thereon than Article X of the Biological Weapons Convention."[99]

After having made clear that non-restriction of free trade is crucial to the Convention, Brazil then concludes in a rather sharply-worded warning that all commitments have a similar binding character, are equal, and that some cannot be treated as a bit more equal than others:

> "The provisions of international treaties are not to be divided into "more important" and "less important", "hard" and "soft" ones. Once the Convention is in force, States Parties that do not comply with a given provision, including those contained in Article XI, will be violating the Convention."[100]

Against this position it is held that there is no positive duty under the CWC to disband the Australia Group, and neither is there any positive obligation to trade in any chemical that some State Party might demand or to share any technological know how. The CWC, so goes the argument, does not foresee a centrally controlled think-tank or stock, which would anyhow be contrary to the very idea of a free market.

Another counter argument used by Australia Group members stresses that the non-proliferation of chemical weapons, and under the BWC the same with regard to biological weapons, is one of the most important provisions under

---

[99] "In case there is a suspicion of non-compliance by an importing State Party, the exporting country that is also a Party to the Convention should bring the issue to the attention of the Executive Council of the Organization. This is not a question which demands unilateral action and should not be treated as a trade issue. On the contrary, suspicion of non-compliance is a question that affects the security concerns of all States Parties to the Convention". And "In other words, a parallel export control regime with schedules and scope exceeding those of the Convention is only admissible if applied and oriented to States not Parties to the Convention. Of course, these States, which voluntarily insist on remaining outside the Convention regime, cannot have recourse to the free trade assurances contained therein". Statement by the delegation of Brazil, at the XIIIth Plenary Session (March 1996) of the Preparatory Commission for the Organization for the Prohibition of Chemical Weapons.

[100] Statement by the delegation of Brazil, *ibid*.

these treaties.[101] Smithson refers to Article XI that "[..]clearly stipulates that efforts to enhance free trade among treaty parties must not be "incompatible with the obligations undertaken under this Convention". She then points to the non-proliferation commitment in Article I of the Convention and concludes that "this wording allows the Australia Group and other unilateral exports controls intended to stem the proliferation of chemical weapons to continue since they are "wholly compatible" with the CWC's principle objectives".[102] The least that can be said against this argument is that the export controls of the Australia Group that are directed at the same non-proliferation goal are not incompatible, but that maintaining them amongst States Parties is not logical for it questions the (effectiveness of the) very non-proliferation system of the CWC with its verification system, by arranging for an additional non-proliferation system alongside the CWC's system. The argument that export controls are integral to the operation of the CWC appears fallacious as the export controls included in the Convention all concern non-State Parties.

What seems reasonable, however, is that until full compliance with the Convention has been assessed and established it would be unrealistic to force States Parties to work on the – unverified - assumption that universal compliance is already in its place from the very first day of the entry into force. Only when it appears that there is full compliance will a review of the respective national regulations in the field of trade in chemicals "to render them consistent with the object and purpose of this Convention"[103] seem imperative, or in the words of what was stated on behalf of the Australia Group, namely, the intent to review its export control policy toward those states that comply fully with the CWC.[104] That such may be a difficult process is apparent from the position taken by the US Senate in its elaborate condition "7" regarding the Australian Group and national export controls as contained in the ratification resolution, whereby it even declared "that the collapse of the informal forum of states known as the "Australia Group", would amount to a fundamental change in circumstances affecting the object and purpose of the Convention",[105] which

[101] Smithson, *supra* n. 94, at 23-24.

[102] Smithson, *ibid*, at 27.

[103] Article XI 2(e).

[104] CD/PV.629 (Geneva: 6 August 1992)(16-7) in Smithson *supra* n. 94, at 20. In this vain the Dutch government stated as regards Article XI that it is being interpreted by members of the Australia Group so that in future, when it appears that States Parties appear to completely comply with their treaty obligations, then export controls that were not based on the treaty, may be either eased or terminated. *Memorie van Toelichting*, Tweede Kamer 1994-1995, 23 910 (R.15 15), nr 3 at 41.

[105] "[..](7). *Continuing Vitality of the Australia Group and National Export Controls. - (A) Declaration.* - The Senate declares that the collapse of the informal forum of states known as the "Australia Group", either through changes in membership or lack of compliance with common export controls, or the substantial weakening of common Australia Group export controls and non-proliferation measures in force on the date of United States ratification would constitute a fundamental change in circumstances affecting the object and purpose of

clearly refers to the doctrine of *rebus sic stantibus*[106] as a ground to be invoked for terminating or withdrawing from the CWC.

4. Supervision

Crucial to the operation of the Convention is an intricate system devised to ensure compliance. In this supervisory system the specially established international organization, the Organization for the Prohibition of Chemical Weapons (OPCW),[107] occupies a central role. Furthermore, States Parties will have to cooperate closely by providing, for instance, declarations, information and clarification. The basic rules for the operation of compliance control can be found in Article VIII on the OPCW, in Article IX on consulation, cooperation and fact-finding, in Article XII on measures to ensure compliance and in the Annex on Verification and the Confidentiality Annex. Supervision not only concerns the destruction of weapons and weapons facillities, but also the production of chemicals.

In order to allow for compliance control of the core obligations to destroy existing chemical weapons, including old and abandoned chemical weapons, and production facilities, first of all an inventory of these weapons, and production and destruction facilities is in order. States Parties will therefore have to start by declaring to the OPCW the "state of affairs" with regard to chemical weapons, and chemical weapons related matters. Such an inventory is also essential to allow for compliance control of future non-production, also when existing stocks and production facilities have not yet been destroyed after the projected 10-year period. For these inventory purposes States Parties will have to declare within 30 days after the entry into force of the Convention whether they own or possess chemical weapons and to indicate the "location, aggregate quantity and detailed inventory"[108] and declare the same with regard to chemical weapons production facilities.[109] These declarations will have to

the Convention". Furthermore is interesting - (B) *Certification requirement*. - Prior to the deposit of the United States instrument of ratification, the President shall certify to Congress that-[..](iii) the Convention preserves the right of State Parties, unilaterally or collectively , to maintain or impose export controls on chemicals and related chemical production technology for foreign policy or national security reasons, notwithstanding Article XI(2); and (iv) each Australia Group member, at the highest diplomatic levels, has communicated to the United States Government its understanding and agreement that export control and non-proliferation measures which the Australia Group has undertaken are fully compatible with the provisions of the Convention, including Article XI(2), and its commitment to maintain in the future such export controls and non-proliferation measures against non-Australia Group members" [...], Ratification Resolution, April 24, 1997, *Congressional Record Senate*, at S3653.

106 As expressed in Article 62 of the Vienna Convention on the Law of Treaties.

107 Article VIII.

108 Article III 1(a); Verification Annex, Part IV (A).

109 Article III 1(c); Verification Annex, Part V.

contain a general plan "for the destruction" of the chemical weapons".[110] For old and abandoned weapons there is a special regime.[111] With regard to the weapons' production facilities the declaration will have to "provide its general plan for the destruction " of any chemical production facility, "specify actions to be taken for the closure of any chemical weapons production facility" and "provide its general plan for any temporary conversion" into a chemical weapons destruction facility.[112] With regard to the destruction of chemical weapons *per se* Article IV provides detailed procedures and Article V does so with regard to the chemical weapons production facilities. A detailed *Declaration Handbook* has been developed providing detailed explanations as well as instructions for the completion of initial, annual and other declarations.[113]

The implementation of the core-obligations - destruction or conversion of weapons production facilities - will be carried out under the close scrutiny of the OPCW, which at this stage introduces the Verification Annex. To begin with, "physical" supervision already starts immediately after the declaration phase, for States Parties will immediately have to "provide access to chemical weapons specified" for the purpose of "systematic verification of the declaration through on-site inspection" by inspectors of the OPCW. This is also the case in the period before destruction because for purposes of systematic on-site verification access will have to be provided. The destruction will have to start within two years after entry into force and will have to have been completed not later than 10 years after entry into force.[114] Detailed plans for the destruction will have to be submitted not later than 60 days before each annual destruction period begins. States Parties will have to make declarations regarding the implementation of these plans and after the destruction process has been completed.[115]

With regard to chemical weapons that are owned or possessed by another State Party a State Party "shall make the fullest efforts to ensure that these chemical weapons are removed from its territory not later than one year" after

---

[110] Article III 1 para. (v).

[111] Old chemical weapons produced before 1925: Article III 1 (b)(i); Verification Annex, Part IV (B). Old chemical weapons produced between 1925-1946 that have deteriorated to such an extent that they can no longer be used as chemical weapons (Article II 5 (b)): Article III 1 (b)(i); Verification Annex, Part IV (B). Abandoned chemical weapons: Article III 1(b)(ii)(iii); Verification Annex, Part IV (B).

[112] Article III 1(c) (v), (vi) and (vii) respectively.

[113] Declaration Handbook for the Convention on the Prohibition of the Development, Production, Stockpiling and Use of Chemical Weapons and on their Destruction, PTS-OPCW, revised 1996-11-14 with appendices to sections A, B, and C and Section F. (Declaration/information concerning old chemical weapons produced between 1925-1946) (draft 17 March 1997).

[114] Article IV, para. 6.

[115] Article IV, para. 7.

the entry into force of the CWC (Article IV, para. 11). The arrangements in Article V with regard to chemical weapons production facilities are structured along the same lines of Article IV concerning chemical weapons. Central of course is the States Parties' duty "to cease immediately all activity" at these plants[116] and start destruction within one year and to finish it not later than 10 years after entry into force. These facilities may, however, temporarily be converted into destruction facilities. "In exceptional cases of compelling need" the Conference of States Parties may allow chemical weapons production facilities to be used for purposes not prohibited under the Convention. All converted facilities shall be subject to systematic verification (V para. 15).

Chapter IV of this contribution deals with the institutional aspects of the OPCW, whereas its functions will be analyzed in chapter V. Both the Convention and its Verification Annex foresee detailed arrangements regarding verification in this respect. As Perry Robinson, however, rightly points out the verification measures set out in the Convention cover only a fraction of the prohibitions enunciated in Article I (1).[117] This leads him to remark that "responsibility for overseeing compliance with the remaining fraction must therefore fall to the individual States parties".[118]

5. *Final clauses*

Of the remaining clauses Article XIII concerns the relationship between the CWC, the 1925 Geneva Protocol and the Biological Weapons Convention, respectively. It stipulates that nothing in the CWC shall be interpreted as in any way limiting or detracting from the obligations assumed by States under the other mentioned instruments.

Article XIV deals with the settlement of disputes concerning "the application or the interpretation" of the CWC. This clause will be dealt with more extensively in para. 6 of Chapter IV.

Article XV concerns the ammendment procedures.

For the Convention and for its Annexes different amendment procedures are applicable, namely *amendments* and *changes* respectively.[119] In the Annexes we find the regulations with regard to the technical and administrative details, which need to be able to be changed relatively easily. In order "to ensure the viability and the effectiveness"[120] of the Convention it therefore foresees a "light" procedure for such proposed changes. Proposed changes of an

---

[116] Article V, para. 4.

[117] J.P. Perry Robinson, The Verification System For The Chemical Weapons Convention, in: Bardonnet (ed.), *supra* n. 4, at 492.

[118] Perry Robinson, *ibid*, at 492.

[119] See Article XV, para. 1.

[120] Article XV, para. 4.

"administrative or technical nature"[121] will be examined thoroughly both by the Director-General for its "possible consequences for the provisions of the CWC and by the Executive Council".[122] If the Executive Council recommends to all States Parties that the proposal be adopted "it shall be considered approved if no State Party objects to it within 90 days after receipt of the recommendation".[123] Changes in the Annexes that are not of an administrative or technical nature need to be made via *amendments*[124] as well as all changes to the Convention. The CWC amendment procedure is special in that it has tried to find a balance between the normal rule that amendments do not bind States Parties that did not participate in amending the treaty and the application to all States Parties of amendments accepted by majorities.[125] Amendments to the Convention shall therefore enter into force when they have been adopted at the Amendment Conference by a positive vote of a majority of all States Parties, with no State Party casting a negative vote and when accepted or ratified by the States Parties casting a positive vote.[126]

This amendment procedure of Article XV CWC therefore "will bind all States Parties, none of them against its declared will, with a requirement for ratification modified to the extent that it applies only to States Parties demonstrating an active interest in the procedure."[127]

Of the remaining articles Article XVII concerns the status of the Annexes, which form an integral part of the Convention, and Article XXII stipulates that the Articles of the Convention are not subject to reservations and that the Annexes shall "not be subject to reservations incompatible with its object and purpose". This leaves Article XVI (Duration and withdrawal), Article XVIII (Signature), Article XIX (Ratification), Article XX (Accession), Article XXI (Entry into force) and the three annexes that have been dealt with so far: the Annex on Chemicals; the Annex on Implementation and Verification (Verification Annex) and the Annex on the Protection of Confidential Information (Confidentiality Annex). The Annex on Chemicals contains the guidelines for

---

[121] Sections A and C of the Confidentiality Annex , Part X of the Verification Annex, and those definitions in Part I of the Verification Annex which relate exclusively to challenge inspections, are excluded from this "light" procedure. See Article XV (4).

[122] Article XV, para. 5 (a)-(d).

[123] "If the Executive Council recommends that the proposal be rejected, it shall be considered rejected if no State Party objects to the rejection within 90 days after receipt of the recommendation", Article XV, para. 5(d).

[124] Krutzsch et al., *supra* n. 4, at 242 comments that "all modifications of the Articles and such modifications of the of the Annexes which are of a more than administrative or technical nature shall be made by amendments". He thereby incorrectly suggests that also changes with regard to the Convention would be possible via the "light" procedure.

[125] See Krutzsch et al., *ibid*, at 241.

[126] See Article XV, especially paras. 1-3.

[127] Krutzsch et al., *supra* n. 4, at 241.

schedules of chemicals as well as the actual schedules of chemicals themselves. The Verification Annex has already been referred to extensively and details the rules relating to the inspections, declarations and so on. It is a sizable document more than twice the size of the Convention. The special case of the Confidentiality Annex with its Confidentiality Commission will be dealt with in Chapter IV paragraph 6 (ii) concerning dispute settlement.

IV. The OPCW: the institutional aspects

1. General functions

Under Article VIII of the CWC States Parties are to establish an international organization - the Organization for the Prohibition of Chemical Weapons (OPCW) - in order to:

> "achieve the object and purpose of this Convention, to ensure the implementation of its provisions, including those for international verification of compliance with it, and to provide a forum for consultation and cooperation among States Parties".[128]

Of these functions the verification of compliance with the core obligations of the Convention is the central one. Running "[..] the most comprehensive verification regime ever devised for a global treaty" will be one of the principal tasks of the OPCW.[129] It is for that reason that the OPCW could be typified as a specialized "single-purpose"[130] organization, the purpose being the implementation of the Convention,[131] with the very specifically related purpose of supervision. That function will be analyzed in Chapter V. This Chapter aims to focus on the institutional framework of this international organization. In order to be able to appraise the special character of the OPCW as an international organization *per se,* this Chapter will focus on some aspects of the institutional structure that all international organizations have in common, namely *the constitution* (para. 2); *membership* (para. 3); *the organs* (para. 4); *legal personality* (para. 5); *decision making* (para. 6); *privileges and immunities* (para. 7) and *dispute settlement* (para. 8). In these paragraphs also some other aspects (inter alia Headquarters Agreement and liability) will also be touched upon.

---

[128] Article VIII, para. 1.

[129] Terrence Taylor, The Chemical Weapons Convention and Prospects for Implementation, 42 *International and Comparative Law Quarterly*, October 1993, at 912.

[130] T. Bernauer, The Organization for the Prohibition of Chemical Weapons (OPCW): Structured, Functions, and Potential Deficiencies, in: Bardonnet (ed.), *supra* n. 4, at 334. Compare also footnote 7.

[131] Compare Krutzsch et al., *supra* n. 4, at 128.

2.The Constitution and the comptences of the organs

The Constitution of the OPCW is contained in Article VIII of the CWC. This means that the CWC general amendment procedure also applies to Article VIII. Also the general rules of treaty interpretation will apply to the Constitution, although the ICJ made it clear in its advisory opinion on the WHO that the constituent treaty of an international organization "can raise specific problems of interpretation "owing, *inter alia*, to their character which is conventional and at the same time institutional".[132] This may lead to special attention when interpreting these constituent treaties.[133] However, given the clear wording of the Convention, its context and object and purpose, it is not expected that problems shall arise with regard to the determination of compteneces. Furthermore, as far as the supplementary means of interpretation are concerned, documentation abounds as regards the preparatory work of the Convention. The experience so far regarding the competences of the organs does not suggest that they have been formulated too narrowly or that there are any grey areas. It therefore seems unlikely that in the near future the doctrine of implied power needs to be applied in order to define more clearly the powers of principal organs. Perphaps also the fact that the OPCW is not a general purpose organization like the United Nations has contributed to this clear delimitation of these competences, for the object and purpose of the CWC are quite clear: banning chemical weapons.

As regards the Convention, one could, however, witness during the PrepCom phase a curious process that may have led to a creeping shift in reading and interpreting its terms and thereby also the Constitution and consequently the competences of the organs. It concerns a process that cannot be explained away as the mere practice of the organization (to be). For some of the participating States Parties were not at the time reading and interpreting the terms of the CWC in accordance with the clear "ordinary meaning to be given to the terms of the treaty in their context and in the light of its object and purpose",[134] but rather used the principle of consensus[135] as a bargaining tool in deciding almost routinely on any issue, like the ones mentioned in the Paris Resolution that had to be decided upon within the framework of the text of the

---

[132] Legality of the use by a state of nuclear weapons in armed conflict (WHO/Nuclear Weapons case), International Court of Justice, Advisory Opnion, 8 July 1996, para. 19.

[133]"...the very nature of the organization created, the objectives which have been assigned to it by its founders, the imperatives associated with the effective performance of its functions, as well as its own practice, are all elements which may deserve special attention when the time comes to interpret these constituent treaties". *Ibid.*

[134] Art. 31 The Vienna Convention on the Law of Treaties.

[135] "All decisions of the Commission should be taken by consensus", Art. 6 The Paris Resolution, *supra* n. 70.

Convention.[136] The Paris Resolution, establishing the PrepCom for the OPCW, describes in detail its tasks which are as diverse as the drafting of "staff rules for recruitment and service conditions" for the personnel of the Technical Secretariat, and the development of draft agreements, provisions and guidelines, such as detailed procedures for verification and for conducting inspections.

By constantly doing this during a preparation process lasting four years, whereby States had to seek agreement on the basis of consensus, unavoidably some compromises crept in, thereby watering down, or changing some of the clear intentions of the States that had agreed to the Convention in 1992. Some of the issues that would appear uncontestable but that according to the Final Report of the PrepCom remained unresolved[137] are illustrative of this process. Take, for instance, the fact that there was no agreement on "the timing of the notification of challenge inspections".[138] According to Article IX, paragraph 15 the Director-General "shall transmit the inspection request to the inspected State Party not less than 12 hours before the planned arrival of the inspection team". The stalemate was caused by the position taken, on the one hand, by States like Iran, India, China and Pakistan, that were of the opinion that there should be earlier notification, for reasons like national holidays or time-zones, with, on the other hand, the postition taken by States like France, Germany, the US, the UK and the Netherlands that notification had to take place in a non-discriminatory manner.

The effect of this process is that the so-called "ordinary meaning" of the Convention is encroachingly being reread in the light of these compromises, thereby effectively reinterpreting the Convention, and thereby also the Constitution of the OPCW. From the point of view of the competences of the organs of the OPCW this development is important to note, as the work in the PrepCom extensively dealt with rules of procedure involving the Technical

---

[136] Illustrative in this respect was an attempt by a few States - Cuba, India, Pakistan and Iran - to hold the adoption of a Draft Final Report of the PrepCom hostage in order to have included in this document not only agreed texts on the issues referred to in the Paris resolution, but also the respective arguments for not agreeing on certain issues. As a result of this attitude the Committee on Preparations for the First Session of the Conference of the States Parties could not agree by consensus on the adoption of such a report, to be approved by the plenary PrepCom in order to present it to the First Conference of States Parties. There was also no agreement on the inclusion in the document of what had already been agreed upon by consensus at the previous fifteen plenary meetings of the PrepCom. Finally, at the final PrepCom a compromise was agreed upon to have included in the Final Document a mere reference to the outstanding issues, as had already been previously suggested during the Committee phase. Compare also Smithson, *supra* n.134, at 6, describing a previous attempt by Pakistan to hold the CWC, as then negotiated, hostage for national policy reasons.

[137] Final Report of the Preparatory Commission for the Organization for the Prohibition of Chemical Weapons to the First Session of the Conference of States Parties and to the First Meeting of the Executive Council, Section Four, unresolved issues pp. 47-53, PC-XVI/37.

[138] *Ibid*, 123, p. 53.

Secretariat or the Executive Council. Sometimes it appeared that pre-Geneva debates were again being opened up. From the point of view of the building phase (gestation period) of an international organization this could be looked upon as merely interesting practice. This process of changing by interpretation the terms of the CWC and thereby also the Constitution of the OPCW took place in a PrepCom that could not be regarded as a "provisional organ", but with "legal capacity" and being something more than a negotiating body. Remarkable, however, is that it concerns a body that was composed of all the signatories, including those that might have no intention whatsoever of ratifying (they already knew that they could not or would not do so), or at least for an indeterminate period like Israel. These latter signatories, in other words, could leave their mark, although it is difficult to pinpoint exactly where. The counter-argument that whatever the case may be, in the end it would be the First Conference of States Parties that would take the formal decisions, is fallacious, for the First Conference could not in two weeks go to the same length as the PrepCom had done in the four years of its operation.[139]

Even if via the "light" amendment procedure changes are brought about in one of the Annexes, it is not to be expected that this would lead to an extension of the powers of the OPCW organs, for all modifications to the Annexes which are more than of an administrative or technical nature have to be made by amendment.[140] The only area in which the OPCW seems to have some room for manoeuvre is in the question of Article X (assistance and protection against chemical weapons).

3. Membership

The principal aim of the negotiators in the Conference on Disarmament was to produce a treaty banning chemical weapons that would be universally acceptable. The OPCW is consequently an open organization. Given the large number of States Parties and of Signatory States[141] to this Convention they have undoubtedly succeeded in this aim of universality. It led, however, in the words of Taylor, to "an element of flexibility, or some would say constructive ambiguity, built into the text without which the Convention would not have been concluded".[142]

---

[139] The same tendency could be seen regarding the issues that could not be resolved during the PrepCom phase (unresolved issues) like equipment-related issues. The Conference adopted the list of approved equipment "in the understanding that the issues contained in paras. 118 and 119 of the Final Report of the PrepCom remain unresolved for the time being", C-I/DEC.71, 23 May 1997.

[140] See Article XV, para. 4 and Krutzsch et al., *supra* n. 4, at 242. Also see Chapter III, para. 5.

[141] As of September 2000 there are 139 States Parties and 35 Signatory States.

[142] Taylor *supra* n. 129, at 913.

All States Parties to the Convention are automatically members of the OPCW. There is therefore no special procedure for a State's admission to membership.[143] The CWC explicitly makes clear that no State Party shall be deprived of its membership.[144] With Krutzsch I am also of the opinion that this also excludes any suspension of membership, for a suspension might have the very negative effect that States Parties wanted to prevent in the first place by excluding deprivation of membership,[145] namely non-universal application of the Convention.[146] Given the object and purpose of this Convention – the total disappearance of chemical weapons - it is clear that this can only be achieved via universal membership. Therefore under no circumstances could it be possible for States Parties to be deprived of their membership as a sanction, for instance for non-payment by a member of its financial contribution, or non-compliance with any other obligation.[147] A different thing altogether is that a State Party may maintain its right to withdraw from the Convention "if it decides that extraordinary events, related to the subject-matter of the Convention, have jeopardized the supreme interests of its country."[148] In the absence of such a clause it could have been held that a State Party would have no right to withdraw from the organization.[149]

4. The Organs of the OPCW

The OPCW has the following organs: the Conference of the States Parties, the Executive Council and the Technical Secretariat.

(i) The Conference of the States Parties

The Conference is the plenary organ of the OPCW and is composed of all members of the Organization. It is the representative organ of the Organization in which all of its members are represented on an equal footing. It meets

[143] Krutzsch et al., *supra* n. 4, at 128.

[144] Article VIII(A)(2).

[145] Krutzsch et al., *supra* n. 4, at 128.

[146] Compare also "Determined [...] to exclude completely the possibility of the use of chemical weapons, through the implementation of the provisions of this Convention [...]" (preamble).

[147] "The rationale for this provision is: a State Party, insensitive for the Organization's urgent appeals to bring itself into compliance with provisions of the Convention, might if stripped of membership, falsely conclude that it was free from obligations undertaken under the convention. In addition, an organization which by virtue of its existence has to strive towards universal adherence, would by a policy of expulsion defeat its main purpose", Krutzsch et al., *ibid*, at 128.

[148] Article XVI, para. 2.

[149] See: H.G. Schermers & N.M. Blokker, *International Institutional Law* (1995), pp. 91-94; N.D. White, *The Law of International Organizations* (1996), at 63.

annually in regular sessions and may furthermore meet in special sessions, for instance at the request of the Executive Council.[150]

It is the principal organ of the Organization.[151] It oversees the implementation of the Convention, and acts in order to promote its object and purpose.[152] In particular, it shall,

> "[t]ake the necessary measures to ensure compliance with this Convention and to redress and remedy any situation which contravenes the provisions of this Convention, in accordance with Article XII"[153]

It is therefore important to note that the Conference is allowed to establish such subsidiary organs as it finds necessary for the exercise of its functions in accordance with the CWC.[154] It oversees, furthermore, the activities of the Executive Council and the Technical Secretariat and may issue guidelines in accordance with the CWC to either of them.[155] "[..]It may make recommendations and take decisions on any questions, matters or issues related to the Convention raised by a State Party or brought to its attention by the Executive Council".[156] The CWC sums up a number of other decisions which the Conference has to take, such as: consideration and adoption of the report, programme and budget of the OPCW,[157] appointment of the Director-General of the Technical Secretariat,[158] election of the members of the Executive Council.[159] Decisions to be taken that stand out are those that it had to consider and approve at its first session, like any draft agreements, provisions and guidelines developed by the PrepCom.

The Conference is furthermore called upon to hold, at regular intervals, review conferences to review the operation of the CWC, taking into account any relevant scientific and technological developments.[160] It is clear from the Convention that the Conference is the authoritative forum to decide upon extraordinary questions or to overcome specific crisis situations connected with compliance disputes.[161]

---

[150] Article VIII, para. 12.
[151] Article VIII, para. 19.
[152] Article VIII, para. 20.
[153] Article VIII, para. 21(k).
[154] Article VIII, para. 21(f).
[155] Article VIII, para. 20.
[156] Article VIII, para. 19.
[157] Article VIII, para. 21(a).
[158] Article VIII, para. 21(d).
[159] Article VIII, para. 21(c).
[160] Article VIII, para. 22.
[161] Krutzsch et al., *supra* n. 4, at 136 (in particular footnote 3). See under Chapter V. In particular see Articles V, para. 13; VIII, paras. 21 (k), 36; IX, paras. 7, 23, 24, 25; XII; XIV paras. 4, 5; Verification Annex: Part IV (A), 22, 26, 34, 58; Part V, 39, 68, 75, 82.

(ii)The Executive Council

The Executive Council is the executive organ of the OPCW with limited membership, which is responsible to the Conference. Its composition was a main point of discussion during the negotiations.[162] A balance had to be struck between the need for a small body that could act effectively and the wish of States Parties to sit frequently on the Council. Furthermore, the interests of States with extensive chemical industries had to be taken into account. Therefore it was decided to have the relatively high number of members, namely 41, to be divided under the five regional groups, taking into account States Parties with the most significant chemical industries. These general principles can be found in paragraph 23 of Article VIII: "In order to ensure the effective functioning of this Convention, due regard being specially paid to equitable geographical distribution, to the importance of chemical industry, as well as to political and security interests [..]". This leads to a mix of regional representation - nine from Africa, nine from Asia, five from Eastern Europe, seven from Latin America and the Caribbean and ten from among Western Europe and other States Parties located in this region. Of these, 41 seats, respectively three, four, one, three, and five shall be the ones "with the most significant national chemical industry in the region".[163] Each State Party has the right, in accordance with the principle of rotation, to serve on the Council. They shall be selected for a period of two years. The Composition and decision-making of the Executive Council "has perhaps been the most controversial and sensitive issue of the negotiations".[164] The final result is built upon the "main elements identified in previous discussions" like the "right of all members to serve on the Board, rotation, election, equitable geographical distribution, importance of chemical industry as well as political and security interests".[165] Krutzsch points to the importance of the PrepCom phase for the smooth functioning of the provisions.[166]

Interestingly, the CWC contains a provision that allows the Conference to review the composition of the Executive Council "taking into account developments related to the principles specified in paragraph 23".[167] Given the

[162] Tweede Kamer, *supra* n. 104, no. 3, p. 34.

[163] Article VIII, para. 23.

[164] Krutzsch et al., *supra* n. 4, at 148. "Although it was the subject of discussions for many years, the efforts to arrive at a balanced and generally acceptable compromise had to be continued until the last minute."

[165] *Ibid*, at 149.

[166] "Since these elements and their interrelationship are not clearly defined, the interpretation of their meaning by common understanding, gentleman's agreement and established practice, starting during the preparation period, will be crucial for the smooth functioning of this provision", *ibid*, at 149.

[167] Article VIII, para. 25. It could be questioned, however, whether this provision allows for

central role of the Executive Council with its substantional powers, one may assume this to be a matter of substance, which therefore in principle has to be decided upon by consensus.

The Executive Council shall carry out the powers and functions entrusted to it under the CWC, as well as those functions delegated to it by the Conference. It shall do so "in conformity with the recommendations, decisions and guidelines of the Conference and assure their proper and continuous implementation."[168] The Council shall promote the effective implementation of the CWC and compliance with it and shall furthermore supervise the activities of the Technical Secretariat, cooperate with the National Authority of each State Party and facilitate consultations and cooperation among the States Parties at their request.[169] Not surprisingly the CWC puts great emphasis on the central role of the Executive Council with regard to questions of compliance and non-compliance.[170] The Executive Council shall consult with the States Parties involved and as appropriate "request the State Party to take measures to redress the situation within a specified time". In case it considers further action to be necessary it shall decide on which measure to take, like informing all States Parties of the issue or matter; bringing the issue or matter to the attention of the Conference or making recommendations to the Conference regarding measures to redress the situation and to ensure compliance.[171] As will be discussed[172] the Executive Council may also bring the issue to the attention of the UN General Assembly and the UN Security Council in cases of "particular gravity and urgency".[173] Another important task of the Executive Council is its role in relation to the conclusion of arrangements and agreements. For it is the Executive Council which shall, on behalf of the OPCW, and subject to the prior approval of the Conference, conclude agreements and arrangements with States and International Organizations.[174] It shall conclude agreements with States Parties concerning the procurement of assistance as foreseen under Article X. It will also have to approve the agreements or arrangements relating to the implementation of verification activities as negotiated by the Technical Secretariat

a change in the composition via the normal rules of decision-making. According to Krutzsch and Trapp an amendment procedure is still necessary: "Amendments of its text must be subject to the procedure generally provided for in Article XV. Paragraph 25 does not dispense with this article", *supra* n. 4 at 152. The contrary argument, however, is why provide in detail for this specific possibility and criteria if it is not meant as an exception to the amendment rule, but as a normal case of amendment. In the latter case this reference is superfluous.

[168] Article VIII, para. 30.

[169] Article VIII, para. 31.

[170] Article VIII, para. 35.

[171] Article VIII, para. 36 (a)(b) and (c).

[172] See under Chapter V, the correction function.

[173] Article VIII, para. 36, final section.

[174] Article VIII, para. 34 (a).

with the States Parties.[175] Like any serious executive body it will also take care of technical matters like submitting to the Conference the draft programme and budget of the OPCW[176] or the draft report of the OPCW on the implementation of the CWC.[177]

(iii)The Technical Secretariat

The Technical Secretariat is the substantial and permanent body which is subordinated to the Conference and the Executive Council[178] and which foresees the necessary technical and administrative know how.[179] Since the Inspectorate is a unit of the Technical Secretariat,[180] it manages the inspection teams. It is the centre for receiving declarations[181] and takes care of the initial and routine inspections. It assesses reports and generally keeps an ear to the ground. The Technical Secretariat, in short, embodies the OPCW as an organization.

> "The Technical Secretariat shall assist the Conference and the Executive Council in the performance of their functions. The Technical Secretariat shall carry out the verification measures provided for in this Convention [..] as well as those functions delegated to it by the Conference and the Executive Council."[182]

The Technical Secretariat shall inform the Executive Council of, inter alia, doubts, ambiguities or uncertainties concerning compliance with this Convention that have come to its notice in the performance of its verification activities and that it has been unable to resolve or clarify through its consultations with thc State Party concerned.[183] Furthermore, it shall negotiate agreements or arrangements relating to the implementation of verification activities with States Parties. It will also play a central and coordinating role with regard to the provision of assistance under Article X of the Convention.[184] Since, according to Bernauer, the functions of the Technical Secretariat were rather vaguely specified in the treaty text, much was left to the PrepCom and the Provisional Technical Secretariat (PTS).[185] In his opinion the problem with regard to the Secretariat pertains not so much to technical issues, but concerns

175 Article VIII, para. 34 (c).

176 Article VIII, para. 32.

177 As well as the report on the performance of its own activities and all such special reports as it deems necessary, or which the Conference requests.(Article VIII, paragraph 32 (b)).

178 Article VIII, D, para. 37.

179 See in general Article VIII paras 38 and 39.

180 Article VIII, para. 42.

181 Article VII, para. 38 (c).

182 Article VIII, para. 37.

183 Article VIII, para. 40.

184 Article VIII, para. 39.

185 Bernauer, *supra* n. 130, at 340.

"the degree to which the Secretariat will be able to act independently and in an activist manner".[186]

The Technical Secretariat shall be headed by a Director-General,[187] who is responsible to the Conference and the Executive Council for the appointment of the staff and the organization of the Technical Secretariat. The Inspectorate shall act under the supervision of the Director-General. The Director-General fulfils an important role with regard to the handling and protection of confidential information.[188]

5. Decisions and decision- making

The two essential types of decisions are the ones taken by the Conference, as the prime representative organ, and those by the Executive Council. Of these two categories of decisions the ones by the Conference are the most important ones, for the Conference not only has the general task of overseeing the implementation of the Convention, it also oversees the activities of the Executive Council and the Technical Secretariat and may issue guidelines in accordance with the CWC to either of them in the exercise of their functions.[189] Furthermore, it elects the members of the Executive Council and appoints the Director-General.[190] The Conference decides on procedural questions by a simple majority of the members present and voting.[191] Matters of substance "should be taken, as far as possible, by consensus". If consensus is not attainable, the Chairman shall defer any vote for 24 hours. During this period he shall do his utmost to facilitate the attaining of consensus. Within this period he shall report to the Conference. If no consensus can be reached at the end of the 24-hour period a majority decision will be taken if the Convention does not specify otherwise. This decision shall be taken by "a two-thirds majority of

---

186 "... that is, to what extent the Secretariat can or will lobby Governments to join the Convention; what role it will play in the process of initiating inspections and evaluating their results; how it will deal with cases where Parties provide incomplete or no information on their relevant behaviour; and how it will handle cases of various forms on non-compliance". Bernauer, *ibid*, at 340.

187 Article VIII, para. 41.

188 The Director-General shall have prime responsibility for ensuring the protection of confidential information and shall establish a stringent regime governing the handling of confidential information by the Technical Secretariat (Confidentiality Annex (A)(2)): See more in particular the Confidentiality Annex and *infra* paragraph 6 (ii) (p 99 et seq.) the case of the Confidentiality Commission.

189 Article VII, para. 20.

190 Article VIII, para. 21 (c), (d).

191 Article VIII, para. 18. Also under the CTBT the Conference of the States Parties of the Comprehensive Nuclear Test-Ban Treaty Organization (CTBTO) (Article II, para. 22). Different is that the adjective "simple" before the word "majority" has been omitted, perhaps a sign that it has become the standard procedure!

members present and voting".[192] The Executive Council shall take decisions on matters of substance by a two-thirds majority of all its members.[193] Decisions on questions of procedure shall be taken by a simple majority of all its members.[194] Decisions taken in accordance with the Convention are binding on the Member States. Remarkable is the fact that two of the organs (including its most important one) of an international organization in the sphere of national (military) security are allowed to take majority decisions! Even more remarkable is that under Article IX, paragraph 17 of the Convention, decisions of the Council *against* carrying out a challenge inspection shall be made by a three-quarters majority of all its members.[195] The required greater majority to block a challenge inspection underlines the central importance that is being attached to this element of challenge inspection. This is understandable because the possibility of a challenge inspection was crucial in order to have the Convention agreed upon in the first place. Furthermore, it underlines the non-discriminatory nature of this Convention by allowing a single vote at both levels for each State Party represented.[196] All of these innovative institutional elements were obviously included in the CWC in order to stimulate universal accession to the Convention, which is essential from the point of view of effective arms control.[197]

6. *Dispute settlement*

(i)General

Although the Convention's central dispute settlement clause as contained in Article XIV was mentioned above[198] and dispute settlement will also be touched upon in Chapter V concerning the creative function, given the central

---

[192] Article VIII, para. 18. Also under the CTBT the Conference of the States Parties of the CTBTO (Article II, para. 22).

[193] Article VIII, para. 29. Accordingly rule 36 of the Rules of Procedure of the Executive Council, C-I/DEC.72, 23 May 1997. Also under the CTBT the Executive Council of the CTBTO (Article II, para. 36).

[194] Article VIII, para. 29. Also under the CTBT the Executive Council of the CTBTO (Article II, para. 36). Different is that the adjective "simple" in front of "majority" has been omitted like is the case with the Conference, see *supra* n.191.

[195] Rule 38 of the Rules of Procedure of the Executive Council, C-I/DEC.72, 23 May 1997.

[196] A member of the Council that is in arrears in the payment of its contribution to the OPCW, however, shall have no vote in the Council "if the amount of its arrears equals or exceeds the amount of the contribution due from it for the preceding two full years unless the Conference permits such a member to vote in accordance with Article VIII, para. 8 of the Convention", rule 35 Rules of Procedure Executive Council, C-I/DEC.72, 23 May 1997.

[197] Compare "general and complete disarmament under strict and effective international control".

[198] See p. 86.

role of the Executive Council and the Conference a few more words are in order in the context of the institutional framework of the OPCW. Article XIV deals with the settlement of disputes concerning "the application or the interpretation"[199] of the CWC. When there is a dispute between States Parties, or between one or more States Parties and the Organization, they shall consult together with a view to the expeditious settlement of the dispute via negotiation or by other peaceful means" of their choice. This apparently refers to the methods of Article 33 of the UN Charter, or more generally to Chapter VI, given the general reference in paragraph 1 of Article XIV to the duty to settle disputes in conformity with the provisions of the Charter. They can furthermore involve the organs of the OPCW and, by mutual consent, submit the dispute to the adjudication of the ICJ.[200] This clause appears to refer to dispute settlement related to treaty technicalities and not to compliance issues. The point of departure is therefore that the above mentioned disputes shall be settled in conformity with the provisions of the UN Charter, in other words via the peaceful settlement techniques contained in Article 33. As will be seen when discussing the supervisory functions of the OPCW, use is made of these techniques from the very first moment in the collection phase. In other words, there is a constant process of dispute settlement.[201]

A dispute may arise at different levels. It may already arise during the review phase of a possible case of non-compliance or it may occur when the Conference has decided on a case. A dispute may also arise regarding a breach of confidentiality. Or it may concern a dispute between the host country and the Organization. A central role is attributed to the two central organs of the OPCW, the Executive Council and the Conference. States Parties may seek the settlement of a dispute via recourse to the appropriate organs of the OPCW.[202] The Executive Council may contribute to the solution of a dispute by whatever method it deems fit, including by offering its good offices.[203] The Conference shall consider questions brought to its attention, and can under Article VIII, paragraph 19 take decisions on any matters or issues related to the Convention brought to its attention by States Parties or by the Executive Council. The Conference may furthermore establish subsidiary organs with tasks related to the settlement of disputes. With the consent of the UN General Assembly the Executive Council or the Conference are empowered to request

---

[199] This formula is taken to include reference to "any legal question arising within the scope of the activities of the Organization" as referred to in Article XIV para. 5 concerning the possiblity of requesting an advisory opinion from the ICJ.

[200] Article XIV, para. 2.

[201] See also E.P.J. Myjer, Supervisory mechanisms and dispute settlement, in: J. Dahlitz, *Avoidance and Settlement of Arms Control Disputes* (1994), at 166. In general 158 et seq.

[202] Article XIV, para. 2. It refers, however, to the appropriate organs "of this Convention", where "of the Organization" would have been more appropriate.

[203] Article XIV, para. 3.

an advisory opinion from the ICJ.[204] In general, however, it can be determined that the CWC is weak as regards judicial dispute settlement.

(ii)The case of the Confidentiality Commission

Given that the CWC is weak as regards judicial dispute settlement, an interesting element of the CWC is the special place of its Confidentiality Commission. The Confidentiality Commission is an autonomous subsidiary organ of the Conference,[205] which is specifically mentioned in the Convention.[206] The fact that the Convention has an Annex specially devoted to the protection of confidential information (the Confidentiality Annex) already underlines the special character of this convention. This not only concerns confidential information in the area of military security, but also confidential business information. Verification of the chemical industries is essential in order to realize the purpose and principles of the CWC. Since, therefore, the civilian chemical industry would be heavily involved in the supervision process (viz. declarations or the inspections of chemical plants) there was strong pressure from the chemical industries to preserve the confidentiality of the information. States Parties and their private industries had to be certain that there would be a sufficient deterrent that the verifying inspectors, the Technical Secretariat and even the States Parties, who had received information, would protect its confidential character.[207] This led to the Confidentiality Annex and the establishment of the Confidentiality Commission. Reference to obligations in this respect can also be found in the Convention in Article VIII, paragraph 5 for the OPCW and in Article VII, paragraph 6 for each State Party.[208] The Annex contains General Principles for the handling of confidential information. This has been detailed in an extensive document: *OPCW Policy on Confidentiality*.[209] It foresees individual secrecy agreements for staff members. The Director General has a central position in case of breach or alleged

---

[204] Article XIV, para. 5.

[205] Confidentiality Annex, D, para. 23. See E.P.J. Myjer, The Settlement of Disputes under the Chemical Weapons Convention and the Case of the Confidentiality Commission, in Bardonnet, *supra* n. 4, at pp.537-553.

[206] Para. 23 of the Annex on the Protection of Confidential Information (Confidentiality Annex) to the CWC.

[207] That this issue is regarded as politically sensitive can be assessed from the fact that also in this area some issues remained unresolved. See PrepCom's Final Report, PC-XVI/37, section four (unresolved issues), paragraph IV (Confidentiality), 115-117, p. 52. See also the debate in the US Senate, *supra* n. 133, p. S 3655-S3656; Also B. Kellman, D.S. Gualteri, E.A. Tanzman, Disarmament and Disclosure: How Arms Control Verification can proceed Without Threatening Confidential Business Information, 36 *Harvard J.Int'l.L.*, pp.71-126.

[208] These requirements are elaborated in the provisions detailing verification procedures like Article VI, para. 10, paras. 56 and 62, Part II of the Verification Annex, and para. 48, Part X, Verification Annex.

[209] C-I/Dec.13/6 May 1997.

breaches of confidentiality. He shall impose punitive and disciplinary measures on staff members who have violated their obligations to protect confidential information. Remarkable is the disclaimer, as discussed, contained in the Annex with regard to the liability of the OPCW in case of a breach of confidentiality committed by members of the Technical Secretariat.[210] The US Senate formulated extensive conditions regarding the protection of confidential information in the ratification resolution.[211] The Confidentiality Commission deals with breaches of confidentiality involving a State Party and the OPCW. Its single task is the settlement of these disputes.

In cases of complaints regarding a breach of confidentiality by the OPCW or by some State Party the Confidentiality Commission may receive a complaint. This Commission, however, is not a kind of joint consultative committee, which we can find in different arms control treaties.[212] It is a real dispute settlement body. The twenty members of the Commission come from different fields of expertise and are appointed by the Conference in their personal capacity for a period of two years. Whenever there is a complaint it is up to the Commission to decide to convene a meeting. According to their extensive operating procedures,[213] drawn up by the Commission and approved by the Conference, there is a refined system for dispute settlement in place, ranging from mediation up to conciliation or even arbitration. Although the Commission can only take binding decisions if the parties so desire, it is essentially a dispute settlement body. And that is what it is supposed to look like. For the Conference was even willing to go along with the proposal by the Commission to appoint the International Bureau of the Permanent Court of Arbitration as an independent Registry to receive the complaints, which otherwise might have to be received by the TS, the very organ against which the complaint might be made.[214] To the author's knowledge this is the first time, and certainly in the area of arms control, that the one international organization (the OPCW) has signed an agreement[215] with another international organization (the Permanent Court of Arbitration) in order to assure the independence of a dispute settlement procedure within a particular regime. And

---

[210] Confidentiality Annex, D, 23. See above.

[211] For instance, in case of a breach of confidentiality the President will have to certify to Congress that the Confidentiality Commission has been established to consider the breach. Ratification Resolution, *Congressional Record Senate,* April 24, 1997, at S 3655.

[212] Compare the Standing Consultative Commission (Article XVII, SALT II), the Verification Commission (Article XIII, INF Treaty), and the Joint Consultative Group (Article XVI, CFE Treaty).

[213] Operating Procedures of the Confidentiality Commission, C-III/DEC.10, published in *The Legal Texts*, *supra* n. 4 at pp.498-512.

[214] In its decision of 5 December 1997 (C-II/DEC.14) the Conference appointed the International Bureau of the Permanent Court of Arbitration in The Hague to serve as the Registry of the Confidentiality Commission. See *The Legal Texts*, *ibid.* at 512.

[215] Registry Agreement between the OPCW and the Permanent Court of Arbitration, dated 9 December 1998. See EC-XII/DEC.6 of 9 October 1998.

this brings in the management aspect, as will be discussed later,[216] because the very appearance of a fair dispute settlement procedure with regard to a possible breach of confidential information may serve as a "confidence-building measure" which may induce not only the States Parties, but also the national chemical industries to cooperate fully with the CWC regime. So within the essentially non-adversarial supervisory system, a potentially adversarial dispute settlement body has been created with detailed operating procedures, although as a matter of course it is primarily equipped with non-judicial techniques. But having said that, it is still adversarial in character.

7. Some general issues

"The organization shall enjoy on the territory and in any other place under the jurisdiction or control of a State Party such *legal capacity* [emphasis added] and such privileges as is necessary for the exercise of its functions",[217] a formulation quite similar to that of Articles 104 and 105 of the UN Charter. Seen in conjunction with paragraph 50, which refers to agreements between the Organization and the States Parties in which the legal capacity, privileges and immunities shall be defined, this reference in the Convention apparently refers to legal capacity at the non-international level.[218] Reference to this capacity does not seem surprising for, as Amerasinghe argues, "[w]ithout personality an organization would not be able to appear in its own right in legal proceedings, whether at the international or non-international level".[219] As regards the international level, as with most international organizations legal personality is not explicitly referred to in the constituent treaty but can nevertheless be presumed. This follows from the functions and powers of the Organization, like the ability to conclude agreements or arrangements[220] and the privileges and immunities for the Director-General and the staff of the Organization.[221] To presume international legal personality is in accordance

---

[216] See p. 127 et seq..

[217] Article VIII, para. 48.

[218] "The legal capacity, privileges and immunities referred to in this Article shall be defined in agreements between the Organization and the States Parties as well as in an agreement between the Organization and the State in which the headquarters of the Organization is seated.[..]", Article VIII, para. 50. See Krutzsch et al., *supra* n. 4, at 169.

[219] "There would also not be a single international person as such having the capacity in its own right to have rights, obligations and powers, whether implied or expressed, both at the international level and at the non-international level. Such rights, obligations and powers would be vested collectively in all the creating States, which may not have been the intention behind the creation of the organization, and also could create unnecessary practical problems, particularly in the area of responsibility, both active and passive." C.F. Amerasinghe, *Principles of the Institutional Law of International Organizations* (1996), at 69.

[220] See Article VIII, paras. 34 and 39 (a).

[221] "Delegates of States Parties, together with their alternates and advisers, representatives

with "the prevalent view", according to which it is implicitly given if there is no specific constitutional attribution.[222] This position finds support in the well-known advisory opinion of the ICJ.[223] It is relatively rare for an intergovernmental organization to state that it has personality "indeed there appears no need for an express provision in the constituent treaty of an organization for it to be deemed to possess personality".[224]

Given that the Constitution of the OPCW makes clear that the OPCW has a certain legal capacity, both at the national and the international level, but at the same time excludes its liability, the question can be raised what is then left of the concept of legal personality if it is at the same time restricted? For, interestingly, as regards a possible breach of confidentiality committed by a member of the Technical Secretariat the Confidentiality Annex makes it quite clear that the OPCW shall not be held liable for such breaches.[225] Since such possible breaches of confidentiality may only occur with regard to the information of Member States, or of facilities under their jurisdiction, there seems to be nothing against States Parties agreeing to have the liability of the OPCW restricted towards themselves. It would, however, have been different if States Parties had restricted the organization's general liability. Still, in this way the created international legal personality appears to be rather unbalanced with, on the one hand, rights but, on the other, fairly restricted duties.

The Organization shall enjoy the usual privileges and immunities on the territory of a State Party and in any place under its jurisdiction or control.[226] The privileges and immunities shall be defined in agreements between the OPCW and the States Parties as well as in the Headquarters Agreement.[227]

---

appointed to the Executive Council together with their alternates and advisers, *the Director-General and the staff of the Organization shall enjoy such privileges and immunities as are necessary in the independent exercise of their functions in connection with the Organization*", Article VIII, para 49 [emphasis added]. Also Krutzsch et al., *supra* n. 4, at 127: "The Organization is equipped with all the attributes of an international legal personality, as contained in Article 104 and 105 of the UN Charter. The Organization is the addressee of rights and obligations provided for by the Convention."

[222] Schermers & Blokker, *supra* n. 149, at 979.

[223] *Reparation for Injuries Suffered in the Service of the United Nations*, ICJ *Rep.* 1949 at 174. See Schermers & Blokker, *ibid.* at 979-980.

[224] White, *supra* n. 149, at 27. Also Amarasinghe, *supra* n. 219 at 78: "International personality is very rarely dealt with explicitly or impliedly in the constitutions of international organizations". See, however, Article 4 of the Rome Statute of the International Criminal Court, wherby the Court is established as an international organization and explicitly granted international legal personality (see Article 4 Rome Satute, A/Conf.183/9).

[225] Confidentiality Annex, D (22).

[226] Article VIII, para. 48

[227] Article VIII, para. 50. OPCW Headquarters Agreement (C-I/DEC.59, 14 May 1997): inter alia, Article 4 (Immunity from legal process); Article 5 (Immunity of property from other actions, inviolability of the archives, samples, equipment, and other material); Article 7 (law and authority in the headquarters); Article 10 (facilities and immunities in respect of

Notwithstanding these regulations, in the Verification Annex[228] detailed arrangements are contained regarding the privileges and immunities of the inspectors and inspection assistants in the carrying out of their inspection duties. During the carrying out of verification activities the immunities of the Director-General and the staff of the TS are accordingly extended.[229]

In its external relations with States and other international organizations under Article VIII para. 34 the OPCW has the capacity to conclude agreements or arrangements. An important example of these is the Relationship Agreement between the United Nations and the OPCW.[230]

V. The supervisory functions of the OPCW

1. General: supervision as a model

In the previous chapters we have looked at the Convention and described its core obligations and we looked at the OPCW as the international organization that is established under this treaty primarily[231] to ensure compliance with these obligations. It aims, in other words, to control compliance with these obligations. Lang refers to compliance control as a relatively new concept, which he does not define, however, but which is rooted in the English term "compliance" and which is linked to the French term "*contrôle*".[232] This is exactly what the concept of supervision is about. More in particular it is about supervision by an international organization in contradistinction to States exercising supervision over each other. The international organization which the OPCW is fulfils a number of sub-functions, all aimed at the overarching goal of supervision of the behaviour of the Member States. This function of supervision is realized via these sub-functions. The techniques applied in these

communications and publications); Article 11 (exemption of the OPCW and its property from taxes and duties); Article 12 (freedom of financial assets from restrictions); Article 13 (exemption from import and export restrictions); Article 14 (transit and residence); Article 15 (permanent missions to the OPCW); Article 16 (privileges and immunities of heads of delegations, permanent representatives to the OPCW and staff members of permanent missions); Article 17 (privileges and immunities of delegates and alternates for and advisers attached to heads of delegation); Article 18 (privileges and immunities of the Director-General and other officials of the OPCW); Article 19 (privileges and immunities of experts).

[228] Verification Annex II, part B.

[229] Article VIII, para. 51.

[230] The Relationship Agreement between the UN and the OPCW, *supra* n. 11.

[231] Also in the sphere of cooperation under Article X the OPCW has a function.

[232] "Compliance-control is a relatively new concept; it is rooted in the English term "compliance" and links it to the term "contrôle", which is the focal point of many French-language writings on this subject", W. Lang, Compliance with Disarmament Obligations, *Zeitschrift für Öffenliches Recht und Völkerrecht*, no. 55/1, 1995, at 69.

sub-functions are all directed to this particular end. "Their main purpose is to evoke compliance behaviour from the subjects of the legal order".[233] The institutional structure of the OPCW regulates the carrying out of these different sub-functions. The OPCW can therefore be held to be first and foremost an international organization that embodies the institutional structure of this supervisory mechanism. This section aims to analyze the sub-functions of this compliance control organization.[234]

Lately much has been written about compliance control, especially by social scientists.[235] Interestingly, it often concerns fields of international law like arms control, trade or environmental protection.[236] No attempt will be made to add more theoretical expositions on compliance control,[237] since the only aim of this section is to analyze the functions of the OPCW in this respect. In order to do so for analytical purposes I will use the concept of supervision, as applied with regard to international economic organizations,[238] with its three separate functions. These functions being the *review function* (judging State behaviour for its conformity with an agreed rule of international law)[239] the *correction function* (the correction of State behaviour, when it is established that a State has violated an international obligation)[240] and the *creative function* (interpretation or clarification of the rules).[241] I have, however, come to the conclusion that for the sake of clarity a fourth function should be added, namely the *collection function*. This function refers to the collection of information, be it the collection of information regarding the behaviour of States Parties, their

---

[233] T.M.R. Chowdhury, *Legal Framework of International Supervision* (Thesis, University of Stockholm (1986)), at xvi.

[234] Also referred to as "monitoring agency", A. Smithson, *supra* n. 94, at 6.

[235] "In the past few years many social scientists interested in cooperation have turned their attention to the problem of compliance in international regulatory regimes. Much of the empirical research in this area has been conducted by a group composed mainly of qualitative political scientists and scholars interested in international law", Downs et al., *infra* n. 237, at 379. An exception in the legal field are the Chayes. See Chayes et al., *supra* n. 69 and *infra* n. 237.

[236] See Lang, *supra* n. 232, at 69. Downs, *infra* n. 237, at 3, 84.
Downs argues that, contrary to what "the managerialists" might argue, "at least with respect to the relationship between enforcement and depth of cooperation, the areas are not as different as one might imagine or as some might hope", *ibid* at 390.

[237] Compare George W. Downs, David M. Rocke, and Peter N. Barsoom, Is the Good News about Compliance Control Good News About Cooperation?, 50 *International Organization*, 3, summer 1996, pp. 379-406; Abram Chayes and Antonia Handler Chayes, On Compliance, 47 *International Organization*, 2, spring, 1993, pp. 175-205.

[238] See P. van Dijk (ed.), *Supervisory Mechanisms in International Economic Organizations* (1984).

[239] But also the accuracy of the information provided.

[240] Compare M. Koskenniemi, Breach of Treaty or Non-Compliance?, Reflections on the Enforcement of the Montreal Protocol, *Yearbook of International Environmental Law*, Vol.3, (1992) at 123-126.

[241] Van Dijk et al., *supra* n. 238 at pp. 11-39.

agents or those legal and natural persons under their jurisdiction. The concept of supervision thus applied appears to provide maximum clarity.[242]

Nollkaemper, writing about environmental law, also makes the distinction between collection of information and its review, where for analytical purposes he divides provisions into three categories corresponding to the three main stages of compliance control by international fora: the *compilation of information* (provisions which aim to ensure that international fora obtain adequate information on the degree to which states comply with their obligations); *review of compliance* (provisions which govern the review of compliance) and *enforcement* (provisions which make it possible that in case of non-compliance obligations are enforced).[243] He does not, however, deal with the creative function separately. Elements thereof can be found in the respective functions like where the review procedure contributes to the clarification of the State's obligations[244] and thereby elucidates the contents of the obligation.

The distinction used by myself is therefore the following: (1) *collection function*; (2) *review function*; (3) *creative function*; and (4) *correction function*. Such a distinction in four (sub-) functions can be applied in various fields of international law,[245] but especially in the field of disarmament and arms control it is indispensable because it allows us better to understand the, for that area, highly developed and pivotal concept of "verification" and to distinguish it from sanctions to be applied in case of a breach of treaty obligations. With regard to verification of arms control agreements Sur, who regards verification as a process,[246] distinguishes three aspects of this process namely: (1) establishments of the facts; (2) their legal assessment; and (3) consequences to be drawn in the event of an established violation. He then presents three possible concepts: the "minimalist concept", which is limited to the hard-core that constitutes establishment of the facts";[247] the "intermediate concept", which incorporates legal assessment;[248] and the "extensive concept", which adds the reactions emanating from the determination of a violation.[249] He is of the opinion that the intermediate concept is the dominant one.

---

[242] See for instance E.P.J. Myjer, The Law of Arms-Control and International Supervision in 3 *LJIL* (1990) at 99-123 / M. Brus et al., The United Nations Decade of International Law (1991), at 99-123; *supra* n. 201, at 149-169 and E.P.J. Myjer, *New Procedures of International Dispute Resolution*, in: ASIL/NVIR Proceedings (1997), at 355-363.

[243] A. Nollkaemper, *The Legal Regime for Transboundary Water Pollution: Between Discretion and Constraint* (1993) p. 256 et seq.

[244] Nollkaemper, *ibid*, at 268.

[245] Like human rights or protection of the environment. On the application of different concepts in the various fields of international law see Lang, *supra* n. 232, at 69.

[246] See *supra* n. 293, at 150.

[247] S. Sur, *A Legal Approach to Verification in Disarmament or Arms Limitation*, Research Paper no. 1 UNIDER (1988), at 8.

[248] Sur, *ibid*, at 8.

[249] Sur, *ibid*, at 8.

Lang, writing about compliance with regard to *disarmament obligations*, in clarifying different notions in this area[250] makes a distinction whereby "verification represents an external approach aimed at checking facts" but not envisaging the consequences of failure to comply.[251] He refers to Sur's three concepts of verification - the minimalist, the intermediate and the extensive - and is of the opinion that *verification* should be restricted to the first two of these variations since problems arising in the third field "... considerably differ from issues of fact finding and legal assessment".[252] Adoption of the extensive concept would then lead back to his (broader) concept of compliance control.[253] This concept of compliance control comes close to that of verification, but also encompasses the consequences in case of non-compliance.

The four functions of supervision as applied by myself come closest to the compliance control concept of Lang and to Sur's extensive concept. However, it disects the different functions and restricts verification to the collection of facts. Furthermore, in distinguishing the correction function it allows one to separate the more political character of the consequences to be drawn, as rightly demonstrated by Sur. With regard to the CWC we find two of these "steps", viz. the collection function and the review function, clearly set out in the four sub-systems that Perry Robinson.[254] distinguishes in the verification system of the Chemical Weapons Convention: 1) *the system of data collection*, whereby "individual States Parties monitor relevant activities within their own jurisdictions"; 2) the system of declarations, whereby prescribed categories of information are reported by individual States Parties to the Technical Secretariat ;[255] 3) *the system of validation*, "which is operated by the Technical secretariat to check the accuracy of State declarations by means of routine on-site inspection"; and 4) *the system of requested inspection*. As will be clear Perry Robinson's system of validation and the system of requested inspection partly coincide with my review function.

---

[250] Notions like compliance control, implementation, application, verification, supervision, monitoring and inspection, Lang, *supra* n. 232, at 69-70.

[251] Lang, *ibid*, at 70.

[252] Lang, *ibid*, at 81.

[253] "Adopting the "extensive concept" would lead back to the broader idea of compliance control already discussed [..]", Lang. *ibid*, at 81.

[254] J.P. Perry Robinson, *supra* n. 117, at 491.

[255] He then continues "which then processes the information and disseminates it to all States Parties", at 491. In my opinion the information will, if necessary, be automatically updated after inspections, as will also be the case after the "validation" and after the challenge inspection.

2. The collection function

This function refers to the actual collecting of all relevant information. A wealth of information is collected within the context of the CWC. This is done both by individual States Parties and by the OPCW respectively. States Parties will have to collect the information they need to declare within their own (national) jurisdictions. They will have to provide this information subsequently to the OPCW via the system of declarations.[256] In principle this information will be validated by the OPCW via routine on-site inspections.[257] Here, indeed, one enters the review function, with the validated information coming back via the collection function as factual information. Furthermore, information will be collected via inspections upon request, which will not take place upon the initiative of the OPCW but rather upon that of the States Parties. States Parties will receive on request, for instance in case they ask for clarification from the OPCW - the Executive Council -[258] the information assembled by the OPCW. With regard to the collection function, Perry Robinson's, sub-systems mentioned in the previous paragraph are illustrative, but not comprehensive since collection of information is also possible outside these systems, e.g. via clarification, on-site monitoring or collation of information. Of the different methods the following are the most prominent:

* national data collection

In order to be able to fulfil its obligation to provide for the requested relevant information States Parties will have to arrange for that nationally. This, in Perry Robinson's words, is *the system of data collection*. With regard to declarations under Article III, State Parties that fall in the "yes" category[259] will normally already have the information required at hand. With regard to Article VI (activities not prohibited under this Convention) in all probability it will mainly concern civilian chemical industries. This information will have to be obtained via national legislation.[260]

---

[256] In order to provide the National Authorities of States Parties to the CWC with detailed explanations on declaration requirements with regard to initial, annual and other declarations a Declaration Handbook has been developed (PTS-OPCW, rev. 1996-11-14).

[257] Notwithstanding initial inspections.

[258] Compare Article IX para. 3.

[259] According to Krutsch the first part of the declaration is a "yes-no" declaration. "Each of the elements *individually* triggers an affirmative or negative declaration, *supra* n. 4 at 48.

[260] Article VII (1) contains the general implementation obligation. Article VI, para. 2 and the Verifacation Annex in Parts VI(D), VII(A), Paragraph VIII(A), IX (A) are specific regarding the declarations.

*via declarations by States Parties[261]

In different articles the CWC details the information (reports) which States Parties will have to submit to the OPCW, and the period within which this will have to be done after the entry into force of the CWC. It concerns information about chemical weapons, on old and abandoned chemical weapons, on chemical weapons production facilities and on other facilities,[262] which under Article III will have to be declared within 30 days after entry into force. For instance, with regard to chemical weapons, inter alia, the precise location and aggregate quantity will have to be declared.[263] With regard to chemical weapons production facilities the requested information concerns any facility under its jurisdiction since 1 January 1946.[264] Furthermore, each State shall submit detailed plans for the destruction of chemical weapons[265] and chemical weapons destruction facilities.[266] With respect to riot control agents "the chemical name, structural formula and Chemical Abstracts Service registry number"[267] will have to be specified. To ensure that toxic chemicals and their precursors are not used for the production of chemical weapons these chemicals, as listed in Schedules 1, 2 and 3, and the related facilities will have to be declared.[268] This means that declarations will not only have to be submitted with regard to weapons and facilities, but also with regard to certain chemicals of which controlled use is allowed for purposes not prohibited under the Convention.[269] Such use, however, is controlled and subject to specific provisions. In order to allow for different degrees of intensity of verification and for the "reporting threshold' (declaration duty) chemicals are ranked in order of risk into three categories, namely Schedule 1, Schedule 2 and Schedule 3 chemicals. Furthermore, there is also the category "discrete organic chemicals". *Schedule 1* lists twelve chemicals that are key to nerve and blister agents[270] and that are unlikely to be of any industrial interest.[271] *Schedule 2*

---

261 See for instance note by the Executive Secretary on the information required from States Parties Immediately or soon after Entry Into Force, PC-XVI/10, 1 April 1997.

262 Article III and Parts IV(A), IV(B) and V of the Verification Annex.

263 Article III, para. (a)(ii).

264 Article III, para. (c).

265 Article IV, para. 7 (a). Furthermore, a State Party shall submit declarations annually regarding the implementation of its plan for the destruction (sub. (b)) and certify not later than 30 days after the destruction process has been completed (sub. (c)).

266 Article V, para. 9 (a) "Not later than 180 days before the destruction of each facility begins").

267 Article III, para. 1 (e).

268 Article VI, para. 7. See for instance regarding the projected activities and anticipated production for the coming year of Schedule 1 activities, Verification Annex, Part VI.16 and 20.

269 States Parties maintain as a principle their right "to develop, produce, otherwise acquire, retain, transfer and use toxic chemicals and their precursors..", Article VI, para. 1.

270 "This category includes all known nerve gasses, mustard agents, lewisites and some key precursors, R.G. Sutherland, The Chemical Weapons Convention: The Problems of

contains fourteen chemicals of significant risk that are not widely used in industry, whereas *Schedule 3* lists seventeen precursors and chemicals that are frequently used in industry, but still pose a risk.[272] Since these categories determine the level of involvement of the civilian chemical industry and becasuse of its complex nature, the following in particular can be said with regard to these categories:

Schedule 1: Because these chemicals present the greatest risk to the CWC's object and purpose,[273] activities with regard to Schedule 1 chemicals are banned, with the exception of permitted activities for a limited number of purposes,[274] which will be closely monitored. Each party is not allowed to have more than 1 tonne of Schedule 1 chemicals. Production exceeding 10 kg can only take place in a single small-scale production facility for research, medical, pharmaceutical and protective purposes.[275] Production facilities for Schedule 1 chemicals fall under the regime of systematic on-site inspections and monitoring with on-site instruments.[276] Also the transfer of Schedule 1 chemicals is subject to severe transfer restrictions.[277] The transfer of these chemicals to non-States Parties is forbidden.[278] The initial declaration will have to take place within 30 days after the entry into force of the CWC; initial declarations on new facilities shall be provided 180 days before operations are to begin.[279] Furthermore, States Parties, will have to make declarations annually concerning the activities of the facility for the previous year.[280]

Schedule 2: There are no production limits for Schedule 2 and 3 chemicals that are being produced commercially, but there are thresholds above which production must be declared.[281] For Schedule 2, the "reporting thresholds"

Implementation, 7 *Pacific Research*, no. 1, 1994, at 8.

271 Sutherland, *ibid* at 8.

272 Smithson, *supra* n. 74 at 7.

273 Kellman et al., *supra* n. 4 at 34.

274 *Ibid*, at 34.

275 See Part VI Verification Annex (Activities not prohibited under this convention in accordance with Article VI. Regime for schedule 1 chemicals and facilities related to such chemicals) under A.1. Para. 11 states that "at facilities approved by the State Party production of chemicals in quantities of more than 100 g per year may be carried out for research, medical or pharmaceutical purposes outside a single small-scale facility in aggregate quantities not exceeding 10 kg per year per facility".

276 See Article VI, para. 3.

277 Kellman et al., *supra* n. 4 at 39.

278 Verification Annex, VI,(B)(3).

279 Verification Annex, Part VI, (d)(13).

280 Verification Annex, Part VI (D)(15).

281 See in particular Verification Annex: Part VII under A.3 (Activities not prohibited under this convention in accordance with Article VI, Regime for schedule 2 chemicals and facilities related to such chemicals) and Part VIII under A.3 (Activities not prohibited under this convention in accordance with Article VI, Regime for schedule 3 chemicals and facilities related to such chemicals). Sutherland, *supra* n. 270 at 8.

range from one kilogram to one tonne. The "inspection threshold", however, is "about tenfold larger".[282] Also Schedule 2 chemicals are subject to export controls. This obligation shall take effect three years after the entry into force of the CWC.[283] During that period "end-user certificates" are required. Declarations will have to be made initially within 30 days after entry into force, and furthermore annually within 90 days after the end of the previous calender year as well as declarations on anticipated activities not later than 60 days before the beginning of the following calendar year. Initial declarations will have to include all plants which have produced at any time since 1946.

Schedule 3: The declaration threshold is thirty tonnes, with an "inspection threshold" of about 200 tonnes.[284] The export controls with regard to Schedule 3 chemicals are less strict. Each State Party shall, however, adopt the necessary measures to ensure that the transferred chemicals shall only be used for purposes not prohibited under the CWC.[285]

Discrete organic chemicals: other chemical plant sites where compounds of these chemicals are made and which contain phosphorus, sulpher or fluorine (PSF) in amounts greater than thirty tonnes will have to be declared, as will plants which produce more than 200 tonnes of unscheduled discrete organic chemicals. Such plants will be liable to CWC inspection after the Convention has been in force for three years.[286] Declarations will have to be made initially within 30 days after the CWC enters into force and annually not later than 90 days after the previous calendar year,[287] as well as declarations on anticipated activities not later than 60 days before the beginning of the following calendar year. Initial declarations will have to include all plants which have produced at any time since 1946.[288]

The duty to declare does not only imply initial declarations, but also annual declarations on past activities as well as on anticipated activities.[289] If the facilities are privately owned, States Parties will have to arrange for the collection of that information via national legislation. To provide the respective National Authority with such information may be made a legal requirement.[290]

---

282 Sutherland, *ibid* at 8.

283 Verification Annex, VII, (B)(31).

284 Verification Annex, Part VIII, B, 12. Sutherland, *supra* n. 270 at 8.

285 Verification Annex, Part VIII, (C)(26).

286 Verification Annex, Part IX, C, 22. Sutherland *supra* n. 270 at 9.

287 Declarations on aggregate national data, on plant sites as well as on past production. See Verification Annex, Part VIII (A).

288 See Verification Annex, Part IX (Regime for other chemical production facilities).

289 See verification annex Part VIII, A (4).

290 See above under "national data collection"; Kellman et al., *supra* n. 4, especially at 41. Compare for the Netherlands the *Uitvoeringswet Verdrag Chemische Wapens*, Tweede Kamer, vergaderjaar 1994-1995, 23 911, nrs. 1-2, especially Articles 4, 5, and 7. Any violation is punishable under the *Economic Offences Act*.

Since the requested information is detailed[291] formats have been developed in order to standardise the information.[292]

*via inspections

As described above the first reports thus obtained will in the first instance be verified via initial inspections[293] by an OPCW inspection team. The purpose of this inspection is not only to verify information, but also to "obtain any additional information needed for planning future verification activities at the facilities, including on-site inspections and continuous monitoring, and for preparing the facility agreements.[294] Of course the very aspect of "verifying information" falls under the review function. The latter aspect - collection of information *per se* - falls under the collection function. The same will be the case for information collected on site during routine or challenge inspections. In accordance with the facility agreements inspectors will receive information, such as, if necessary, "[..]samples taken at their request from any devices, bulk containers and other containers at the destruction facility or the storage facility thereat".[295]

Under the CWC four different kinds of verification inspections can be distinguished:

- systematic verification of chemical weapons and their production facilities through on-site inspection and monitoring with on-site instruments;[296]

---

[291] Compare regarding chemical weapons: "The declaration of chemical weapons by a State Party pursuant to Article III, para. 1 (a) (ii), shall include the following: (a) The aggregate quantity of each chemical declared; (b) The precise location of each chemical weapons storage facility, expressed by: (i) Name; (ii) Geographical coordinates; and (iii) A detailed site diagram, including a boundary map and the location of bunkers/storage areas within the facility; (c) The detailed inventory for each chemical weapons storage facility including: (i) Chemicals defined as chemical weapons in accordance with Article II; (ii) Unfilled munitions, sub-munitions, devices and equipment defined as chemical weapons; (iii) Equipment specially designed for use directly in connection with the employment of munitions, sub-munitions, devices or equipment specified in sub-para. (ii); (iv) Chemicals specifically designed for use directly in connection with the employment of munitions, sub-munitions, devices or equipment specified in sub-para. (ii)." Verification Annex, Part IV (A)(1).

[292] In order to provide the National Authorities of States Parties to the CWC with detailed explanations on declaration requirements with regard to initial, annual and other declarations a Declaration Handbook has been developed (PTS-OPCW, rev. 1996-11-14: *Declaration Handbook related to Industrial Declarations.*)

[293] "Each declared facility subject to on-site inspection pursuant to Articles IV (chemical weapons, author), V (chemical weapons production facilities, author), and VI (Activities not prohibited under this convention, author), shall receive an inspection promptly after the facility is declared", Verification annex, Part III, A (1); Verification Annex Part IV (A) D (38).

[294] Verification Annex, Part III, A (1).

[295] Verification Annex (A), IV D 70(c).

[296] See: Article IV, para. 3 (chemical weapons); Article V, para. 3 (chemical weapons

- routine inspections of certain chemical facilities;[297]
- challenge inspections;[298]
- investigations in case of alleged use of chemical weapons.[299]

Of these types of inspection the first two primarily concern data control. That will not necessarily be the case with the challenge inspection and investigations in case of alleged use.

There are two categories of inspections, namely the *initial* and the *routine inspections* at the initiative of the Organization, as well as the *challenge inspections* at the request of States Parties. The purpose of the initial inspection is "to verify information provided and to obtain any additional information needed for planning future verification activities at the facility, including on-site inspections and continuous monitoring with on-site instruments" and to prepare the facility agreements.[300] Facility agreements are agreements between the Organization and States Parties relating to specifically declared facilities subject to on-site verification pursuant to Articles IV, V and VI.[301]

(1)initial and routine inspections
All declared locations at which chemical weapons are stored or destroyed, as well as all chemical weapons production facilities shall receive an initial inspection promptly after the facility has been declared.[302] For each declared facility that is subject to on-site inspections[303] a facility agreement will be concluded with the Organization. These facilities are subject to systematic verification through "on-site inspection and monitoring with on-site instruments".[304] The destruction of these weapons, which will have to take place within a period of two to ten years after the entry into force of the Convention, and one to ten years for the production facilities respectively, will be closely monitored. The routine inspections will take place at short notice and not less than 24 hours in advance of the planned arrival of the inspection team at the point of entry.[305] Old and abandoned weapons are subject to a different regime.

Initial inspections will also take place with regard to the "second line" - not chemical weapons as such - of chemical substances, namely chemicals that are used to make pharmaceuticals, pesticides, fertilizers and other everyday

---

production facilities); Article VI, para. 3 (Schedule 1 chemicals and facilities).

[297] Article VI, paras. 2, 4, 5 and 6.

[298] Article IX, para. 8 ("of any facility or location").

[299] Article X, paras. 8-11.

[300] Verification Annex, Part III under A.1.

[301] Verification Annex, Definitions, 7.

[302] Part III, A 1, Verification Annex.

[303] Pursuant to Articles IV, V and VI, para. 3.

[304] Article IV, para. 3 and Article V, para. 3.

[305] Part III, C 17, Verification Annex.

commercial products, but which can also be used to make chemical weapons.[306]

(2)Challenge inspections

Challenge inspections, remarks Kellman, "are the Convention's safety net".[307] "For the sole purpose of clarifying and resolving any questions concerning possible non-compliance" with the provisions of the CWC each State Party has the right to request an on-site challenge inspection of any facility or location in the territory or in any other place under the jurisdiction or control of any other State Party.[308] These inspections will have to be conducted anywhere without delay by an inspection team designated by the Director-General. The State Party to be inspected will not be notified less than 12 hours before the planned arrival of the inspection team at the point of entry.[309] Within 12 hours after having received the inspection request the Executive Council may "decide by a three-quarter majority of all its members against carrying out the challenge inspection if it considers the inspection request to be frivolous, abusive or clearly beyond the scope" of the CWC.[310] States Parties are under the obligation to keep the inspection request within the scope of the CWC and "shall refrain from unfounded inspection requests, care being taken to avoid abuse".[311] The request shall contain all appropriate information on the basis of which concern has arisen regarding possible non-compliance with the CWC. Therefore it is expected that "[t]hese inspections are not regular, nor, presumably frequent".[312]

For its part the inspected State Party shall have "the right and obligation to make every reasonable effort to demonstrate its compliance with this Convention and, to this end, to enable the inspection team to fulfil its mandate".[313] The inspection team and the inspected State Party need to come to an agreement on the requested perimeter of the inspection site.[314] Access, however, is "managed"[315] ostensibly which "allows inspectors enough access to determine whether the site is indeed involved in prohibited activity while also allowing the facility under inspection to protect sensitive information unrelated to the Convention".[316] Accordingly, in the Verification Annex it is stated

[306] Smithson, *supra* n.74, at 7.
[307] Kellman et al., *supra* n. 4, at 131.
[308] Article IX, para. 8.
[309] Article IX para. 15.
[310] Article IX, para. 17
[311] Article IX, para. 9.
[312] Kellman et al., *supra* n. 4, at 131.
[313] Article IX, para. 11 (a).
[314] Verification Annex, Part X, (B)(14)-(21).
[315] Declared facilities under Articles IV, V, and VI use different managed access procedures. See Verification Annex, X (c)(52); Kellman et al., *supra* n. 4, at 140.
[316] Smithson, *supra* n. 74, at 32.

that "[..] The inspected State Party has the right under managed access to take such measures as are necessary to protect national security".[317] But also that these provisions "may not be invoked by the inspected State Party to conceal evasion of its obligations not to engage in activities prohibited under this Convention"! This means that the extent of access to any particular place or places within the site, the exact nature of inspection activities, and the information that the host officials are to provide to the inspection team are subject to negotiations between host officials and the inspection team.[318]

*via monitoring with on-site instruments
Monitoring with on-site instruments is possible with regard to chemical weapons[319] that are stored at some facility, chemical weapons production facilities[320] and with regard to Schedule 1 chemicals.[321] Accordingly, arrangements have to be made in the facility agreement.

*via compilation
The Technical Secretariat with its specialized knowledge, complete overview of the declarations, its highly advanced information system and other information (for instance, results of scientific research), will generate "new" information of its own accord.

In conclusion it can be said that under the CWC a wealth of information is collected. That, in itself, is not sufficient. There is, for example, no automatic assurance that the information collected nationally will be correct.

> "The success or failure of routine verification will therefore largely be determined by how conscientiously States Parties conduct their national monitoring in the first place, and otherwise prepare themselves for submitting full and accurate declarations. If garbage is what they feed into the verification system, then garbage is what will come out of it, no matter how skilful and dedicated the OPCW Technical Secretariat may be."[322]

---

[317] Verification Annex, Part X (41).

[318] Smithson, *supra* n. 74, at 32.

[319] Verification Annex IV (A) D 42 ("The systematic verification shall be initiated as soon as possible after the declaration of chemical weapons is submitted and shall continue until all chemical weapons have been removed from the storage facility. It shall in accordance with the facility agreement, combine on-site inspections and monitoring with on-site instruments"); 51; 59.

[320] Verification Annex Part V, C (46);(56);(60)(83) (concerns the conversion of chemical weapons production facilities to purposes not prohibited under the CWC).

[321] Verification Annex Part VI E (22) ("The facility shall be subject to systematic verification through on-site inspection and monitoring with on- site instruments") and the same with regard to other facilities referred to in paras. 10 and 11(29).

[322] Perry Robinson, *supra* n. 117, at 491.

What therefore has to be done is to assess a) whether the information provided is correct and b) whether that information confirms a State Party's compliance with the Convention. In other words, whether that information reflects State behaviour, or behaviour for which a State is responsible, and whether that information conforms to the norm. That assessment will take place within the review function.

3. The Review Function

In general the "review function" refers to judging State behaviour as regards its conformity with an agreed rule of international law. This also includes an assessment of the accuracy of the information provided. In our case it concerns the question whether States Parties fulfil their obligations under the CWC. In general the review will take place via three stages involving the three organs of the OPCW, namely, and in this order, via the TS, the Executive Council and the Conference. The methods to be applied appear to be of a non-judicial dispute settlement character. The normal situation, however, is that there is no problem with the information provided and that information confirms a State Party's compliance with the Convention. In that case there is no need for the TS to involve either the Executive Council or the Conference and this is where the review ends. With regard to the information to be assessed, a distinction can be made as regards the way in which this information is obtained because certain information has to be handed in as a hard and fast rule ("routinely") while other information is obtained in special cases.

The following situations can be distinguished:

routine

- information provided in declarations has to be compared with the results of initial and routine inspections. Assessed has to be the "actual state of affairs". This has to be weighed against the norms of the Convention. This should lead to either a "yes compliance" or "no non-compliance" situation. If it would result in an "uncertain/don't know situation", additional information may then be necessary or something is inherently wrong with the collection mechanism;[323]

[323] From this should be distinguished the situation whereby it appears that incorrect information had been provided, but that on the basis of correct information the State Party has acted in conformity with the norm, in other words: only the declaration was mistaken.

special

- information obtained via challenge inspections confirms, via the same assessment procedure as in the routine situation, a breach of treaty norms;
- a case of actual use is established;

The organs of thc OPCW are involved in reviewing in the following way:

* The role of the TS

The Convention does not contain a separate article exclusively devoted to the review function. Even Article VIII paragraph 40 regarding the role of the Technical Secretariat in informing

> "[..] the Executive Council of any problem that has arisen with regard to the discharge of its functions, *including doubts, ambiguities or uncertainties about compliance* with this Convention that have come to its notice in the performance of its verification activities and that it has been unable to resolve or clarify through its consultations with the State Party concerned" [emphasis added]

is not exclusively devoted to compliance problems. "Information on *specific cases concerning compliance* will be only a portion of the Activities stipulated in this Article".[324] According to Krutzsch "any problem", in this paragraph, has a rather broad meaning and "also relates to shortcomings in organization and structure of the TS, budgetary problems as well as inexpedient verification procedures or instruments".[325] He is of the opinion that with regard to "doubts, ambiguities or uncertainties about compliance", in Article VIII, Paragraph 40 as quoted above, "uncertainties" is the most important and objective term, the meaning of which covers the other two terms.[326] Interestingly, paragraph 40 contains an important qualification, for the Executive Council will only have to be informed when the TS has been unable to resolve or clarify those uncertainties through its consultations with the State Party. It can therefore be held that the first stage in the review process already takes place during the collection phase, when the TS tries to resolve or clarify uncertainties. In order to be able to do so, almost "by definition" a measuring against specific norms needs to take place. It will thereby use dispute settlement techniques like asking for clarification and making use of the technical fact-finding by the inspectors and (designated) laboratories. The TS, however, will have to decide on whether or not it is satisfied within the confines of the TS, rendering it a non-public, and

---

[324] Krutzsch et al., *supra* n. 4, at 165.
[325] Krutzsch et al., *ibid*, at 165.
[326] Krutzsch et al., *ibid*, at 165.

therefore non-transparent, procedure. The actual decisionmakers, however, are international civil servants. And only when the TS is not satisfied will the Executive Council be informed. This leads one to wonder whether this review stage will be documented and whether it will be accessible to States Parties, for instance when they ask for clarification under Article IX under Paragraph 3. A similar reference to "uncertainties" is contained in the Verification Annex, Part II, paragraphs 64 and 65 concerning the inspection reports.[327]Also here elements of a (provisional) review are evident when the inspectors have to decide which "facts are relevant to compliance".[328] It is of course during the reporting phase by the inspector that actual doubts about compliance may (begin to) grow. The final report[329] together with observations (in other words not only factual information) that an inspector may attach to the report will immediately be submitted to the inspected State Party. "Any written comments which the inspected State Party may immediately make on its findings shall be annexed to it."[330] This report is then presented to the Director-General of the TS within 30 days after the inspection. The Director-General, on his part, shall approach the inspected State Party for clarification "should the report contain uncertainties".[331] If these cannot be removed "or the facts established are of a nature to suggest that obligations under this Convention have not been met"[332] the Director-General shall inform the Executive Council.

* The role of the Executive Council

Other instances[333] whereby information relevant for consideration under Article VIII paragraphs 35-36 will be brought to the attention of the Executive Council are: the case of a challenge inspection, when the Director-General has to transmit the final report of the inspection team promptly to the Executive Council[334] and the above mentioned case of the Verification Annex[335] part II, paragraph 65,[336] which according to Krutzsch should be regarded as being included under

---

[327] Krutzsch and Trapp obviously find it an "empty" requirement for they refer to it as "[t]he requirement of fruitless efforts aimed at the solution of uncertainties..", *ibid*, at 165.

[328] Verification Annex, part II, para. 62.

[329] "Including information as to the manner in which the State Party inspected cooperated with the inspection team", Verification Annex, part II, paragraph 62.

[330] Verification Annex, Part II, para. 63.

[331] " [..] or should cooperation between the National Authority and the inspectors not measure up to the standards required [..]", Verification Annex, part II, para. 64. It is not clear why this reference was included. In order to have the national authorithy punished?

[332] Verification Annex, Part II, para. 65.

[333] Krutzsch et al., *supra* n. 4, at 157-158.

[334] Article IX, para. 21. In paras. 22-25 in particular the review is detailed.

[335] Verification Annex, Part II, para. 65.

[336] Krutzsch et al., *supra* n. 4, at 165: "For consistency, the interpretation of paragraph 35

Article VIII paragraph 35. In these cases the Executive Council is involved in the review of inspection reports. Other cases that involve the Executive Council are when States Parties request the Executive Council to assist in the clarification of situations which may be considered ambiguous or give rise to a concern about the possible non-compliance of another State Party;[337] when it is requested to obtain clarification from another State Party;[338] or in case a State Party requests assistance in the clarification of a situation that has given rise to its possible non-compliance.[339] The Executive Council shall consider any issue or matter within its competence affecting the Convention and its implementation "including concerns regarding compliance, and cases of non-compliance".[340] Whereas under Article VIII paragraph 31 - under *powers and functions* - the general task of the Executive Council of promoting adherence with the Convention is set out ("[..] *shall promote* the effective implementation of, and compliance with, this Convention"[..]), paragraph 35 is about actual or potential breaches ("[..] *shall consider* any issue [..] affecting this Convention, including concerns regarding compliance [..]").[341] This is elaborated upon in paragraph 36. What then are the "review" methods to be applied by the Executive Council? In contradistinction to the TS-phase, and not withstanding the essential protection of confidential information, it will be done via a semi-public procedure, for the Executive Council with its 41 members is a representative organ of the OPCW.[342] Like in the case of the Director-General who can seek clarification (see above) the Executive Council "shall consult" with the States Parties involved and, as appropriate, request the State Party to take measures to redress the situation within a specified period.[343] With the exception of consultation - a non-judicial dispute settlement technique - no specific method for review is suggested by the Convention. It may be assumed therefore that the objective facts established by the TS and the (technical) assessment made by it, which has led to doubts about compliance, together with the ensuing comments by States Parties that are not considered to be satisfatcory form the basis ("the file of the case") for a review by the Council. Furthermore, it may be assumed that the norm to be applied is uncontested and if not, that also the opinion of the legal council of the Organization would be

---

should also cover the content of the provision of Verification Annex, Part II, paragraph 65."

[337] Article IX, para. 3.

[338] Article IX, para. 4.

[339] Article IX, para. 5.

[340] Article VIII, para. 35.

[341] Emphasis added.

[342] Compare the case of the United Nations Commission on Human Rights with its 43 members: "..although the procedure under Resolution 1503 is confidential, it is certainly not secret. Every communication is seen in summary by the forty-three government representatives on the Commission.", A.H. Robertson & J.G. Merrills, *Human Rights in the World*(1992), at 76

[343] Article VIII, para. 36.

included. But who, one might wonder, then weighs this opinion on the level of the Executive Council? The Convention is silent on this point.[344] This clearly involves the creative function.

This information will then have to lead the Executive Council to a decision, a matter of substance, therefore to be taken by a two-thirds majority.[345] Here we find a mix of review and correction as the Executive Council may opt for an extended review by the Conference or by the UN GA or SC. Even in the case whereby it recommends a particular course it may be assumed that an extended review first takes place within the context of the Conference. The measures[346] to be applied are:

(a) inform all States Parties of the issue or matter;
(b) bring the issue to the attention of the Conference;
(c) make recommendations to the Conference regarding measures to redress the situation and to ensure compliance.

Informing all States Parties of the matter (*sub. a*) is designed to attract the attention of the membership of the OPCW to the case. It can also be regarded as a "moral sanction".[347] The difference between *sub. b* and *sub. c* may be that in the case of *sub.b* "… the Conference's action may be required, be it that the Council was unable to come to a conclusion on how to assess a contested behaviour ... .[348] In the case of *sub. c* the Council has been able to decide on a course of action. Krutzsch is of the opinion that "[s]uch action would be required if the authority of the Conference and concerted actions of the members of the Organization are needed to overcome the resistance of the State Party involved to bring its behaviour into harmony with its obligations under the Convention".[349] A more simple explanation may be that it concerns a situation in which the Council has already asked the State Party to take measures to redress a situation and it is the Conference and not the Executive Council that is empowered under Article XII to decide on the necessary

---

[344] Also the Rules of Procedure of the Executive Council do not elaborate on this. It has to be assumed that questions concerning compliance will be dealt with just as any other question which the Executive Council has to consider. Rule 12 refers to meeting at short notice under these circumstances. Furthermore, rule 18 makes clear that each matter "brought to the attention of the Council by the Director-General or proposed for inclusion in the agenda by any member of the Organization, the United Nations or a State or an international organization with which the Organization has a relationship agreement *shall be accompanied by an explanatory memorandum and, if possible, by basic documents or by a draft decision or recommendation*", C-I/DEC.72, 23 May 1997. The least that one may assume is that the explanatory memorandum, the draft decision or recommendation will have passed the desk of the legal advisor (TS) of the OPCW.

[345] Article VIII, para. 29.

[346] Article VIII, para. 36.

[347] Krutzsch et al., *supra* n. 4 at 160.

[348] "[..]or that the decision of the principal organ is needed on a problem of general importance", *ibid.* at 160.

[349] *Ibid*, at 160.

measures. In cases of "particular gravity" the Executive Council may bring the matter, including relevant information and conclusions, directly to the GA and the SC.

The rather open way of reviewing is illustrated in the case of a challenge inspection where the Convention rather vaguely stipulates that the Executive Council "shall review" the inspection report and the comments made thereto "*in accordance with its powers and functions*".[350] It should be remembered, however, that it is the Conference that decides on the powers and functions both of the Executive Council and the TS.[351]

* The role of the Conference

Under "powers and functions" of the Conference in Article VIII the central position of the Conference regarding compliance is established: "The Conference shall review compliance with this Convention." This is not surprising for the Conference is the principal organ of the OPCW at which each member is represented. Furthermore, the Conference, being the principal organ of the OPCW, may take decisions on "any questions, matters or issues related to this Convention raised by a State Party or brought to its attention by the Executive Council".[352] For that it shall take the necessary measures to ensure compliance and redress and remedy any situation in contravention of the CWC.[353] It appears that the Conference is completely free to organize this review stage. It could even decide to establish a subsidiary organ for this purpose.[354]

On the basis of what information will the Conference take its decisions? If we take the case of the "challenge inspection" to guide us, it will have a varied "file" at its disposal. This will not only contain the factual findings of the inspector as well as an assessment by the inspection team "of the degree and nature of access and cooperation granted for the satisfactory implementation of the challenge inspection"[355] but also the comments made by the requesting State Party, the inspected State Party and those by other States Parties.[356] Furthermore, in considering the necessary measures under Article XII the Conference "shall take into account all information and recommendations[357]

---

[350] Article IX, para. 22.
[351] Article VIII, para. 19.
[352] Article VIII, para. 19.
[353] Article VIII, para. 21 (k).
[354] Article VIII, para. 21 (f).
[355] Article IX, para. 21.
[356] Article IX, para. 21.
[357] It is not clear from the wording of Article XII whether or not a recommendation is essential before the Conference can decide on this matter. The most logical seems to be that the Conference also can decide without any recommendation and that the Conference "[..]

submitted on the issues by the Executive Council".[358] When reviewing the case before it decides on any such measure the Conference will therefore also have the opinion of the Executive Council to hand, as otherwise it could not recommend measures in cases of non-compliance. No effective review therefore seems to be possible without a proper hearing and having received a complete file, in other words essential elements for due process.

4. The correction function

The next question is what can actually be done to correct a State Party's behaviour if the conclusion is that it has breached the Convention? In that respect the supervisory system under the CWC does not seem so much different from general international law for it appears rather weak on actual enforcement. It is, however, important to note that the CWC actually addresses the question of reactions in the event of a breach, be it decisions of a binding or of a recommendatory character, and that it concerns reactions by the compliance control organization: the OPCW. Article XII deals with "measures to redress a situation and to ensure compliance including sanctions". Referring to the negotiations of the Convention Krutzsch mentions that although several attempts were made to draw up a list of possible sanctions these failed, but that it became clear that an organization "for the implementation of a disarmament treaty" did not have economic services or benefits available, like an organization for economic assistance and co-operation and development to restrict or suspend.[359] To start with, a State Party may not be deprived of its membership in the Organization as a sanction,[360] which is not surprising given that it is essential to preserve the universal character of the Convention.[361] Accordingly a member should be allowed to be able to fulfil its major rights under this Convention under Article IX. However, in cases where a State Party has been requested by the Executive Council to take measures to redress a situation "raising problems with regard to compliance" and fails to accommodate such a request, the Conference could restrict or suspend the State Party's right and privileges under the Convention until it is in compliance with the CWC.[362] Within the system of the Convention this appears as the crucial sanction.

---

the Executive Council", (Krutzsch et al., *supra* n.4, at 222).

[358] Article XII, para. 1.

[359] Krutzsch et al., *supra* n. 4 at 224.

[360] Article VIII, para. 2. This also includes suspension of membership. See Krutzsch, *ibid*, at 128.

[361] Also Krutzsch et al., *supra* n. 4 at 128 "[..]an organization which by virtue of its existence has to strive towards universal adherence, would by a policy of expulsion defeat its main purpose". Furthermore, they give as the rationale that a State Party stripped of its membership might falsely conclude that it was free from its obligations under the Convention.

[362] Article XII, para. 2. See Krutzsch et al., *ibid*, at 223.

Which rights and privileges under the Convention are of sufficient weight to give it such prominence?

- The case which first springs to mind revolves around Article XI on economic and technological developments, especially the suspension of "the right to participate in the fullest possible exchange of chemicals, equipment and scientific and technical information relating to the development and application of chemistry for purposes not prohibited under this Convention" (para. 2(b)), as well as a recommendation to Member States for restrictions in trade concerning chemicals, equipment and know how under Article XI paragraph 2 (c).[363] The heated debates during the PrepCom about the obligations under Article XI at least suggest the contentious character of any such measures.
- Another sanction would be the suspension of the rights to assistance and protection against chemical weapons under Article X.
- Also as a sanction one might treat a State Party as a non-treaty Party as far as the transfer of chemicals is concerned, viz. non-trade in Schedule 2 chemicals, because three years after entry into force only the transfer of chemicals to States Parties is permitted.[364] Also Schedule 1 chemicals may only be transferred to another State Party for the objectives indicated in the Verification Annex.[365] And with regard to Schedule 3 chemicals, States Parties shall adopt measures that ensure that the transferred chemicals shall only be used for non-prohibited purposes,[366] whereby after five years after entry into force States Parties shall consider the need to establish "other measures" regarding the transfer of Schedule 3 chemicals to States not Party to the Convention!
- In breaching its duty to maintain the confidential character of information received a suspension of the right to receive confidential information, for instance under Article IX paragraph 3, seems logical.
- In cases where "serious damage to the object and purpose" of the CWC may result from activities prohibited under the CWC, in particular the ones mentioned by Article I, the Conference may "recommend collective measures to States Parties in conformity with international law."[367] This clearly points to

---

[363] See, Krutzsch et al., *ibid*, at 224. "The right to participate in the fullest possible exchange of chemicals etc. pursuant to Article XI, para. 2 (b), can be restricted with regard to Schedule 2 chemicals when a State Party fails to comply with the provisions of the Verification Annex, Part VII, paragraphs 31 and 32, concerning the transfers of such chemicals to States not Party to this Convention", Article IX, para. 23 allows for financial compensation for the costs of challenge inspections in case of abuse. Krutzsch et al. (at 224) also mention the financial costs resulting from non-cooperation with the inspection team under the Verification Annex, Part II 35 and 36. They do not, however, provide any basis therefor.

[364] Verification Annex, Part VII, C, para. 31.

[365] Verification Annex, Part VI, B, 3.

[366] Verification Annex, Part VIII, C, 26.

[367] Article XII, para. 3.

the recommendation to States Parties of countermeasures not contrary to international law like retorsion. These measures, however, are of a non-binding recommendatory character,[368] for instance a recommendation "monitored by the verification mechanism of the Organization"[369] to withhold from the non-complying State Party the export of certain chemicals or equipment, or technical knowledge. The Conference and the Executive Council here seem to have a maximum of flexibility, as long as these recommendations fit the purpose and principles of the Convention and are not contrary to international law.[370] This even seems not to exclude the recommendation of classic sanctions under international law in not directly related areas.[371]

- And "in cases of particular gravity" the Conference shall (the only time "shall" is mentioned in Article XII, author) bring the issue together with the file on the matter to the attention of the General Assembly and the Security Council. A similar provisional correction could already be undertaken by the Executive Council "in case of particular gravity and *urgency*".[372] In the Relationship Agreement between the OPCW and the UN both cases are specifically mentioned. In these cases the OPCW shall notify the Secretary-General of the UN, who shall bring the question to the attention of the General Assembly and the Security Council which will act as appropriate, in accordance with their own mandates. Of course this reference to the UN General Assembly or Security Council cannot create any competence for these organs that they do not already have under the Charter. These measures should be regarded as complementary to the aforementioned ones under the Convention on which the Conference decides in close cooperation with the Executive Council. The Relationship Agreement between the UN and the OPCW, however, assures that the UN will give the matter proper consideration and that the OPCW will provide the UN with any additional information which may be necessary.[373] Consideration by the Security Council may lead to

---

368 M. Kamto, Discussion in: Bardonnet (ed.), *supra* n. 4, at 403: "As for recommendations under Article XII, para. 3, they fall within the category of classic non-binding recommendations". Mahiou, however, mentions "even if it is not known whether the word "recommendation" is used in Article XII in its usual sense or whether it means that there is an obligation", *ibid*, at 402.

369 Krutzsch et al., *supra* n.4, at 226.

370 According to Krutzsch et al. "in conformity with international law" "carries the message that the prerogatives of the UN Security Council should be respected", *ibid* n. 4, at 225. I am of the opinion, however, that the simple meaning is that such measures should not be contrary to international law.

371 For instance via reprisals. On countermeasures under Article XII see A. Rosas, Reactions in the Event of Breach, in Bardonnet (ed.), *supra* n. 4, at 577-589.

372 Article VIII, para. 36. Emphasis is added.

373 "1. The United Nations and the OPCW, recognising the need to work jointly to achieve mutual objectives, and with a view to facilitating the effective exercise of their responsibilities, agree to cooperate closely within their respective mandates and to consult on

decisions of the Security Council under Chapter VII of the UN Charter, like sanctions or if necessary enforcement actions to redress a situation.

5. The creative function

This function of the OPCW could be regarded as the tool to assist any of the other functions discussed, because in any of these functions a rule may need to be clarified. Often a rule of law needs to be clarified before the collection, review and correction function can become operative. It may appear that what is meant is a technique to interpret a rule of law comparable to the rules contained in Articles 31-33 of the Vienna Convention on the Law of Treaties which deal with the interpretation of treaties. But the quintessential difference is that there is an ongoing process within the context of an international organization in the execution of its principal task of compliance control, or supervision of States Parties' commitments under the CWC. Therefore one of the supervisory functions of the OPCW is the shaping of the law. Bernauer seems to refer to this same function when he remarks: "[o]ne of the most important functions of international organizations is to serve as fora where the parties can engage in the interpretation and modification of agreements and decide on actions to be taken in the implementation process".[374] As we have seen when discussing the other supervisory functions, there is a constant referral back and forth between States Parties and the OPCW. Thereby a constant use is being made of diplomatic dispute settlement techniques like consultation, or clarification (compare Article IX), both of which are forms of negotiation. More in general it can be held that this wide use of dispute

matters of mutual interest and concern. To that end, the United Nations and the OPCW shall cooperate with each other in accordance with the provisions of their respective constituent instruments.

2. Cooperation between the United Nations and the OPCW, in particular, shall require that:

(a) cases of particular gravity and urgency which, in accordance with paragraph 36 of Article VIII of the Convention, shall, including relevant information and conclusions, be brought directly to the attention of the General Assembly and the Security Council by the Executive Council, through the Secretary-General in accordance with the existing United Nations procedures;

(b) cases of particular gravity which, in accordance with paragraph 4 of Article XII of the Convention, shall, including relevant information and conclusions, be brought to the attention of the General Assembly and the Security Council by the Conference of the States Parties through the Secretary-General in accordance with the existing United Nations procedures;

[...]

3. The OPCW, within its competence and in accordance with the provision of the Convention, shall cooperate with the General Assembly and the Security Council by furnishing them, at the request of either, such information and assistance as may be required in the exercise of their respective responsibilities under the United Nations Charter.

[...]", Article II, Relationship Agreement between the UN and the PCW, *supra* n.11.

[374] Bernauer, *supra* n. 130, at 335.

settlement techniques is characteristic of the system of supervision under the CWC. Not surprisingly (in this vain) also disputes concerning "the application or the interpretation" of the CWC will have to be settled in conformity with the provisions of the UN Charter, viz. Article 33 or more generally Chapter VI. Also disputes between two or more States Parties or between the OPCW and one or more States Parties concerning the interpretation or application of the CWC will according to Article XIV have to be settled via negotiation or other means of their choice, including recourse to appropriate organs. This appears also to refer to the subsidiary organs that the Conference by virtue of Article XIV, paragraph 4 may establish[375] (or entrust) with the task of settlement of disputes brought to its attention by the Executive Council or raised by States Parties. Elsewhere[376] I have argued that given the structure of Article XIV and of its close link with Article 33 (1) of the Charter it is obvious that these tasks seem to refer to fact finding, conciliation and arbitration, modes of settlement contained in Article 33 (1) of the Charter but not explicitly mentioned in Article XIV. Given the strong provisions of the CWC with regard to *collection* there does not appear to be any direct necessity for the establishment of a subsidiary organ for fact finding; with regard to the creative function it is not even necessary. All the more so for the effective execution of the creative function of the OPCW some institutional basis for conciliation or arbitration, either *ad hoc* or semi-permanent via a subsidiary organ is in order, as this will provide the necessary institutional basis for these two modes of dispute settlement.

States Parties may, by mutual consent, also refer a dispute to the ICJ. Given that only States may be parties before the Court[377] this excludes disputes involving the OPCW. Under Article XIV, paragraph 5 both the Conference and the Executive Council may request the ICJ for an advisory opinion on "any legal question within the scope of the activities of the Organization". For this, however, on each occasion authorization is needed by the General Assembly of the UN.[378]

---

[375] On the basis of Article VIII, para. 21 (f).

[376] Myjer, *supra* n. 205, at p. 541.

[377] Article 34, Statute of the International Court of Justice.

[378] This is an interesting feature, for the OPCW is apparently not to be regarded as a specialized agency with a general authorization under Article 96 (compare L.M. Goodrich and E. Hambro, *Charter of the United Nations, Commentary and Documents* (1946), at 267) but as an "independent autonomous international organization", that will be dependent on authorization from the GA in each separate case. Compare the Relationship Agreement UN-OPCW (*supra* n. 11): "The UN recognizes that the OPCW, by virtue of the Convention, shall function as an independent, autonomous international organization in the working relationship with the UN established by this Agreement", (Article I, para. 2), and also the position taken by the Legal Advisor of the OPCW, when discussing the Headquarters Agreement. At that time Pakistan insisted that an explicit reference would be made in it concerning the

Furthermore, the Executive Council may contribute by whatever means it considers appropriate, including offering its good offices.[379]

VI. CWC supervision as a management model and the quantum leap in the institutional law of arms control

1. General

Are there, apart from the few specific characteristics mentioned, other reasons to regard the OPCW as an international organization so special that it was not only used to model the CTBTO upon, but that also the IAEA was looking at the system of the CWC for answers to improve its function as well as the States Parties to the BWC? The answer seems to lie in the fact that the OPCW is more than a simple verification organization. For even though we are dealing with what could be called a single purpose organization,[380] the single purpose is, however, of a rather broad nature. It is not only fulfilling a single aspect of the process of supervision, viz. the verification by the inspectors and the TS of compliance by States Parties with the Convention. The OPCW represents an organization, whereby the technical verification via inspections is only one aspect. The sum of the different stages of supervision offers more in terms of effective supervision than suggested by the respective sub-functions apart, for all four - collection, review, correction and creation - are woven together. From the very first moment that States Parties hand in their declarations and the initial inspections take place, there is a constant referral back and forth providing additional information and explanation. There is contact between the suspicious and the suspected State Party asking for clarification, which may ultimately culminate in a challenge inspection, not as a favour but as a right. It

---

adjudication of the ICJ. In its reply the Legal Advisor did not agree for he was of the view that "due to the Article 96 of the UN Charter (only organs of the UN and specialized agencies are entitled to request advisory opinions) the OPCW will not receive general authorisation and will be obliged to ask the General Assembly in each *separate case* (emphasis added) to consider its application and to give authorisation to request the advisory opinion". (PC-XVI/A/2). Since he thought this to be a too cumbersome and time-consuming mechanism, he did not want to recommend this as a dispute settlement mechanism in the Headquarters Agreement. It would, however, be interesting to hear whether also the GA would agree to that and under which paragraph the possibility for these separate requests would then fall. For Article 96, para. 1 refers to the GA or SC requesting such an advisory opinion and Article 96 para. 2 concerns other organs of the UN and specialized agencies. The UN/OPCW Relationship Agreement is not clear in that respect: "The UN and the OPCW agree that each such request for an advisory opinion shall first be submitted to the GA, which will decide upon the request in accordance with Article 96 of the Charter," (Article VII, para. 2), *supra* n. 11.

[379] Article XIV, para. 3.

[380] A special organization to perform specific functions. See Schermers & Blokker, *supra* n. 149 at 43.

involves active participation in all stages, be it for fact finding, review or correction purposes, by the different organs of the OPCW. And in all of these stages use is made of dispute settlement techniques in order to ensure compliance within the system of the Convention. Via the different functions of the OPCW it appears possible to maximize States Parties' compliance. All of this happens within the framework of this specialized international organization, that indeed has a single purpose, this being control over compliance, in all its aspects, with the central norms of the Chemical Weapons Convention. The interesting aspect is that compliance is primarily being controlled within the system by making use of methods of dispute settlement, and less by making use of the more traditional coercive methods to enforce compliance. This process is constantly in operation, whereby via the element of information and clarification compliance is constantly being assessed.[381] This whole process is somehow reminiscent of *musyawarah,*[382] an Indonesian indigenous way of decision-making via deliberation and discourse.

The CWC system of supervision adheres to Chowdhury's observation that

> "[..] the effectiveness of a legal order is not exclusively dependent on the effectiveness of sanctions; effectiveness and availability of the techniques and procedures for detection of breach are equally important".[383]

This is the case since it represents a comprehensive system of continuous control whereby from the very first moment dispute settlement techniques are used. Of these the fact finding via on-site inspection is of course of primordial importance.

The CWC with the OPCW thereby resemble a self-contained regime.[384] This leaves us, however, with some of the pertinent questions raised by Koskenniemi in his challenging article on the comparable enforcement of commitments under environmental law,[385] how special non-compliance

---

[381] Den Dekker (*supra* n. 13) in his current research is developing a model of supervision, which partly explains the constancy, by pointing out that the element of control is constantly in operation. Regardless of the clarification of possible disputes, the "run of the mill" verification continues.

[382] Literally: 1. meeting, conference; 2. discussion, deliberation. It is closely linked with local law (*adat*), which is based on decisions taken in the village council after a process of deliberation (*musyawarah*) and consensus seeking (*mufakat*)", J. Van Reenen, *Central Pillars of the House* (thesis Leyden, 1996), at 35.

[383] Chowdhury, *supra* n. 233, at xvi.

[384] Compare the discussion on self-contained regimes in L.A.N.M. Barnhoorn and K.C. Wellens (ed.), *Diversity in Secondary Rules and the Unity of International Law* (1995).

[385] "Recent treaties have set up bodies for monitoring and information gathering, reporting and inspection of party performance. Such bodies rarely possess formal power for

procedures relate to using traditional remedies for breach of treaties. For, after all, he argues, a breach of an international obligation is an internationally wrongful act, and wrongfulness gives rise to responsibility:

> "As far as traditional law is concerned, this is the long and the short of "non-compliance": Breach entails wrongfulness; wrongfulness calls for responsibility which in turn may be realized either through recourse to third-party settlement or, in certain circumstances, by taking counter-measures against a non-performing party. Where, then, is the need for specific provisions on non-compliance?"[386]

2. The management model

With this conclusion on the type of compliance control model the CWC system of supervision represents we have entered the quite specific debate on compliance control by regime theorists[387] for this characterisation of the OPCW appears to correspond to the "management model" - in contradistinction to the "coercive model"[388]- of the managerial school[389]- as developed by social scientists and of which, amongst lawyers, the Chayes'[390] are proponents - that considers "arrangements featuring enforcement as a means of eliciting compliance"[391] as not of much use in international society. "Those compliance problems that do exist are best addressed as management rather than enforcement problems."[392] Instances of apparent non-compliance are problems to be solved, rather than violations that have to be punished.[393] Downs and co. who establish a connection between the depth of cooperation represented by a given treaty and the amount of enforcement that is needed[394] are of the opinion that "this suggests that evaluating the importance of enforcement by examining the level of compliance is misleading".[395] Instead we need to worry about the possibility that:

---

enforcement, but instead rely on their "capacity to bring to bear a form of community pressure and international accountability". Koskenniemi, *supra* n. 240, p.123.

[386] Koskenniemi, *ibid*, at 125.

[387] On regime theory and international law see for instance A. Hurrell, International Society and the Study of Regimes: A Reflective Approach, in: R.J. Beck et al., *International Rules, Approaches from International Law and International Relations* (1996).

[388] See review of Chayes, by Harold Hongju Koh, in 91 *AJIL* (1997), at 389-391.

[389] Downs, *supra* n. 237, at 379 refers to this group of social scientists as the managerial school.

[390] Chayes, *supra* n. 69. See inter alia also Chayes & Chayes, On compliance, *supra* n. 237, pp 175-205.

[391] O. Young quoted in Downs, *supra* n. 237, at 381.

[392] *Ibid*, at 379.

[393] *Ibid*, at 381.

[394] *Ibid*, 382 et seq.

[395] *Ibid*, at 387.

> "[..] both the high rate of compliance and relative absence of enforcement threats are due not so much to the irrelevance of enforcement as to the fact that states are avoiding deep cooperation [..] because they are unwilling or unable to pay the costs of enforcement."[396]

The most prominent aspects of the CWC regime, as described above, fall into place and can be explained by looking at it through the prism of the management model, like the discursive nature of the compliance control model, as well as its intrinsically transparent character. Taking a closer look at some of the central elements of Chayes' management strategy, in particular at the elements of *transparency*, *dispute settlement*, *capacity building* and the uses of *persuasion*, is illustrative. There is the element of ensuring transparency via, for instance, the development of data on "the performance of the parties as to the principal treaty norms and on the general situations of concern to the regime",[397] mostly done via self-reporting, and verification. Under the CWC the first element is found in the *collection function* of the OPCW, the second element in the *review function*. Dispute settlement under the management strategy may concern situations "where ambiguity or vagueness in treaty language creates compliance problems [..]".[398] Albeit via binding procedures or not, what counts is that treaty regimes foresee an "authoritative interpretation of controverted provisions".[399] This is exactly what happens under the *creative function*. Capacity building refers to technical, bureaucratic or financial assistance where it concerns difficulties of domestic enforcement of measures adopted in compliance with international environmental obligations.[400] In the case of the CWC reference could, for instance, be made to the establishment and maintenance of permanent stockpiles of emergency goods and humanitarian assistance by States Parties (against chemical weapons) in accordance with Article X paragraph 7 (b) and (c), or to training courses for National Authorities that have been voluntarily organized. Furthermore, it can be held that the whole process of supervision in itself leads to greater transparency.[401] "These disparate elements - transparency, dispute settlement, capacity building - [..] can be considered to be parts of a management strategy. They merge into a broader process of "jawboning" - the effort to *persuade* the miscreant to change its ways - that is the characteristic method by which international regimes seek to induce compliance".[402] It is this element of persuasion that can be traced back in the different functions of the OPCW, like when information is

[396] *Ibid*, at 387.
[397] Chayes, *supra* n. 69, at 23.
[398] *Ibid*, at 24.
[399] *Ibid*, at 24.
[400] *Ibid*, at 25.
[401] In Article X(4) where it concerns the provision of information reference is even made to "transparency" ("for the purposes of increasing *transparency*"). (Emphasis added).
[402] Chayes, *supra* n. 69, at 25.

exchanged and clarification is being asked for, culminating as a last resort in the *correction function*. Compliance further seems to benefit from the two levels of management, namely at the international level by the OPCW and by the States Parties and at the national level by the respective National Authorities, which leads to the greater "interwoveness" of rules and procedures between these two levels. The focus on management to ensure compliance, instead of on coercive strategies, compensates under the CWC regime for the lack of a real enforcement mechanism, although I have to agree with Hongju Koh that management and the elements of coercion are not alternatives, but complement one another,[403] which is the way correction via the UN should be looked upon.

The Chayes' refer to a *New Sovereignty*. According to Hongju Koh they "suggest that sovereignty now means not freedom *from* external interference, but freedom *to* engage in international relations as members of international regimes. A state's sovereignty thus becomes contingent upon its *ongoing web* [emphasis added] of international ties and obligations".[404] And here we enter the institutional law of arms control, that appears to be beginning to be shaped via the compliance control models of an OPCW kind like the CTBTO,[405] which hang together within the broader context of the outer boundaries of the international law of military security - only arms to allow for quintessential exceptions (both conventional and customary) to the use of force, namely the use of force for collective security and for self-defence.[406] Compliance control models of the OPCW type seem to offer the best possible opportunity to realize compliance with the central treaty norms regarding chemical disarmament. The least that can be said is that given the delicate nature of national security and States' disinclination to allow for inroads on their sovereignty, this seems at present the maximum system of supervision which is attainable. This leads me to conclude that the OPCW with its specifically organized supervisory functions can be regarded as a model for future compliance

[403] Hongju Koh, *supra* n. 388 at 391. Compare A. Mahiou, Discussion in: Bardonnet (ed.), *supra* n. 4, at 402 in particular. This power of the sanction is extremely important even if it is not known whether the term "recommendation" is used in Article XII in its usual sense or whether it means that there is an obligation. Kamto, *supra* n. 369, however, is of a different opinion: "As for recommendations under Article XII, para. 3, they fall within the category of classic non-binding recommendations."

[404] Hongju Koh, *ibid* at 390. "The process [of persuasion, author] works because modern states are bound in a tightly woven fabric of international agreements, organizations, and institutions that shape their relations with one another and penetrate deeply into their internal economics and politics. The integrity and reliability of this system are of overriding importance for most states, most of the time", Chayes, *supra* n. 69 at 26.

[405] Or the one discussed with regard to the BWC, namely an organization for the Prohibition of Biological Weapons (OPBW), the effect on IAEA and so on. See p. 64.

[406] See also Introduction p.3.

control in the area of arms control. Given the multiplication of international organizations with this special compliance control function, thereby creating for States in the sphere of international security a web of "international ties and obligations",[407] one feels tempted to typify it as the prototype for an (essential) international arms control organization. In comparing it with the *International Disarmament Organization* as proposed by the Netherlands at the United Nations Special Session on Disarmament,[408] several similarities are apparent.

3. An International Disarmament Organization

For this UN Special Session on Disarmament the Netherlands tabled a working paper on the establishment of an international disarmament organization. In it "...an international disarmament organization is envisaged as the operational framework for the implementation of international arms control and disarmament treaties, with functions mainly in the field of verification. In addition it is thought that such an organization could be instrumental to the preparation and organization of review conferences already provided for in several disarmament treaties and could serve as a clearinghouse for information on disarmament."[409] The suggested approach was to initially set up an international disarmament organization for the implementation of a particular disarmament treaty, and then gradually to give it more functions "dependent on emerging needs and taking into account experience gained".[410] With regard to the possible functions for such an organization a possible future chemical weapons convention was mentioned, which would "probably provide for rather extensive notification and verification procedures" and with regard to a treaty banning nuclear tests,"[a]n international seismic system will in all probability be established to exchange and process seismic data", which would make necessary a consulatative organ with respect to technical and organizational problems of the seismic system.[411] As a first step it is then proposed that in the final document of the Special Session the Secretary-General of the UN "is requested to seek the views of member States with respect to the functions and organization of a possible

[407] Hongju Koh, *supra* n. 388, at 391.

[408] Tenth Special Session of the General Assembly, New York, 23 May-1 July 1978 (First Special Session devoted to disarmament). See Final Document of the Tenth Special Session of the General Assembly of 30 June 1978 (A/RES/S – 10/2) 125 (GG). Also A/S – 10/AC.1/37, para. 186.

[409] Study on the establishment of an international disarmament organization, Netherlands working paper, 5 April 1978, reproduced in: Ministerie van Buitenlandse Zaken (Netherlands Ministry of Foreign Affairs) no. 122 (1979), *Verslag over de Tiende Bijzondere Zitting van de Algemene Vergadering der Verenigde Naties*, at p. 97.

[410] *Ibid.*

[411] *Ibid.*

international disarmament organization...".[412] This proposal with regard to the implementation of disarmament agreements failed to be included in the Final Document,[413] however, because of Soviet Resistance to the Dutch proposal, which was procedural in nature.[414]

When comparing the OPCW with this proposed international disarmament organization the most noticeable similarity is that it also foresaw a permanent organization to streamline the consultations[415] and the implementation measures, with functions mainly in the field of verification and that it was also supposed to serve as a clearing-house for information on disarmament.[416] The proposal was then to start with a single disarmament treaty and to gradually expand it by also giving it certain tasks concerning other treaties. Looking at the OPCW this may occur in the future, but the need to build one single Disarmament Organization seems less pressing today not only because of the highly developed information systems (technology), but also because of the fact that experience has taught us that it is better to have a few active and streamlined organizations, than one single organization which, like the UN, may be considered to be top-heavy. Perhaps the above mentioned web of ties and obligations in the field of arms control or - more generallly - in the field of security, by States with different organizations of the OPCW type and between such organizations themselves offers the best guarantee for compliance. Given the present state of the art in international law where international security is concerned, or more explicitly the international law of military security, and especially with regard to the law of arms control, the CWC with its OPCW

---

[412] *Ibid.*

[413] See *supra* n. 408.

[414] Ministry of Foreign Affairs, *supra* n. 409 at 4. Also earlier, in 1973, both the Netherlands (CCD/PV 617 and CCD/410 of 13 July 1973) and Sweden (Document CCD/PV 601 of 13 April 1973) and CCD/PV 610 of 5 July 1973) had already expressed detailed views on this subject in the Conference of the Committee on Disarmament. Interestingly "*[T]he standing disarmament organ, as proposed by the Netherlands, would firstly be entrusted with the verification of a treaty banning chemical weapons*. However, it was envisaged from the beginning that such an organ could take upon itself other tasks, such as the verification of other arms control and disarmament treaties as well as the organization of review conferences provided for such treaties.In the absence of prospects, at that time, for substantial multilateral disarmament agreements as well as for other reasons, the ideas put forward by Sweden and the Netherlands were not pursued to any further degree", *ibid*, at p. 97. (Emphasis added).

[415] *Ibid*, at 98.

[416] Regarding this clearing-house function it is further elaborated: "(f). Relevant information with respect to the implementation of arms control and disarmament agreements could be combined in one organization. Data on various disarmament measures, such as for instance stockpile-destruction, seismic data, results of inspections and fact-finding missions could be stored with one organization which would act as a clearing-house for information on all implementation efforts in the field of disarmament", *ibid*, at 98.

adds a new dimension by presenting some very specific outlines for the institutional law of arms control. As such, the OPCW can be regarded as constituting a quantum leap in the institutional law of arms control.

VII. Concluding remarks

1. The relevance of initial organizational practice

Before drawing some general conclusions it should be stressed that these will primarily be based on an analysis of a theoretical model, as presented in the previous chapters when charting the CWC, the OPCW and analyzing the supervisory functions of the OPCW. As is often the case with any analysis of theoretical models the total picture may seem rather overly neat and tidy, whereas State and organizational practice may be less perfect and may lead to undesired consequences. For a proper assessment of a given regime, therefore, such practice should also be taken into consideration. The CWC regime, however, is still too much in its infancy to have already accumulated enough practice to be able to weigh properly how it will function in real terms.[417] There are, however, already some indications that the non-fulfilment by States Parties of some basic procedural obligations may affect the very delicate compliance process in all its aspects and make the management process less transparent and thereby it will undoubtedly suffer. This can be demonstrated by the example of the initial practice concerning handing in the necessary declarations, which is illustrative of possible undesired consequences. It thereby concerns the crucial and supposedly simple task of actually handing in declarations ("not later than 30 days after the Convention enters into force") for which States Parties had all the time to prepare (given that the CWC was signed in January 1993 and entered into force in May 1997). These declarations, however, remain sluggishly forthcoming. According to the report for the Fourth Conference on the implementation of the convention, by the end of 1998 one third of the States Parties had still failed to hand in the declarations that were due.[418] The report notes that this issue had become "a point of serious political concern for the OPCW by the end of 1998." Earlier, in his opening statement to the Third Conference, Director-General Bustani voiced his frustration in unequivocal terms by explicitly mentioning the

---

[417] As a sequel to their Commentary on the CWC (Krutzsch et al. supra n. 4) recently a first commentary on verification in practice by Krutszch and Trapp was published: W. Krutzsch and R. Trapp, Verification Pratice under the Chemical Weapons Convention. (1999)

[418] "By the end of 1998 a total of 86 States Parties had submitted their initial declarations to the Organization. While all of the declared chemical weapons possessor States and, with one notable exception, all States with a sizable chemical industry, had submitted their declarations to the OPCW in the period under review, approximately one third of States Parties had still failed to report their declarable activities to the Organization." C-IV/5, 2 July 1999, p. 2.

United States[419] and by urging it to submit declarations with regard to its chemical industry as it had blocked any inspection of the American chemical (civilian) industry. This led States Parties that had already fulfilled their obligations to grumble about the frequency of the inspections of their facilities[420] and voices were even heard to place budgetary constraints on the number of inspections of Schedule 2 facilities. The possible negative impact of a non-declaration by a leading country on the delicate structure of supervision, for instance non-compliance by other States Parties that would welcome this as an excuse, may explain the rather strongly worded call by the Director-General when he expressed "a feeling of uneasiness in relation to what appears to be the temptation, on the part of some States Parties, to use this current situation to place artificial limits on the number of industry inspections".[421] He urged States Parties to continue to demonstrate understanding and political generosity of spirit and not to hold "the verification regime of the Convention [..] hostage to this issue".[422] The Director-General's message therefore seems to have had a wider purpose aimed at all States Parties by stressing that it is "becoming critically important to close the remaining gaps in the verification regime, caused by the absence of declarations and by incomplete declarations. If the present situation is allowed to persist, confidence in the regime will begin to erode [..]".[423]

---

[419] "The stated source of this dissatisfaction with industry inspections is the fact that the United States of America, the State Party with the largest chemical industry in the world, has - due to legislative difficulties - not submitted declarations with respect to its chemical industry under Article VI of the Convention, and has not exposed its chemical industry to inspections. Fortunately, the primary cause of this problem, the absence of national implementing legislation for the Convention in the United States of America, has now been removed. In order to establish the "level playing field" foreseen in the Convention, it is, however, essential for the Government of the United States of America to take the necessary action to ensure that it can meet its obligations with respect to its chemical industry declarations at the earliest opportunity. I urge the Government of the United States of America, therefore, to take whatever action is necessary to achieve this goal soon." Statement by the Director-General to the Conference of the States Parties at its Third Session, C-III/DG.12, 16 November 1998. By the time of the Fifth Conference the US was pleased to state that it had "(…) at last submitted long-overdue Article VI declarations". (C-V/NAT.2, 18 May 2000).

[420] "It is an open secret that, for some national chemical industries and their respective governments, the first experience of industry verification was less than satisfactory, not because of the quality of the inspections which they received, but due to the uneven application of the verification regime across States Parties. In the interests of the Convention, it is imperative that this situation be redressed as soon as possible, and I believe that there are now good chances that this will happen", *ibid.*

[421] *Ibid.*

[422] "..I also urge other States Parties with a concern in relation to this issue, in particular those which have so far borne the bulk of the industry inspections, to continue to demonstrate understanding and political generosity of spirit. In particular, I would ask them not to hold the verification regime of the Convention, and the OPCW Programme of Work and Budget, hostage to this issue". *Ibid.*

[423] *Ibid.* In a statement to the First Committee of the UN (19 October 1990), the Director-

Also other instances similar to these, where States Parties not completely fulfil their commitment, may harm the supervisory mechanism.[424] Some States Parties may, for instance, still have difficulties in fully complying, for instance regarding challenge inspections, as a result of national constitutional impediments, or slowly forthcoming or inadequate national implementation legislation.[425] Observations like these, however, do not lead to the conclusion that the actual process of supervision does not function or is ineffective. At this stage - the CWC only entered into force in April 1997 - and on the basis of the (open) information available, one cannot yet answer this question. One is, however, reminded that even a refined theoretical model may encounter difficulties in practice.

The outlook, however, is positive, for there is already an international organization in place and operational and if one only goes by the sheer size of the number of inspections the system seems to work well.[426] But given the almost universal membership it also points at some of the limitations of this inherently transparent compliance control model.

2. General Conclusions

— Looking at its structure as an international organization the OPCW does not seem so remarkable: it was created by States Parties via a treaty, containing its constitution, describing clearly both its functions as well as the tasks and competences of the respective organs. Of these organs the Conference as the plenary is the classic representative one, the Executive Council the executive one and the Technical Secretariat the classic permanent body foreseeing both the technical and administrative support structure. Given the necessary universal application of the Convention, the OPCW is an open organization of which all States Parties are automatically members. The organization enjoys privileges and immunities, with special arrangements for the inspectors in carrying out their duties. Given the subject matter of the Convention and

General of OPCW stated when referring to what might happen if the current situation were to continue for "yet another year": "I have no doubt that the very soul of the Convention's verification regime would be at stake".

[424] "It is also my sincere hope[..] that, in the very near future the United States of America will take action to rectify those aspects of its implementing legislation - in relation to the issues of challenge inspections, out of country analysis and low concentration thresholds - which, in our eyes and in the eyes of many, are not in accordance with the spirit of the Convention." *Ibid.*

[425] States Parties, however, are bound to comply fully with the CWC, which may not be subject to reservations (Article XXII). On the issue of national implementation see M. Bothe, National Implementation of the CWC: Some Legal Considerations, in Bothe et al., supra n. 4, in particular pp. 545-546 (on the relationship between treaties and the constitution) and pp. 551-552 (on the need for appropriate implementation legislation).

[426] For only 1998 the 200 inspectors of the OPCW made a total of 261 inspections of 198 sites in 26 States Parties, amounting to 16,927 inspector days! C-IV/5, 2 July 1999.

specifically the element of challenge inspection the extensive arrangements in this respect are functional and essential for the fulfilment of its purposes and functions.[427] Furthermore, the OPCW can be regarded to have both an internal and an external legal personality, with ensuing rights, like a treaty-making capacity,[428] and duties. A special feature in this respect is the fact that the liability of the OPCW for any breach of confidentiality committed by a member of the TS is excluded.[429] Special, and essential from the point of view of arms control, is the fact that no State Party can be deprived of its membership, for instance as a reaction to non-compliance. With regard to decision making we have noted the possibility of decision making by a two-thirds majority, which is especially remarkable in the area of security. Furthermore, that which has stood out is the three-quarters majority which is required to block a challenge inspection and the non-discriminatory character of allowing each State Party an equal vote, all aimed at achieving the aspect of universality.

— From the dogmatic point of view of the law of international organizations the OPCW does not therefore have many characteristics that make it stand out as an international organization. After all, within that area of the law one already finds all forms of transfer of state power to an international organization, whereby the ultimate form of transfer is the creation of a supranational international organization in a certain area. However, given the fact that arms control commitments deal with the security interests of States, and thereby impact on a State's security concept, allowing for compliance control in this very security area is by its very nature a delicate issue. It

---

[427] See Amarasinge, *supra* n. 219, at 370.

[428] Compare "The Executive Council shall: (a) Conclude agreements or arrangements with States and international organizations..."(Article VIII, para. 34). See for instance the OPCW Headquarters Agreement (C-I/DEC.59, of 14 May 1997) or the draft Relationship Agreement between the United Nations and the OPCW. See *supra* n. 11. On the possession of personality by international organizations and treaty-making capacity see White, *supra* n. 149 at 28: "[..] although the possession of personality by international organizations may produce certain common core features in the sense of rights, principally treaty-making capacity, privileges and immunities, limited *locus standi* before international tribunals and capacity to bring claims, and duties in the sense of the "responsibility of the organization for its own illegal acts, the extent of the personality of a particular organization depends on its constituent document [..]", at 28. Also I. Brownlie, *Principles of Public International Law* (1990), at 683-684: "The existence of legal personality does not of itself support a power to make treaties, and everything depends on the terms of the constituent instrument of the organization."

[429] This, however, does not exclude the responsibility of the OPCW. (Compare *supra* n. 149 Schermers & Blokker at 991). It deals with a complicated question that touches upon Member States' liability which was the issue in the case of the insolvent Tin Council. See Schermers & Blokker, *ibid*, at 990 et seq, in particular 993-994 and 1009-1010. On responsibility and liability also see extensively Amerasinghe, *supra* n. 219. With regard to the Tin Council especially at 259 et seq.

therefore appears remarkable that the CWC allows for such a substantial encroachment into States Parties' national sovereignty by allowing for on-site monitoring, on-site routine inspections and even on-site challenge inspections, which at after all take place within States Parties' domestic jurisdiction. It may then seem even more remarkable that although the primary organs - the Executive Council and the Conference - primarily aim to achieve decisions by consensus, they *can* take decisions by a two-thirds majority. One observes therefore, in other words, that in the supervision of States Parties' compliance with the material obligations of the CWC, responsibility is primarily allocated to the international organization and its organs rather than to States Parties separately. These apparently paradoxical commitments, however, emanate from the very fact that it concerns commitments in the area of security. States Parties were only willing to allow for such a fundamental encroachment upon their sovereignty, as well as the substantial financial costs this supervisory mechanism entails, because of the very fact that in the area of arms control they need maximum certainty that all States Parties will comply. This could be classified as a principle of arms control law.

— Under the CWC a supervisory mechanism has been developed whereby a central role is allocated to the OPCW. In all respects its role is that of a supervisory organization *pur sang* and is not restricted to that of a verification organization. As a model it has several similarities with the 1978 Dutch proposal for an *International Disarmament Organization*. It could even be argued that the OPCW goes further and is more comprehensive in the supervisory functions it exercises.

— The supervisory system in the case of the CWC, with its central role for the OPCW, demonstrates essentially a non-adversarial process whereby there is a mix between, on the one hand, States Parties which are bound to declare a certain state of affairs with, on the other, organs of this international organization which have a reviewing capacity. But not only does the organization actively review, the States Parties also do so when asking for clarification or initiating a challenge inspection. Characteristic of this supervisory system is that in this process with regard to all of the supervisory functions (collection, review, correction, creative) there is constant referral back and forth to the States Parties in question, be it the inspected or the requesting State, and also between the different phases of this process of supervision. Within this process all elements like the declarations, the clarifications or the inspections are essential.

— This process acts as a constant "guardian" of the collective security interests of the States Parties and will undoubtedly have a beneficial effect on the prevention of formal disputes. This is important, for the CWC is weak as regards judicial dispute settlement.

— The supervision model under the CWC actually presents an example of compliance management in the sense of Chayes & Chayes, which is cooperative rather than adversarial in character. Applying this model makes the most prominent aspects of the CWC regime, like its non-adverserial and transparant character fall into place. It also explains the very strength of the CWC model, whereby the different stages of supervision offer more in terms of effective supervision than suggested by the respective sub-functions on their own, as all four functions are interwoven.

— The OPCW's Confidentiality Commission, with its special Registry Agreement, is at the same time illustrative of how essential it is, if only from the point of view of confidence building, also to have a proper - potentially adverserial and coercive - dispute settlement system in place.

COMMENTS

Dieter Fleck

The invitation to comment on Dr. Myjer's paper has offered me the privilege to be one of its first readers. So I should like to take this opportunity to open our discussion by congratulating the author on a most comprehensive, carefully researched and very timely study of the law of international organizations.

The Organization for the Prohibition of Chemical Weapons (OPCW) which is now formally established may be expected to play an active role in implementing the Convention, verifying and supporting its compliance by States Parties and assisting in the avoidance and peaceful settlement of disputes. Dr. Myjer's study very distinctly shows that certain functions of the OPCW require further legal consideration.

Although I have some interest in the topic as a government expert who concluded one of the first support arrangements with the Preparatory Commission for the OPCW in March 1997, the following observations are personal. Let me first discuss a few more limited questions and then focus on Dr. Myjer's assessment of the OPCW as a "quantum leap" in the international law of arms control.

I can see some difficulties with a reference Dr. Myjer made to "self-defence *ex* Article 51 of the UN Charter" (p. 4), since the legal roots of self-defence cannot be exclusively located in the Charter. Article 51 refers to self-defence as an inherent right which did not require a new definition in the Charter. As the International Court of Justice stated in the *Nicaragua* case, it is difficult to see how the "natural" or "inherent" right of self-defence can be other than of a customary nature, "even if its present context has been confirmed and influenced by the Charter". Furthermore, for a study so closely related to legal aspects of international security it should not be taken as mere semantics if I may suggest to broaden the concept of "military security" used in several parts of the study (e.g. pp. 2-4). Considering the overall political aspects involved, we should not confine ourselves to military aspects but should rather speak of international security in general. For a proper assessment of the work of the OPCW a broad notion of international security remains very essential.

When discussing privileges and immunities, Dr. Myjer expressed the opinion that they should be defined in agreements between the OPCW and the States Parties as well as in the Headquarters Agreement (pp. (102, 103). While

E.P.J. Myjer (ed.), Issues of Arms Control Law and the Chemical Weapons Convention, 141–144.

this is certainly very valid as far as the Headquarters Agreement is concerned,[1] I would submit that the observance by the States Parties of privileges and immunities of the Organization under Article VIII (48-51) CWC, and of inspectors and inspection assistants under Part B of the Verification Annex are not and should not be made subject to special agreements, since the provisions referred to are sufficient and any effort to supplement or even modify them might lead to a weakening of the protection of the personnel concerned in critical situations.

Turning to liability, Dr. Myjer stated that the Confidentiality Annex makes it quite clear that the OPCW shall not be held liable for a breach of confidentiality committed by a member of the Technical Secretariat (p. 103). While I would have difficulties in interpreting the Confidentiality Annex in this way, I would agree with the opinion expressed in the same context (p. 137), that there would still be responsibility on the part of the OPCW, unless liability is excluded under special agreements. I would also add that as a matter of principle all States Parties to the OPCW remain fully liable for claims that cannot be settled by the OPCW within its budget.

Apart from these minor observations on the draft as it was presented, I fully support Dr. Myjer's assessment of the OPCW as a single purpose organization with both an internal and external legal personality, with due regard to the complexity of its purpose in all its facets. The factual material presented in the study is, indeed, very useful to understand the nature and quality of this new international body. As far as its main functions are concerned, it might be discussed whether the distinction used in the study (p. 106 et seq.), i.e.:
(a) collection function;
(b) review function;
(c) creative function; and
(d) correction function;
should not be seen in three rather than four main aspects, considering the creative and correction functions in one context. This would not only correspond to the ideas developed by Sur,[2] who distinguishes between (a) *establishment of facts* (collection function), (b) their *legal assessment* (review function) and (c) *consequences to be drawn* in the event of an established violation (creative and corrective functions); it would perhaps even come closer to the expected working procedure of the OPCW for which the effectiveness and availability of techniques and procedures for detecting breach, consultation and discourse to be developed under Articles VIII-XI CWC, may be as important as the effectiveness of measures to redress a

---

[1] OPCW Headquarters Agreement (C-I/DEC.59, 14 May 1997).

[2] S. Sur, *A Legal Approach to Verification in Disarmament or Arms Limitation*, Research Paper no. 1 UNIDER (1988), at 8.

situation and to ensure compliance, including sanctions, in accordance with Article XII.

In this respect, the process described by Dr. Myjer (p. 128) as being reminiscent of *musyawarah,* an Indonesian indigenous way of decision making via deliberation and discourse, may be one of his most far-reaching visions of the practice to be expected by the OPCW. It would, indeed, be a most welcome development, if the new Organization could follow this line in its present and future practice. The "management model", as coined by the Chayes[3] in contradistinction to the "coercive model", may be considered as being the key to its success. Where former legal theories of international organization had drawn a distinction between co-ordinating and subordinating (to include supranational) functions, the OPCW may well help to overcome such bipolar thinking by offering arguments and procedures to rationalize international co-operation by developing arguments and establishing procedures which sovereign States cannot neglect in their relations *inter se.*

The overall assessment of the OPCW will also depend on such important practical issues as its relationship with the United Nations, budget problems relating to both general and specific expenditure, recruitment of personnel, standards of behaviour for such personnel, the administrative structure, acceptance of its services by States, the success of its creative functions and, last but not least, information handling which will be of particular importance for the performance of the OPCW. I assume that some of these issues will be addressed by the following speaker and I do appreciate the presence in this discussion of so many distinguished experts working professionally and full-time for the implementation of the Convention.

A clear picture of how the OPCW practice will develop in the long term, which is necessary to ensure the destruction of existing stocks and to establish confidence-building in compliance even in critical areas, is of course not yet available. In this respect, much will depend on the conviction by all the parties concerned that international co-operation in implementing the CWC will serve national security better than recourse to loopholes, grey areas or even circumventions.

Thus it still remains to be seen to what extent Dr. Myjer's vision (p. 127) can be put into practice, that the OPCW may not only by its design but also in its practice will serve as a model for the forthcoming Comprehensive Nuclear Test Ban Treaty Organization, to be established in Vienna under the Treaty of 24 September 1996, that it can furthermore provide answers to improve the functioning of the International Atomic Energy Agency and that eventually it will offer solutions to establish a system of compliance for the Biological Weapons Convention. His idea, however, that given the present state of international law, a web of ties and obligations in the field of arms control may

---

[3] Abraham Chayes & Antonia Handler Chayes, *On compliance.* International Organization 47, 2, Spring 1993, pp 175-205.

be more effectively supported by a few active and lean organizations rather than one single body, is a very appealing one which, as Dr. Myjer's study itself, will be significant for further work on the law of international organizations and its development.

COMMENTS

by Johan Rautenbach[1]

I Introduction

The main thrust of Eric Myjer's paper "The Organization for the Prohibition of Chemical Weapons: closer towards an international arms control organization? - a quantum leap in the institutional law of arms control", as I understand it is to analyse whether the OPCW can be characterised as a fully fledged supervision organization, or whether it is merely a verification organization. Does the OPCW have the capacity to only judge State behaviour in complying with the legal rules contained in the CWC (collection function and review function) or does it have a wider capacity? Does it have the capacity not only to interpret and clarify the legal rules, and thus to determine to some extent the scope of the rules against which the behaviour will be tested (creative function), but also to do that which is necessary to correct State behaviour if it is established that the behaviour is not in conformity with the rules contained in the CWC (correction function)? Closely tied to this is the question of whether the OPCW has any unique features of a sufficiently distinctive and innovative nature so that it could serve as a model for other disarmament undertakings.

Myjer's conclusion is that the OPCW has the capacity to exercise a corrective function[2] - albeit not in the traditional coercive style but in the so-called "management" style.[3] The management process operates in a staged process; from development of information, identification of questionable behaviour and identification of sources for such behaviour, to the examination of a State's capacity to comply, assistance to redress any under capacity, threat or invocation of dispute settlement procedures and modification of treaty rules to accommodate the non-compliance conduct.[4] Clearly the OPCW fits this model as a glove and I therefore agree with the conclusion.

Both Myjer and Koh make the point that the so-called management model is not necessarily an alternative approach, but rather complementary to the coercive model. Koh even goes so far as to imply that the management model

---

[1] All opinions expressed in the comments are the author's own and do not necessarily reflect the position of the OPCW or any State.

[2] pp. 130-131.

[3] The concept developed by Abram and Antonia Chayes in their book *The New Sovereignty: Compliance with International Regulatory Agreements* (1995).

[4] See Harold Hongju Koh's review of the Chayes' book in 91 AJIL pp. 389 - 391.

E.P.J. Myjer (ed.), Issues of Arms Control Law and the Chemical Weapons Convention, 145–153.

often succeeds only because there is the possibility of sanctions, even though they might be rare or remote. I can agree with the statement that the ultimate possibility of coercive measures remains a great incentive for the managerial model to be effective. In the case of the CWC one should not rule out the effect of considerations such as being perceived as a responsible member of the multilateral process and the lack of eagerness to be the subject of discussion in the United Nations Security Council and General Assembly.

I would like to draw your attention to two issues flowing from Eric Myjer's conclusion that the OPCW has a supervisory capacity and not only a verification capacity. The first is a practical example of the persuasion model at work in the OPCW. The second would be to look a little further, maybe in a somewhat provocative way, to see how his conclusion can bring a breath of fresh air to the stale debate on Article XI/Australia Group.

II Practical persuasion at work

At the beginning of the First Session of the Conference of the States Parties ("FSCSP") 165 States had signed the Chemical Weapons Convention ("Convention"). Of these only 88 had ratified it at that time, and it had entered into force for 87.[5] During the Conference one additional State deposited its instrument of ratification.

The FSCSP was thus confronted with the fact that the Convention had not entered into force for a number of States that were active in the preparatory phase, including one of the two declared chemical weapons possessor States. Added to this was the fact that many of the issues dealt with during the preparatory phase had remained unresolved. Although States Parties would legally have been entitled to address all unresolved issues and take action on them, this would not necessarily have taken into account the known national positions of non-States Parties.

Two possibilities were open to States Parties. One would have been the approach that States which had not ratified the CWC had acted at their own peril, and that they would subsequently not be able to escape the sanctions in the CWC aimed at non-States Parties. Relevant sanctions here are not only limitations on the transfer of chemicals but, more importantly (at this stage of the development of the OPCW), the fact that States that ratify later will be confronted with detailed interpretations of, and procedures for, the implementation of the CWC. The negative side of this would have been that it could serve as a disincentive for such States to ratify the CWC in that they might find it difficult to comply with such interpretations and procedures,

---

[5] Article XXI(2) of the Convention provides that for States whose instruments of ratification or accession are deposited subsequent to the entry into force of this Convention - i.e. 29 April 1997 - it shall enter into force on the 30th day following the date of deposit of their instrument of ratification or accession.

particularly in those cases where their positions were known from the preparatory phase. Non-ratification might be a preferred option to sacrificing some vital national interests. It was quite clear to all that the question of the effect of this on the often stated aim of universality of the Convention and the OPCW, had to be addressed.

States Parties opted for the persuasion approach: allow non-States Parties sufficient flexibility to make their positions clear, but without so much influence that the impetus for ratification becomes nullified.

In practical terms this boiled down to two main issues in respect of working procedures. The first was the rights of non-States Parties regarding participation in meetings during the FSCSP. The second was how to address the unresolved issues that the FSCSP did not resolve during that Session itself.

1. The rights of non-States Parties regarding participation in meetings during the FSCSP

This issue came up during the finalisation of the Rules of Procedure of the Conference (which was itself an unresolved issue at the end of the preparatory phase). The two relevant rules developed and adopted by the Conference were:

> *Rule 29* **Signatory States**
>
> Any State signatory to the Convention which has not yet deposited its instrument of ratification in accordance with Article XXI, paragraph 2, of the Convention shall be entitled, subject to prior written notification to the Director-General, to participate, without taking part in the adoption of decisions, whether by consensus or by vote, in the deliberations of the Conference. This means that Signatory States shall be entitled to appoint observers to attend plenary meetings of the Conference other than those designated private meetings; to deliver statements at such meetings; to receive the documents of the Conference and to submit its views in writing to delegations.
>
> *Rule 52* **Public and private meetings**
>
> Plenary meetings of the Conference shall be held in public unless declared private. Meetings of subsidiary bodies, including committees, shall be held in private unless designated otherwise. All decisions of the Conference taken at a private meeting shall be announced at an early public meeting. At the close of each private meeting of committees and other subsidiary bodies, the presiding officer may issue a communiqué through the Director-General.

The following elements are contained in these two rules:

- Plenary meetings of the Conference shall be public unless declared private;
- Meetings of subsidiary bodies shall be private unless designated otherwise;
- All decisions of the Conference taken at a private meeting shall be announced at an early public meeting;
- Signatory States shall be entitled to attend public meetings;
- Signatory States shall be entitled to deliver statements at public plenary meetings of the Conference;
- Signatory States shall be entitled to receive the documents of the Conference; and
- Signatory States shall be entitled to circulate documents containing their views to delegations.

Due to the particular nature of the FSCSP, States Parties considered it appropriate to have some limited informal understandings on the application of Rule 29 for the duration of the FSCSP only. These understandings were as follows:

- Contracting States[6] would have the right to participate in the debate in the Committee of the Whole without taking part in the adoption of decisions, whether by consensus or by vote;
- Signatory States would be allowed to attend meetings of the Committee of the Whole. This is a clear extension of signatory States' rights under Rule 52;

---

[6] Article 2(1)(f) of the Vienna Convention on the Law of Treaties defines "Contracting State" as a State which has consented to be bound by the treaty, whether or not the treaty has entered into force. The FSCSP used the term to refer to those States which deposited their instruments of ratification after entry into force and for which the Convention would enter into force on the 30th day following the date of deposit of their instrument of ratification - thus after the conclusion of the Conference.

- Signatory States could provide written submissions, expressing their views in advance of meetings of the Committee of the Whole, to the Secretariat for distribution;

- The Chairman of the Committee of the Whole would announce in advance agenda items under consideration for a particular meeting of the Committee of the Whole;

- For the remainder of the Conference, there would be a number of Plenary meetings to review decisions recommended by the Committee of the Whole. At the beginning of the Plenary meeting there would be a possibility for all delegations, including Signatory States, to make statements under agenda item 12: "General Debate". Such Plenaries could take place immediately preceding a meeting of the Committee of the Whole. This understanding, together with the previous two, clearly afforded Signatory States an opportunity to bring their views to the attention of States Parties at a point in time that would afford it maximum consideration;

- When the Chairman convenes a meeting of the Plenary on a specific subject on which decisions are to be made, only States Parties would have the right to request the floor. This was aimed at the provision in Rule 29 that provides that participation of non-States Parties should be without taking part in the adoption of decisions, whether by consensus or by vote. The making of statements on a specific subject on which decisions are to be made (particularly by consensus) might be construed as taking part in the adoption of such decision.

2. Addressing the unresolved issues that the FSCSP did not resolve during that Conference itself

The FSCSP did not address or finalise any of the substantive issues that were left unresolved by the Commission. It dealt only with those issues that were essential from a procedural perspective during the Session itself and issues necessary for the setting up of the organization. For the same reasons mentioned in paragraph 2 above, it was necessary for the FSCSP to find a mechanism to address the unresolved issues in a manner that would enhance the prospects of the universality of the CWC and the OPCW.

The FSCSP adopted a procedure[7] to address the unresolved issues during the first inter-sessional period between the close of the First Session in May

[7] See Conference Decision C-I/DEC.70, dated 22 May 1997.

and the opening of the Second Session in December. The procedure consists of the following nine elements:

- Because of the nature of the unresolved issues and their impact on the immediate implementation of the Convention, every effort shall be made to complete work on all of the unresolved issues listed in the Final Report of the Preparatory Commission (document PC-XVI/37). In this context, the procedures described apply only during the period between the First and Second Sessions of the Conference of the States Parties.

- The unresolved issues shall be addressed through a flexible, informal and transparent consultation process.

- Particular attention shall be given to issues requiring resolution in accordance with the time-lines stipulated by the Convention, as well as to other issues identified by the States Parties or the Director-General as requiring urgent resolution.

- The Chairman of the Committee of the Whole shall designate facilitators and shall assign issues to them. The facilitators shall operate under the general guidance of the Chairman of the Committee of the Whole but shall otherwise decide themselves how to proceed on the issue or issues assigned to them. The Secretariat shall provide appropriate support to them. The facilitators shall keep the Chairman of the Committee of the Whole informed about the progress of the consultations.

- The facilitators shall make proposals to the Committee of the Whole at the Second Session of the Conference of States Parties. Each proposal shall be accompanied by a report issued by the facilitator in his or her name, describing the consultation process and the rationale for the proposal submitted.

- In addition, an issue may be brought to the Executive Council when the implementation of the Convention requires its immediate resolution or urgent action. When such an issue overlaps with the work of a facilitator, the facilitator's work shall be taken into account. The Director-General may also inform the Executive Council of any practical experience which the Technical Secretariat has gained. The Executive Council's action in this regard shall be without prejudice to any future decision of the Conference.

- The Executive Council shall monitor the functioning of the procedure for addressing unresolved issues. To this end, the Executive Council may invite the Chairman of the Committee of the Whole to inform the Council about the progress made in the consultations of the facilitators.
- The facilitators shall make every reasonable effort to ensure that all States Parties have an opportunity to participate in the resolution of the issues.

- Signatory States shall be given a reasonable opportunity to express their views during the facilitators' consultation process.

By developing the above working methods, States Parties used persuasion to limit possible obstacles to ratification by some signatory States. There was, however, some element of coercion as well, in that the limited informal understandings were reached as regards the First Session of the Conference and the first inter-sessional period only.

III Can Article IX resolve Article XI?

As I have stated before,[8] I agree with Eric Myjer when he makes the point that the OPCW is a supervisory organization and not only a verification organization. It is also so that the CWC does not have much to offer in the line of immediately apparent coercive sanctions. The rights that can be restricted or suspended in terms of Article XII(2) would seem few. It does not have services and benefits as economic treaties have. It is so that Articles X and XI offer some elements in this regard, but that would only be of use in the case of States Parties that are net recipients of such benefits. The argument can be made that for a State Party which is breaching one of its basic obligations regarding the production, etc., of chemical weapons, this would be a small price to pay. There are also the possibilities regarding limiting transfer of scheduled chemicals and refusing access to information mentioned by Myjer.[9]

There might be more. I want to postulate, in a somewhat provocative way, that the obligations of States Parties under the CWC are also an individual State Party's rights. The managerial model for corrective action gives us a hint here. The CWC creates not only a verification regime, but a supervision regime. This would imply that it not only verifies compliance but that it also offers a mechanism for resolving disputes regarding non-compliance.

Article IX is central to this. It provides for consultations, co-operation and fact finding through a process of either requesting clarification or through challenge inspections. At first glance it would seem like onerous obligations

---

[8] See paragraph 2 above.

[9] See his contribution to this volume at pp. 122-125.

for a State Party to undertake. My postulation is that this offers the strongest right of all to an individual State Party. A State Party has the right to be asked for clarification or to be inspected if any other State Party raises any concern regarding non-compliance by the first State Party with its obligations under the CWC.

Paragraph 5, an often forgotten paragraph, of Article IX, as well as paragraph 6, read as follows:

> 5. A State Party shall also have the right to request the Executive Council to clarify any situation which has been considered ambiguous or has given rise to a concern about its possible non-compliance with this Convention. The Executive Council shall respond by providing such assistance as appropriate.
>
> 6. The Executive Council shall inform the States Parties about any request for clarification provided in this Article.

A State Party accused of non-compliance here has a powerful tool to prove compliance. It would be entitled to request the Executive Council to have the Director-General conduct an immediate inspection to clarify whether any non-compliance has taken place. Should non-compliance not be proved, other States Parties will be informed thereof by the Executive Council in a way that is much more credible than simple denial by the accused State Party.

So, what does this have to do with Article XI? At the risk of over-simplifying the situation, the position where the debate on Article XI has ground to a halt during the preparatory phase is more or less as follows. One group of States argued that Article XI(2)(c) clearly prohibits the maintenance of restrictions other than those provided for in the CWC against another State Party. Any restrictions implemented as a result of the Australia Group activities would therefore be in violation of this article. Another group of States argued that Article XI does not place any obligation on them to discard free market principles and to trade where they would not normally trade. Secondly, they make the argument that the non-proliferation commitment undertaken by States Parties in terms of Article I would allow them to restrict trade in cases of concern regarding non-compliance, at least until it is clear that the measures under the CWC are effective. Without commenting on these arguments, it is here that my postulation regarding the rights of a State Party under Article IX becomes relevant.

Should a State Party be of the opinion that there is sufficient concern about another State Party's compliance that it is obliged, in terms of its obligations under Article I, to take non-proliferation measures, a strong case can be made that in terms of Article IX it cannot do so without first utilising the persuasion mechanism contained in the CWC. This would imply that every State Party that is suspected of non-compliance should have the opportunity to either clarify an ambiguity through the provision of information or, if this is not sufficient, to request action by the Executive Council in terms of paragraphs 5 and 6 of Article IX to prove its compliance.

Paragraphs 1 and 2 of Article IX, after all contain the following mandatory (added, editor) language:

> 1. States Parties **shall consult** and co-operate, directly among themselves, or through the Organization or other appropriate international … on any matter which may be raised relating to the object and purpose, or the implementation of the provisions, of this Convention. (Emphasis added.)
>
> 2. Without prejudice to the right of any State Party to request a challenge inspection, States Parties **should, whenever possible, first make every effort** to clarify and resolve, through exchange of information and consultations among themselves, any matter which may cause doubt about compliance with this Convention, or which gives rise to concerns about a related matter which may be considered ambiguous …(Emphasis added.)

This approach has benefits for both sides of the divide. On the one hand, any State Party that is confronted with a situation that in its opinion would place it at risk regarding its own compliance with its obligations under Article I could take the necessary action in a transparent manner that will enhance compliance by all States Parties. The whole aim of having a treaty of this nature is after all to ensure compliance. Coercion is only a means to an end and not an end in itself. The benefit of this for States Parties on the other side of the argument is that it clearly separates action taken by other States Parties based on concerns regarding compliance and those based on other (maybe economic or political) reasons.

On a personal basis I would thus like to draw the conclusion that Article IX offers a way forward to resolve the current (lack of progress in the) discussions on Article XI.

COMMENTS

Thilo Marauhn

Eric P.J. Myjer has presented a comprehensive analysis of the institutional framework of the Chemical Weapons Convention. In commenting on his paper I want to confine myself to five aspects which I consider to be of major importance in evaluating the contribution of the Chemical Weapons Convention to the institutional law of arms control.

I.

There are various elements in the CWC regime which may be described as persuasive. It is necessary to distinguish between those mechanisms designed to ensure universal participation and others aiming at facilitating and promoting compliance with the provisions of the Convention:

Among the first category of treaty stipulations are the provisions restricting trade in chemicals with non-parties, in particular those included in Part VII, paragraphs C.31 and 32, and Part VIII, paragraphs C.26 and 27, of the Verification Annex. These provisions ensure that exports of Schedule 2 chemicals to non-parties after an interim period of three years after the entry into force of the Convention are prohibited. During this interim period transfers of Schedule 2 chemicals to non-parties are admissible, but subject to certain controls. Exports of Schedule 3 chemicals to non-parties remain admissible subject to a detailed end-user certificate. Five years after the entry into force of the Convention, the Conference of States Parties will have to consider the need to establish other measures regarding transfers of Schedule 3 chemicals to non-parties.

As for the other category of treaty provisions, routine verification is the primary means to ensure compliance under the Convention. Remaining gaps in the overall verification system are filled by challenge inspections and investigations of alleged CW use. The pertinent provisions of the Convention are a device for generating the confidence of parties that the benefits of complying with the obligations of the CWC outweigh the costs. Whereas verification in case of suspected or alleged non-compliance is calculated to threaten any non-compliance with discovery, the routine verification arrangements of the Convention are designed to increase transparency in order to diminish misperceptions of activities not prohibited under the Convention and to enable *bona fide* parties to demonstrate their compliance.

E.P.J. Myjer (ed.), Issues of Arms Control Law and the Chemical Weapons Convention, 155–158.

II.

Given the recent trend towards legalism in arms control and disarmament law and the development of what Eric Myjer calls the institutional law of arms control, the question arises whether every new treaty necessitates new international institutions for its implementation. It is not just the utilisation of existing organizations which may be discussed, but also the establishment of a new, (single) central institution. Compliance control in the context of arms control and disarmament, however, has the following peculiarity:

A prerequisite for effective compliance control is that the procedures and institutions are oriented as far as possible towards the substantive obligations in the treaty under consideration. A largely treaty-specific procedural architecture is therefore required, a separate "tailor-made" regime for every treaty. The establishment of a new, centralised institution would run counter to these considerations. On the other hand, cost-efficiency factors can militate against a proliferation of international bodies and institutions. However, the various organizations may co-operate and, in a reciprocal way, draw upon their experiences. This primarily applies to technical bodies such as secretariats, not to political organs such as Conferences of the Parties. The heterogeneous membership of the various conventions alone necessitates the specific creation of these political bodies for each convention. In addition, these bodies must take into account the peculiarities of individual treaties when deciding on measures to be taken in response to the outcome of the legal evaluation in compliance control.

III.

When looking at the institutional law of arms control, in particular at the OPCW, it is important to remember the close interrelationship between substantive and procedural obligations. The Chemical Weapons Convention is the first multilateral treaty whose objective is the total elimination of a whole class of weapons, and it is aimed at and designed to ban chemical weapons *effectively*. Looking at the negotiations leading to the conclusion of the CWC it goes without saying that it was one of the major concerns of the negotiators not to draft an international instrument which - though legally binding - would have little impact and remain pure paperwork.

This meant that there had to be something more than a set of substantive obligations. There had to be provisions dealing with law enforcement and compliance. However, it would not have been sufficient to rely on traditional enforcement methods of international law such as state responsibility, reprisals, retorsion and eventually sanctions through the United Nations. States only in rare and extreme circumstances resort to these traditional instruments of law enforcement. It may even be argued that arms control and disarmament law cannot and does not in fact depend on these enforcement techniques. This is the reason why the CWC relies heavily on a complex organizational structure which is aptly described as a supervisory mechanism.

IV.

In every supervisory mechanism we have to distinguish two elements: first, the procedural steps structuring such a mechanism, and second, general procedural principles applicable throughout the whole process which range from what has been called "compliance information systems", including reporting and fact finding, to reactions in the event of non-compliance.

While the CWC and other international arms control and disarmament agreements include precise stipulations as to the procedural steps to be taken, most of them suffer from a lack of well-designed procedural principles. Procedural steps under the CWC begin with national data collection and declarations required of the parties. In the context of routine verification the following steps may be defined: the initiation of the procedure, a decision on jurisdiction and admissibility, the definition of applicable standards and the formulation of the verification and inspection mandates, the ascertainment of facts by way of continuous monitoring, on-site inspections and sampling, then factual and legal evaluation, and, finally, the decision on whether or not to take measures to redress a situation.

When discussing procedural principles, the following has to be borne in mind. The tension inherent in the development of arms control and disarmament law, namely the interrelationship between national sovereignty and international co-operation comes to a point when compliance control is at issue: interferences with national sovereignty are inherent in any international control mechanism. Such interferences are only acceptable for states if their sovereign rights are given due respect. There are hardly any explicit references to the sovereign rights of States Parties in the context of any compliance control mechanism. However, numerous provisions of the pertinent agreements reflect the need for balancing national sovereignty and international scrutiny. Within the context of the CWC one may identify the following general principles for the performance of verification procedures: the principle of procedural co-operation, the right to be heard, the principle of proportionality, and the protection of confidential information.

V.

Turning finally to the relationship between national or multilateral export control regimes and the Convention's mechanism of compliance control, I agree with Eric Myjer that there are good arguments for giving routine verification preference over the exercise of national or multilateral measures.

However, it is important to distinguish between export prohibitions and export control. It may be useful at this point to recall what the chairman of the Ad Hoc Committee, Adolf Ritter von Wagner, said when explaining the final draft of the CWC. In addressing Art. XI, para. 2(c), he pointed out that "the notion of consistency with the object and purpose of the Convention is referring, according to the relevant wording in the Preamble, to both: 'to exclude completely the possibility of use of chemical weapons, through the implementation of this Convention' as well as 'to promote free trade in chemicals'. Thus, in the view of the Chairman, to the extent that successful implementation of the Convention realises the objective 'to exclude completely the possibility of use of chemical weapons' other restrictions specifically designed to curb the spread of chemical weapons lose their legitimacy under this Convention. At the same time the Chairman feels - against the background of the object and purpose of this Convention - that the sovereign right of States Parties to maintain export control for non-CW-related purposes is not affected by this paragraph" (CD/CW/WP. 414, 30).

SUMMARY OF DISCUSSION

(The Organization for the Prohibition of Chemical Weapons: closer towards an international arms control organization?, A quantum leap in the institutional law of arms control).

Prof Green[1]

Mr Chairman, if we are going to rely on traditional methods for coercive measures, then I would not be hopeful with regard to the practice. "Good faith" of States Parties needs to be enforced from time to time. In this context, we should look at the importance of Article 51 of the UN Charter and the inherent right of self-defence.

I recall the recent 1996 Advisory Opinion of the International Court of Justice on the (il)legality of the use or the threat of use of nuclear weapons. In its opinion, the Court states clearly that for the ultimate decision in circumstances where survival of the State is at stake, the inherent right to self-defence is the guiding principle. This begs the question how the ICJ would view a similar question in case of chemical weapons. My guess, therefore, would be that the real issue at stake is the illegality of the use, rather than the ban of chemical weapons. From a practial point of view also, achieving illegality of the use is recommendable. This is what the international community as a whole and OPCW in particular should aim for.

Dr Marauhn

Mr Chairman, the ICJ Advisory Opinion is based on the fact that there is no Convention on nuclear weapons, while there is now one for chemical weapons. I therefore disagree with Prof Green on the applicability of the ICJ Opinion to this issue.

On the Chayes model, I would like to point out that this model encompasses a management-approach within a process model. Where is the lawyer in this process, what is his role in this model? I would suggest that the approach by Dr Rautenbach seems to hold a perpetually pragmatic view. The lawyer is a safeguard for the rights and obligations of the Organization and the States Parties. At the same time, the lawyer provides procedural safeguards by applying general principles of law.

---

[1] University Professor Emeritus, Honorary Professor of Law, University of Alberta, Canada

E.P.J. Myjer (ed.), Issues of Arms Control Law and the Chemical Weapons Convention, 159–160.

Mr Kisselev[2]
Mr Chairman, I take exception to the statement by Dr Rautenbach on the role of persuasion and coercion provisions in the CWC. Signatory States such as the Russian Federation were not party to discussions on the interpretation and establishment of the Rules and Procedures of the OPCW. We should be aware that the OPCW may offer or set an example , but it is still in its early stages.

More specifically, I would like to refer to the comments on Article IX and Article XI of the CWC. It is my firm belief that in case of non-compliance with the provisions of Article XI, any State which believes its rights have been infringed can invoke Article IX to seek redress.

Dr Rautenbach
Mr Chairman, let me just say that I find Mr Kisselev's idea of invoking the provisions of Article IX in a situation of non-compliance with Article XI interesting and challenging. For instance, Iraq is a rather unwilling participant in the exercise of arms control. This would be an interesting test case. I would also like to express my agreement with Dr Marauhn on the role of the lawyers within the OPCW. He is right on the mark.

Dr Fleck
Mr Chairman, I would like to make a few remarks. First, international law is a means to rationalize politics. Second, OPCW indeed still has a long way to go. My guess is that it will take at least another ten years or so before chemical weapons will have been abolished.

Thirdly, international cooperation includes other organizations functioning in the arena of arms control. For example, the already existing International Atomic Energy Agency is very active towards North Korea. On the basis of the Convention on Biological Weapons and the Comprehensive Test Ban Treaty, two new organizations are still to be established. This expansion of activities in the arms control arena demands more than ever a broad perception of security.

Utrecht, 2 July 1997
Reporter: Tim Sneek

---

[2] At the time Counsellor and Deputy Head of Delegation of the Russian Federation to the OPCW

CONVENTION ON THE PROHIBITION OF THE DEVELOPMENT, PRODUCTION, STOCKPILING AND USE OF CHEMICAL WEAPONS AND ON THEIR DESTRUCTION*

(Corrected version in accordance with Depositary Notification C.N.246.1994.TREATIES-5 and the corresponding Procès-Verbal of Rectification of the Original of the Convention, issued on 8 August 1994)

* http://www.opcw.org

PREAMBLE

The States Parties to this Convention,

Determined to act with a view to achieving effective progress towards general and complete disarmament under strict and effective international control, including the prohibition and elimination of all types of weapons of mass destruction,

Desiring to contribute to the realization of the purposes and principles of the Charter of the United Nations,

Recalling that the General Assembly of the United Nations has repeatedly condemned all actions contrary to the principles and objectives of the Protocol for the Prohibition of the Use in War of Asphyxiating, Poisonous or Other Gases, and of Bacteriological Methods of Warfare, signed at Geneva on 17 June 1925 (the Geneva Protocol of 1925),

Recognizing that this Convention reaffirms principles and objectives of and obligations assumed under the Geneva Protocol of 1925, and the Convention on the Prohibition of the Development, Production and Stockpiling of Bacteriological (Biological) and Toxin Weapons and on their Destruction signed at London, Moscow and Washington on 10 April 1972,

Bearing in mind the objective contained in Article IX of the Convention on the Prohibition of the Development, Production and Stockpiling of Bacteriological (Biological) and Toxin Weapons and on their Destruction,

Determined for the sake of all mankind, to exclude completely the possibility of the use of chemical weapons, through the implementation of the provisions of this Convention, thereby complementing the obligations assumed under the Geneva Protocol of 1925,

Recognizing the prohibition, embodied in the pertinent agreements and relevant principles of international law, of the use of herbicides as a method of warfare,

Considering that achievements in the field of chemistry should be used exclusively for the benefit of mankind,

Desiring to promote free trade in chemicals as well as international cooperation and exchange of scientific and technical information in the field of chemical activities for purposes not prohibited under this Convention in order to enhance the economic and technological development of all States Parties,

Convinced that the complete and effective prohibition of the development, production, acquisition, stockpiling, retention, transfer and use of chemical weapons, and their destruction, represent a necessary step towards the achievement of these common objectives,

Have agreed as follows:

ARTICLE I

GENERAL OBLIGATIONS

1. Each State Party to this Convention undertakes never under any circumstances:

    (a) To develop, produce, otherwise acquire, stockpile or retain chemical weapons, or transfer, directly or indirectly, chemical weapons to anyone;

    (b) To use chemical weapons;

    (c) To engage in any military preparations to use chemical weapons;

    (d) To assist, encourage or induce, in any way, anyone to engage in any activity prohibited to a State Party under this Convention.

2. Each State Party undertakes to destroy chemical weapons it owns or possesses, or that are located in any place under its jurisdiction or control, in accordance with the provisions of this Convention.

3. Each State Party undertakes to destroy all chemical weapons it abandoned on the territory of another State Party, in accordance with the provisions of this Convention.

4. Each State Party undertakes to destroy any chemical weapons production facilities it owns or possesses, or that are located in any place under its jurisdiction or control, in accordance with the provisions of this Convention.

5. Each State Party undertakes not to use riot control agents as a method of warfare.

ARTICLE II

DEFINITIONS AND CRITERIA

For the purposes of this Convention:

1. "Chemical Weapons" means the following, together or separately:

    (a) Toxic chemicals and their precursors, except where intended for purposes not prohibited under this Convention, as long as the types and quantities are consistent with such purposes;

(b) Munitions and devices, specifically designed to cause death or other harm through the toxic properties of those toxic chemicals specified in subparagraph (a), which would be released as a result of the employment of such munitions and devices;

(c) Any equipment specifically designed for use directly in connection with the employment of munitions and devices specified in subparagraph (b).

2. "Toxic Chemical" means:

Any chemical which through its chemical action on life processes can cause death, temporary incapacitation or permanent harm to humans or animals. This includes all such chemicals, regardless of their origin or of their method of production, and regardless of whether they are produced in facilities, in munitions or elsewhere.

(For the purpose of implementing this Convention, toxic chemicals which have been identified for the application of verification measures are listed in Schedules contained in the Annex on Chemicals.)

3. "Precursor" means:

Any chemical reactant which takes part at any stage in the production by whatever method of a toxic chemical. This includes any key component of a binary or multicomponent chemical system.

(For the purpose of implementing this Convention, precursors which have been identified for the application of verification measures are listed in Schedules contained in the Annex on Chemicals.)

4. "Key Component of Binary or Multicomponent Chemical Systems" (hereinafter referred to as "key component") means:

The precursor which plays the most important role in determining the toxic properties of the final product and reacts rapidly with other chemicals in the binary or multicomponent system.

5. "Old Chemical Weapons" means:

(a) Chemical weapons which were produced before 1925; or

(b) Chemical weapons produced in the period between 1925 and 1946 that have deteriorated to such extent that they can no longer be used as chemical weapons.

6. "Abandoned Chemical Weapons" means:

Chemical weapons, including old chemical weapons, abandoned by a State after 1 January 1925 on the territory of another State without the consent of the latter.

7. "Riot Control Agent" means:

Any chemical not listed in a Schedule, which can produce rapidly in humans sensory irritation or disabling physical effects which disappear within a short time following termination of exposure.

8. "Chemical Weapons Production Facility":

(a) Means any equipment, as well as any building housing such equipment, that was designed, constructed or used at any time since 1 January 1946:

(i) As part of the stage in the production of chemicals ("final technological stage") where the material flows would contain, when the equipment is in operation:

(1) Any chemical listed in Schedule 1 in the Annex on Chemicals; or

(2) Any other chemical that has no use, above 1 tonne per year on the territory of a State Party or in any other place under the jurisdiction or control of a State Party, for purposes not prohibited under this Convention, but can be used for chemical weapons purposes;

or

(ii) For filling chemical weapons, including, inter alia, the filling of chemicals listed in Schedule 1 into munitions, devices or bulk storage containers; the filling of chemicals into containers that form part of assembled binary munitions and devices or into chemical submunitions that form part of assembled unitary munitions and devices, and the loading of the containers and chemical submunitions into the respective munitions and devices;

(b) Does not mean:

(i) Any facility having a production capacity for synthesis of chemicals specified in subparagraph (a) (i) that is less than 1 tonne;

(ii) Any facility in which a chemical specified in subparagraph (a) (i) is or was produced as an unavoidable by-product of activities for purposes not prohibited under this Convention, provided that the chemical does not exceed 3 per cent of the total product and that the facility is subject to declaration and inspection under the Annex on Implementation and Verification (hereinafter referred to as "Verification Annex"); or

(iii) The single small-scale facility for production of chemicals listed in Schedule 1 for purposes not prohibited under this Convention as referred to in Part VI of the Verification Annex.

9. "Purposes Not Prohibited Under this Convention" means:

(a) Industrial, agricultural, research, medical, pharmaceutical or other peaceful purposes;

(b) Protective purposes, namely those purposes directly related to protection against toxic chemicals and to protection against chemical weapons;

(c) Military purposes not connected with the use of chemical weapons and not dependent on the use of the toxic properties of chemicals as a method of warfare;

(d) Law enforcement including domestic riot control purposes.

10. "Production Capacity" means:

The annual quantitative potential for manufacturing a specific chemical based on the technological process actually used or, if the process is not yet operational, planned to be used at the relevant facility. It shall be deemed to be equal to the nameplate capacity or, if the nameplate capacity is not available, to the design capacity. The nameplate capacity is the product output under conditions optimized for maximum quantity for the production facility, as demonstrated by one or more test-runs. The design capacity is the corresponding theoretically calculated product output.

11. "Organization" means the Organization for the Prohibition of Chemical Weapons established pursuant to Article VIII of this Convention.

12. For the purposes of Article VI:

(a) "Production" of a chemical means its formation through chemical reaction;

(b) "Processing" of a chemical means a physical process, such as formulation, extraction and purification, in which a chemical is not converted into another chemical;

(c) "Consumption" of a chemical means its conversion into another chemical via a chemical reaction.

ARTICLE III

DECLARATIONS

1. Each State Party shall submit to the Organization, not later than 30 days after this Convention enters into force for it, the following declarations, in which it shall:

(a) With respect to chemical weapons:

(i) Declare whether it owns or possesses any chemical weapons, or whether there are any chemical weapons located in any place under its jurisdiction or control;

(ii) Specify the precise location, aggregate quantity and detailed inventory of chemical weapons it owns or possesses, or that are located in any place under its jurisdiction or control, in accordance with Part IV (A), paragraphs 1 to 3, of the Verification Annex, except for those chemical weapons referred to in sub-subparagraph (iii);

(iii) Report any chemical weapons on its territory that are owned and possessed by another State and located in any place under the jurisdiction or control of another State, in accordance with Part IV (A), paragraph 4, of the Verification Annex;

(iv) Declare whether it has transferred or received, directly or indirectly, any chemical weapons since 1 January 1946 and specify the transfer or receipt of such weapons, in accordance with Part IV (A), paragraph 5, of the Verification Annex;

(v) Provide its general plan for destruction of chemical weapons that it owns or possesses, or that are located in any place under its jurisdiction or control, in accordance with Part IV (A), paragraph 6, of the Verification Annex;

(b) With respect to old chemical weapons and abandoned chemical weapons:

(i) Declare whether it has on its territory old chemical weapons and provide all available information in accordance with Part IV (B), paragraph 3, of the Verification Annex;

(ii) Declare whether there are abandoned chemical weapons on its territory and provide all available information in accordance with Part IV (B), paragraph 8, of the Verification Annex;

(iii) Declare whether it has abandoned chemical weapons on the territory of other States and provide all available information in accordance with Part IV (B), paragraph 10, of the Verification Annex;

(c) With respect to chemical weapons production facilities:

(i) Declare whether it has or has had any chemical weapons production facility under its ownership or possession, or that is or has been located in any place under its jurisdiction or control at any time since 1 January 1946;

(ii) Specify any chemical weapons production facility it has or has had under its ownership or possession or that is or has been located in any place under its jurisdiction or control at any time since 1 January 1946, in accordance with Part V, paragraph 1, of the Verification Annex, except for those facilities referred to in sub-subparagraph (iii);

(iii) Report any chemical weapons production facility on its territory that another State has or has had under its ownership and possession and that is or has been located in any place under the jurisdiction or control of another State at any time since 1 January 1946, in accordance with Part V, paragraph 2, of the Verification Annex;

(iv) Declare whether it has transferred or received, directly or indirectly, any equipment for the production of chemical weapons since 1 January 1946 and specify the transfer or receipt of such equipment, in accordance with Part V, paragraphs 3 to 5, of the Verification Annex;

(v) Provide its general plan for destruction of any chemical weapons production facility it owns or possesses, or that is located in any place under its jurisdiction or control, in accordance with Part V, paragraph 6, of the Verification Annex;

(vi) Specify actions to be taken for closure of any chemical weapons production facility it owns or possesses, or that is located in any place under its jurisdiction or control, in accordance with Part V, paragraph 1 (i), of the Verification Annex;

(vii) Provide its general plan for any temporary conversion of any chemical weapons production facility it owns or possesses, or that is located in any place under its jurisdiction or control, into a chemical weapons destruction facility, in accordance with Part V, paragraph 7, of the Verification Annex;

(d) With respect to other facilities:

Specify the precise location, nature and general scope of activities of any facility or establishment under its ownership or possession, or located in any place under its jurisdiction or control, and that has been designed, constructed or used since 1 January 1946 primarily for development of chemical weapons. Such declaration shall include, inter alia, laboratories and test and evaluation sites;

(e) With respect to riot control agents: Specify the chemical name, structural formula and Chemical Abstracts Service (CAS) registry number, if assigned, of each chemical it holds for riot control purposes. This declaration shall be updated not later than 30 days after any change becomes effective.

2. The provisions of this Article and the relevant provisions of Part IV of the Verification Annex shall not, at the discretion of a State Party, apply to chemical weapons buried on its territory before 1 January 1977 and which remain buried, or which had been dumped at sea before 1 January 1985.

ARTICLE IV

CHEMICAL WEAPONS

1. The provisions of this Article and the detailed procedures for its implementation shall apply to all chemical weapons owned or possessed by a State Party, or that are located in any place under its jurisdiction or control, except old chemical weapons and abandoned chemical weapons to which Part IV (B) of the Verification Annex applies.

2. Detailed procedures for the implementation of this Article are set forth in the Verification Annex.

3. All locations at which chemical weapons specified in paragraph 1 are stored or destroyed shall be subject to systematic verification through on-site inspection and monitoring with on-site instruments, in accordance with Part IV (A) of the Verification Annex.

4. Each State Party shall, immediately after the declaration under Article III, paragraph 1 (a), has been submitted, provide access to chemical weapons specified in paragraph 1 for the purpose of systematic verification of the declaration through on-site inspection. Thereafter, each State Party shall not remove any of these chemical weapons, except to a chemical weapons destruction facility. It shall provide access to such chemical weapons, for the purpose of systematic on-site verification.

5. Each State Party shall provide access to any chemical weapons destruction facilities and their storage areas, that it owns or possesses, or that are located in any place under its jurisdiction or control, for the purpose of systematic verification through on-site inspection and monitoring with on-site instruments.

6. Each State Party shall destroy all chemical weapons specified in paragraph 1 pursuant to the Verification Annex and in accordance with the agreed rate and sequence of destruction (hereinafter referred to as "order of destruction"). Such destruction shall begin not later than two years after this Convention enters into force for it and shall finish not later than 10 years after entry into force of this Convention. A State Party is not precluded from destroying such chemical weapons at a faster rate.

7. Each State Party shall:

(a) Submit detailed plans for the destruction of chemical weapons specified in paragraph 1 not later than 60 days before each annual destruction period begins, in accordance with Part IV (A), paragraph 29, of the Verification Annex; the detailed plans shall encompass all stocks to be destroyed during the next annual destruction period;

(b) Submit declarations annually regarding the implementation of its plans for destruction of chemical weapons specified in paragraph 1, not later than 60 days after the end of each annual destruction period; and

(c) Certify, not later than 30 days after the destruction process has been completed, that all chemical weapons specified in paragraph 1 have been destroyed.

8. If a State ratifies or accedes to this Convention after the 10-year period for destruction set forth in paragraph 6, it shall destroy chemical weapons specified in paragraph 1 as soon as possible. The order of destruction and procedures for stringent verification for such a State Party shall be determined by the Executive Council.

9. Any chemical weapons discovered by a State Party after the initial declaration of chemical weapons shall be reported, secured and destroyed in accordance with Part IV (A) of the Verification Annex.

10. Each State Party, during transportation, sampling, storage and destruction of chemical weapons, shall assign the highest priority to ensuring the safety of people and to protecting the environment. Each State Party shall transport, sample, store and destroy chemical weapons in accordance with its national standards for safety and emissions.

11. Any State Party which has on its territory chemical weapons that are owned or possessed by another State, or that are located in any place under the jurisdiction or control of another State, shall make the fullest efforts to ensure that these chemical weapons are removed from its territory not later than one year after this Convention enters into force for it. If they are not removed within one year, the State Party may request the Organization and other States Parties to provide assistance in the destruction of these chemical weapons.

12. Each State Party undertakes to cooperate with other States Parties that request information or assistance on a bilateral basis or through the Technical Secretariat regarding methods and technologies for the safe and efficient destruction of chemical weapons.

13. In carrying out verification activities pursuant to this Article and Part IV (A) of the Verification Annex, the Organization shall consider measures to avoid unnecessary duplication of bilateral or multilateral agreements on verification of chemical weapons storage and their destruction among States Parties.

To this end, the Executive Council shall decide to limit verification to measures complementary to those undertaken pursuant to such a bilateral or multilateral agreement, if it considers that:

(a) Verification provisions of such an agreement are consistent with the verification provisions of this Article and Part IV (A) of the Verification Annex;

(b) Implementation of such an agreement provides for sufficient assurance of compliance with the relevant provisions of this Convention; and

(c) Parties to the bilateral or multilateral agreement keep the Organization fully informed about their verification activities.

14. If the Executive Council takes a decision pursuant to paragraph 13, the Organization shall have the right to monitor the implementation of the bilateral or multilateral agreement.

15. Nothing in paragraphs 13 and 14 shall affect the obligation of a State Party to provide declarations pursuant to Article III, this Article and Part IV (A) of the Verification Annex.

16. Each State Party shall meet the costs of destruction of chemical weapons it is obliged to destroy. It shall also meet the costs of verification of storage and destruction of these chemical weapons unless the Executive Council decides otherwise. If the Executive Council decides to limit verification measures of the Organization pursuant to paragraph 13, the costs of complementary verification and monitoring by the Organization shall be paid in accordance with the United Nations scale of assessment, as specified in Article VIII, paragraph 7.

17. The provisions of this Article and the relevant provisions of Part IV of the Verification Annex shall not, at the discretion of a State Party, apply to chemical weapons buried on its territory before 1 January 1977 and which remain buried, or which had been dumped at sea before 1 January 1985.

ARTICLE V

CHEMICAL WEAPONS PRODUCTION FACILITIES

1. The provisions of this Article and the detailed procedures for its implementation shall apply to any and all chemical weapons production facilities owned or possessed by a State Party, or that are located in any place under its jurisdiction or control.

2. Detailed procedures for the implementation of this Article are set forth in the Verification Annex.

3. All chemical weapons production facilities specified in paragraph 1 shall be subject to systematic verification through on-site inspection and monitoring with on-site instruments in accordance with Part V of the Verification Annex.

4. Each State Party shall cease immediately all activity at chemical weapons production facilities specified in paragraph 1, except activity required for closure.

5. No State Party shall construct any new chemical weapons production facilities or modify any existing facilities for the purpose of chemical weapons production or for any other activity prohibited under this Convention.

6. Each State Party shall, immediately after the declaration under Article III, paragraph 1 (c), has been submitted, provide access to chemical weapons production facilities specified in paragraph 1, for the purpose of systematic verification of the declaration through on-site inspection.

7. Each State Party shall:

(a) Close, not later than 90 days after this Convention enters into force for it, all chemical weapons production facilities specified in paragraph 1, in accordance with Part V of the Verification Annex, and give notice thereof; and

(b) Provide access to chemical weapons production facilities specified in paragraph 1, subsequent to closure, for the purpose of systematic verification through on-site inspection and monitoring with on-site instruments in order to ensure that the facility remains closed and is subsequently destroyed.

8. Each State Party shall destroy all chemical weapons production facilities specified in paragraph 1 and related facilities and equipment, pursuant to the Verification Annex and in accordance with an agreed rate and sequence of destruction (hereinafter referred to as "order of destruction"). Such destruction shall begin not later than one year after this Convention enters into force for it, and shall finish not later than 10 years after entry into force of this Convention. A State Party is not precluded from destroying such facilities at a faster rate.

9. Each State Party shall:

(a) Submit detailed plans for destruction of chemical weapons production facilities specified in paragraph 1, not later than 180 days before the destruction of each facility begins;

(b) Submit declarations annually regarding the implementation of its plans for the destruction of all chemical weapons production facilities specified in paragraph 1, not later than 90 days after the end of each annual destruction period; and

(c) Certify, not later than 30 days after the destruction process has been completed, that all chemical weapons production facilities specified in paragraph 1 have been destroyed.

10. If a State ratifies or accedes to this Convention after the 10-year period for destruction set forth in paragraph 8, it shall destroy chemical weapons production facilities specified in paragraph 1 as soon as possible. The order of destruction and procedures for stringent verification for such a State Party shall be determined by the Executive Council.

11. Each State Party, during the destruction of chemical weapons production facilities, shall assign the highest priority to ensuring the safety of people and to protecting the environment. Each State Party shall destroy chemical weapons production facilities in accordance with its national standards for safety and emissions.

12. Chemical weapons production facilities specified in paragraph 1 may be temporarily converted for destruction of chemical weapons in accordance with Part V, paragraphs 18 to 25, of the Verification Annex. Such a converted facility must be destroyed as soon as it is no longer in use for destruction of chemical weapons but, in any case, not later than 10 years after entry into force of this Convention.

13. A State Party may request, in exceptional cases of compelling need, permission to use a chemical weapons production facility specified in paragraph 1 for purposes not prohibited under this Convention. Upon the recommendation of the Executive Council, the Conference of the States Parties shall decide whether or not to approve the request and shall establish the conditions upon which approval is contingent in accordance with Part V, Section D, of the Verification Annex.

14. The chemical weapons production facility shall be converted in such a manner that the converted facility is not more capable of being reconverted into a chemical weapons production facility than any other facility used for industrial, agricultural, research, medical, pharmaceutical or other peaceful purposes not involving chemicals listed in Schedule 1.

15. All converted facilities shall be subject to systematic verification through on-site inspection and monitoring with on-site instruments in accordance with Part V, Section D, of the Verification Annex.

16. In carrying out verification activities pursuant to this Article and Part V of the Verification Annex, the Organization shall consider measures to avoid unnecessary duplication of bilateral or multilateral agreements on verification of chemical weapons production facilities and their destruction among States Parties.

To this end, the Executive Council shall decide to limit the verification to measures complementary to those undertaken pursuant to such a bilateral or multilateral agreement, if it considers that:

(a) Verification provisions of such an agreement are consistent with the verification provisions of this Article and Part V of the Verification Annex;

(b) Implementation of the agreement provides for sufficient assurance of compliance with the relevant provisions of this Convention; and

(c) Parties to the bilateral or multilateral agreement keep the Organization fully informed about their verification activities.

17. If the Executive Council takes a decision pursuant to paragraph 16, the Organization shall have the right to monitor the implementation of the bilateral or multilateral agreement.

18. Nothing in paragraphs 16 and 17 shall affect the obligation of a State Party to make declarations pursuant to Article III, this Article and Part V of the Verification Annex.

19. Each State Party shall meet the costs of destruction of chemical weapons production facilities it is obliged to destroy. It shall also meet the costs of verification under this Article unless the Executive Council decides otherwise. If the Executive Council decides to limit verification measures of the Organization pursuant to paragraph 16, the costs of complementary verification and monitoring by the Organization shall be paid in accordance with the United Nations scale of assessment, as specified in Article VIII, paragraph 7.

ARTICLE VI

ACTIVITIES NOT PROHIBITED UNDER THIS CONVENTION

1. Each State Party has the right, subject to the provisions of this Convention, to develop, produce, otherwise acquire, retain, transfer and use toxic chemicals and their precursors for purposes not prohibited under this Convention.

2. Each State Party shall adopt the necessary measures to ensure that toxic chemicals and their precursors are only developed, produced, otherwise acquired, retained, transferred, or used within its territory or in any other place under its jurisdiction or control for purposes not prohibited under this Convention. To this end, and in order to verify that activities are in accordance with obligations under this Convention, each State Party shall subject toxic chemicals and their precursors listed in Schedules 1, 2 and 3 of the Annex on Chemicals, facilities related to such chemicals, and other facilities as specified in the Verification Annex, that are located on its territory or in any other place under its jurisdiction or control, to verification measures as provided in the Verification Annex.

3. Each State Party shall subject chemicals listed in Schedule 1 (hereinafter referred to as "Schedule 1 chemicals") to the prohibitions on production, acquisition, retention, transfer and use as specified in Part VI of the Verification Annex. It shall subject Schedule 1 chemicals and facilities specified in Part VI of the Verification Annex to systematic verification through on-site inspection and monitoring with on-site instruments in accordance with that Part of the Verification Annex.

4. Each State Party shall subject chemicals listed in Schedule 2 (hereinafter referred to as "Schedule 2 chemicals") and facilities specified in Part VII of the Verification Annex to data monitoring and on-site verification in accordance with that Part of the Verification Annex.

5. Each State Party shall subject chemicals listed in Schedule 3 (hereinafter referred to as "Schedule 3 chemicals") and facilities specified in Part VIII of the Verification Annex to data monitoring and on-site verification in accordance with that Part of the Verification Annex.

6. Each State Party shall subject facilities specified in Part IX of the Verification Annex to data monitoring and eventual on-site verification in accordance with that Part of the Verification Annex unless decided otherwise by the Conference of the States Parties pursuant to Part IX, paragraph 22, of the Verification Annex.

7. Not later than 30 days after this Convention enters into force for it, each State Party shall make an initial declaration on relevant chemicals and facilities in accordance with the Verification Annex.

8. Each State Party shall make annual declarations regarding the relevant chemicals and facilities in accordance with the Verification Annex.

9. For the purpose of on-site verification, each State Party shall grant to the inspectors access to facilities as required in the Verification Annex.

10. In conducting verification activities, the Technical Secretariat shall avoid undue intrusion into the State Party's chemical activities for purposes not prohibited under this Convention and, in particular, abide by the provisions set forth in the Annex on the Protection of Confidential Information (hereinafter referred to as "Confidentiality Annex").

11. The provisions of this Article shall be implemented in a manner which avoids hampering the economic or technological development of States Parties, and international cooperation in the field of chemical activities for purposes not prohibited under this Convention including the international exchange of scientific and technical information and chemicals and equipment for the production, processing or use of chemicals for purposes not prohibited under this Convention.

ARTICLE VII

NATIONAL IMPLEMENTATION MEASURES

General undertakings

1. Each State Party shall, in accordance with its constitutional processes, adopt the necessary measures to implement its obligations under this Convention. In particular, it shall:

   (a) Prohibit natural and legal persons anywhere on its territory or in any other place under its jurisdiction as recognized by international law from undertaking any activity prohibited to a State Party under this Convention, including enacting penal legislation with respect to such activity;

   (b) Not permit in any place under its control any activity prohibited to a State Party under this Convention; and

   (c) Extend its penal legislation enacted under subparagraph (a) to any activity prohibited to a State Party under this Convention undertaken anywhere by natural persons, possessing its nationality, in conformity with international law.

2. Each State Party shall cooperate with other States Parties and afford the appropriate form of legal assistance to facilitate the implementation of the obligations under paragraph 1.

3. Each State Party, during the implementation of its obligations under this Convention, shall assign the highest priority to ensuring the safety of people and to protecting the environment, and shall cooperate as appropriate with other States Parties in this regard.

Relations between the State Party and the Organization

4. In order to fulfil its obligations under this Convention, each State Party shall designate or establish a National Authority to serve as the national focal point for effective liaison with the Organization and other States Parties. Each State Party shall notify the Organization of its National Authority at the time that this Convention enters into force for it.

5. Each State Party shall inform the Organization of the legislative and administrative measures taken to implement this Convention.

6. Each State Party shall treat as confidential and afford special handling to information and data that it receives in confidence from the Organization in connection with the implementation of this Convention.

It shall treat such information and data exclusively in connection with its rights and obligations under this Convention and in accordance with the provisions set forth in the Confidentiality Annex.

7. Each State Party undertakes to cooperate with the Organization in the exercise of all its functions and in particular to provide assistance to the Technical Secretariat.

ARTICLE VIII

THE ORGANIZATION

A. GENERAL PROVISIONS

1. The States Parties to this Convention hereby establish the Organization for the Prohibition of Chemical Weapons to achieve the object and purpose of this Convention, to ensure the implementation of its provisions, including those for international verification of compliance with it, and to provide a forum for consultation and cooperation among States Parties.

2. All States Parties to this Convention shall be members of the Organization. A State Party shall not be deprived of its membership in the Organization.

3. The seat of the Headquarters of the Organization shall be The Hague, Kingdom of the Netherlands.

4. There are hereby established as the organs of the Organization: the Conference of the States Parties, the Executive Council, and the Technical Secretariat.

5. The Organization shall conduct its verification activities provided for under this Convention in the least intrusive manner possible consistent with the timely and efficient accomplishment of their objectives. It shall request only the information and data necessary to fulfil its responsibilities under this Convention. It shall take every precaution to protect the confidentiality of information on civil and military activities and facilities coming to its knowledge in the implementation of this Convention and, in particular, shall abide by the provisions set forth in the Confidentiality Annex.

6. In undertaking its verification activities the Organization shall consider measures to make use of advances in science and technology.

7. The costs of the Organization's activities shall be paid by States Parties in accordance with the United Nations scale of assessment adjusted to take into account differences in membership between the United Nations and this Organization, and subject to the provisions of Articles IV and V. Financial contributions of States Parties to the Preparatory Commission

shall be deducted in an appropriate way from their contributions to the regular budget. The budget of the Organization shall comprise two separate chapters, one relating to administrative and other costs, and one relating to verification costs.

8. A member of the Organization which is in arrears in the payment of its financial contribution to the Organization shall have no vote in the Organization if the amount of its arrears equals or exceeds the amount of the contribution due from it for the preceding two full years. The Conference of the States Parties may, nevertheless, permit such a member to vote if it is satisfied that the failure to pay is due to conditions beyond the control of the member.

B. THE CONFERENCE OF THE STATES PARTIES

Composition, procedures and decision-making

9. The Conference of the States Parties (hereinafter referred to as "the Conference") shall be composed of all members of this Organization. Each member shall have one representative in the Conference, who may be accompanied by alternates and advisers.

10. The first session of the Conference shall be convened by the depositary not later than 30 days after the entry into force of this Convention.

11. The Conference shall meet in regular sessions which shall be held annually unless it decides otherwise.

12. Special sessions of the Conference shall be convened:

(a) When decided by the Conference;

(b) When requested by the Executive Council;

(c) When requested by any member and supported by one third of the members; or

(d) In accordance with paragraph 22 to undertake reviews of the operation of this Convention.

Except in the case of subparagraph (d), the special session shall be convened not later than 30 days after receipt of the request by the Director-General of the Technical Secretariat, unless specified otherwise in the request.

13. The Conference shall also be convened in the form of an Amendment Conference in accordance with Article XV, paragraph 2.

14. Sessions of the Conference shall take place at the seat of the Organization unless the Conference decides otherwise.

15. The Conference shall adopt its rules of procedure. At the beginning of each regular session, it shall elect its Chairman and such other officers as may be required. They shall hold office until a new Chairman and other officers are elected at the next regular session.

16. A majority of the members of the Organization shall constitute a quorum for the Conference.

17. Each member of the Organization shall have one vote in the Conference.

18. The Conference shall take decisions on questions of procedure by a simple majority of the members present and voting. Decisions on matters of substance should be taken as far as possible by consensus. If consensus is not attainable when an issue comes up for decision, the Chairman shall defer any vote for 24 hours and during this period of deferment shall make every effort to facilitate achievement of consensus, and shall report to the Conference before the end of this period. If consensus is not possible at the end of 24 hours, the Conference shall take the decision by a two-thirds majority of members present and voting unless specified otherwise in this Convention. When the issue arises as to whether the question is one of substance or not, that question shall be treated as a matter of substance unless otherwise decided by the Conference by the majority required for decisions on matters of substance.

Powers and functions

19. The Conference shall be the principal organ of the Organization. It shall consider any questions, matters or issues within the scope of this Convention, including those relating to the powers and functions of the Executive Council and the Technical Secretariat. It may make recommendations and take decisions on any questions, matters or issues related to this Convention raised by a State Party or brought to its attention by the Executive Council.

20. The Conference shall oversee the implementation of this Convention, and act in order to promote its object and purpose. The Conference shall review compliance with this Convention. It shall also oversee the activities of the Executive Council and the Technical Secretariat and may issue guidelines in accordance with this Convention to either of them in the exercise of their functions.

21. The Conference shall:

(a) Consider and adopt at its regular sessions the report, programme and budget of the Organization, submitted by the Executive Council, as well as consider other reports;

(b) Decide on the scale of financial contributions to be paid by States Parties in accordance with paragraph 7;

(c) Elect the members of the Executive Council;

(d) Appoint the Director-General of the Technical Secretariat (hereinafter referred to as "the Director-General");

(e) Approve the rules of procedure of the Executive Council submitted by the latter;

(f) Establish such subsidiary organs as it finds necessary for the exercise of its functions in accordance with this Convention;

(g) Foster international cooperation for peaceful purposes in the field of chemical activities;

(h) Review scientific and technological developments that could affect the operation of this Convention and, in this context, direct the Director-General to establish a Scientific Advisory Board to enable him, in the performance of his functions, to render specialized advice in areas of science and technology relevant to this Convention, to the Conference, the Executive Council or States Parties. The Scientific Advisory Board shall be composed of independent experts appointed in accordance with terms of reference adopted by the Conference;

(i) Consider and approve at its first session any draft agreements, provisions and guidelines developed by the Preparatory Commission;

(j) Establish at its first session the voluntary fund for assistance in accordance with Article X;

(k) Take the necessary measures to ensure compliance with this Convention and to redress and remedy any situation which contravenes the provisions of this Convention, in accordance with Article XII.

22. The Conference shall not later than one year after the expiry of the fifth and the tenth year after the entry into force of this Convention, and at such other times within that time period as may be decided upon, convene in special sessions to undertake reviews of the operation of this Convention. Such reviews shall take into account any relevant scientific and technological

developments. At intervals of five years thereafter, unless otherwise decided upon, further sessions of the Conference shall be convened with the same objective.

C. THE EXECUTIVE COUNCIL

Composition, procedure and decision-making

23. The Executive Council shall consist of 41 members. Each State Party shall have the right, in accordance with the principle of rotation, to serve on the Executive Council. The members of the Executive Council shall be elected by the Conference for a term of two years. In order to ensure the effective functioning of this Convention, due regard being specially paid to equitable geographical distribution, to the importance of chemical industry, as well as to political and security interests, the Executive Council shall be composed as follows:

(a) Nine States Parties from Africa to be designated by States Parties located in this region. As a basis for this designation it is understood that, out of these nine States Parties, three members shall, as a rule, be the States Parties with the most significant national chemical industry in the region as determined by internationally reported and published data; in addition, the regional group shall agree also to take into account other regional factors in designating these three members;

(b) Nine States Parties from Asia to be designated by States Parties located in this region. As a basis for this designation it is understood that, out of these nine States Parties, four members shall, as a rule, be the States Parties with the most significant national chemical industry in the region as determined by internationally reported and published data; in addition, the regional group shall agree also to take into account other regional factors in designating these four members;

(c) Five States Parties from Eastern Europe to be designated by States Parties located in this region. As a basis for this designation it is understood that, out of these five States Parties, one member shall, as a rule, be the State Party with the most significant national chemical industry in the region as determined by internationally reported and published data; in addition, the regional group shall agree also to take into account other regional factors in designating this one member;

(d) Seven States Parties from Latin America and the Caribbean to be designated by States Parties located in this region. As a basis for this designation it is understood that, out of these seven States

Parties, three members shall, as a rule, be the States Parties with the most significant national chemical industry in the region as determined by internationally reported and published data; in addition, the regional group shall agree also to take into account other regional factors in designating these three members;

(e) Ten States Parties from among Western European and other States to be designated by States Parties located in this region. As a basis for this designation it is understood that, out of these 10 States Parties, 5 members shall, as a rule, be the States Parties with the most significant national chemical industry in the region as determined by internationally reported and published data; in addition, the regional group shall agree also to take into account other regional factors in designating these five members;

(f) One further State Party to be designated consecutively by States Parties located in the regions of Asia and Latin America and the Caribbean. As a basis for this designation it is understood that this State Party shall be a rotating member from these regions.

24. For the first election of the Executive Council 20 members shall be elected for a term of one year, due regard being paid to the established numerical proportions as described in paragraph 23.

25. After the full implementation of Articles IV and V the Conference may, upon the request of a majority of the members of the Executive Council, review the composition of the Executive Council taking into account developments related to the principles specified in paragraph 23 that are governing its composition.

26. The Executive Council shall elaborate its rules of procedure and submit them to the Conference for approval.

27. The Executive Council shall elect its Chairman from among its members.

28. The Executive Council shall meet for regular sessions. Between regular sessions it shall meet as often as may be required for the fulfilment of its powers and functions.

29. Each member of the Executive Council shall have one vote. Unless otherwise specified in this Convention, the Executive Council shall take decisions on matters of substance by a two-thirds majority of all its members. The Executive Council shall take decisions on questions of procedure by a simple majority of all its members. When the issue arises as to whether the question is one of substance or not, that question shall be treated as a matter of substance unless otherwise decided by the Executive Council by the majority required for decisions on matters of substance.

Powers and functions

30. The Executive Council shall be the executive organ of the Organization. It shall be responsible to the Conference. The Executive Council shall carry out the powers and functions entrusted to it under this Convention, as well as those functions delegated to it by the Conference. In so doing, it shall act in conformity with the recommendations, decisions and guidelines of the Conference and assure their proper and continuous implementation.

31. The Executive Council shall promote the effective implementation of, and compliance with, this Convention. It shall supervise the activities of the Technical Secretariat, cooperate with the National Authority of each State Party and facilitate consultations and cooperation among States Parties at their request.

32. The Executive Council shall:

(a) Consider and submit to the Conference the draft programme and budget of the Organization;

(b) Consider and submit to the Conference the draft report of the Organization on the implementation of this Convention, the report on the performance of its own activities and such special reports as it deems necessary or which the Conference may request;

(c) Make arrangements for the sessions of the Conference including the preparation of the draft agenda.

33. The Executive Council may request the convening of a special session of the Conference.

34. The Executive Council shall:

(a) Conclude agreements or arrangements with States and international organizations on behalf of the Organization, subject to prior approval by the Conference;

(b) Conclude agreements with States Parties on behalf of the Organization in connection with Article X and supervise the voluntary fund referred to in Article X;

(c) Approve agreements or arrangements relating to the implementation of verification activities, negotiated by the Technical Secretariat with States Parties.

35. The Executive Council shall consider any issue or matter within its competence affecting this Convention and its implementation, including concerns regarding compliance, and cases of non-compliance, and, as

appropriate, inform States Parties and bring the issue or matter to the attention of the Conference.

36. In its consideration of doubts or concerns regarding compliance and cases of non-compliance, including, inter alia, abuse of the rights provided for under this Convention, the Executive Council shall consult with the States Parties involved and, as appropriate, request the State Party to take measures to redress the situation within a specified time. To the extent that the Executive Council considers further action to be necessary, it shall take, inter alia, one or more of the following measures:

(a) Inform all States Parties of the issue or matter;

(b) Bring the issue or matter to the attention of the Conference;

(c) Make recommendations to the Conference regarding measures to redress the situation and to ensure compliance.

The Executive Council shall, in cases of particular gravity and urgency, bring the issue or matter, including relevant information and conclusions, directly to the attention of the United Nations General Assembly and the United Nations Security Council. It shall at the same time inform all States Parties of this step.

D. THE TECHNICAL SECRETARIAT

37. The Technical Secretariat shall assist the Conference and the Executive Council in the performance of their functions. The Technical Secretariat shall carry out the verification measures provided for in this Convention. It shall carry out the other functions entrusted to it under this Convention as well as those functions delegated to it by the Conference and the Executive Council.

38. The Technical Secretariat shall:

(a) Prepare and submit to the Executive Council the draft programme and budget of the Organization;

(b) Prepare and submit to the Executive Council the draft report of the Organization on the implementation of this Convention and such other reports as the Conference or the Executive Council may request;

(c) Provide administrative and technical support to the Conference, the Executive Council and subsidiary organs;

(d) Address and receive communications on behalf of the Organization to and from States Parties on matters pertaining to the implementation of this Convention;

(e) Provide technical assistance and technical evaluation to States Parties in the implementation of the provisions of this Convention, including evaluation of scheduled and unscheduled chemicals.

39. The Technical Secretariat shall:

(a) Negotiate agreements or arrangements relating to the implementation of verification activities with States Parties, subject to approval by the Executive Council;

(b) Not later than 180 days after entry into force of this Convention, coordinate the establishment and maintenance of permanent stockpiles of emergency and humanitarian assistance by States Parties in accordance with Article X, paragraphs 7 (b) and (c). The Technical Secretariat may inspect the items maintained for serviceability. Lists of items to be stockpiled shall be considered and approved by the Conference pursuant to paragraph 21 (i) above;

(c) Administer the voluntary fund referred to in Article X, compile declarations made by the States Parties and register, when requested, bilateral agreements concluded between States Parties or between a State Party and the Organization for the purposes of Article X.

40. The Technical Secretariat shall inform the Executive Council of any problem that has arisen with regard to the discharge of its functions, including doubts, ambiguities or uncertainties about compliance with this Convention that have come to its notice in the performance of its verification activities and that it has been unable to resolve or clarify through its consultations with the State Party concerned.

41. The Technical Secretariat shall comprise a Director-General, who shall be its head and chief administrative officer, inspectors and such scientific, technical and other personnel as may be required.

42. The Inspectorate shall be a unit of the Technical Secretariat and shall act under the supervision of the Director-General.

43. The Director-General shall be appointed by the Conference upon the recommendation of the Executive Council for a term of four years, renewable for one further term, but not thereafter.

44. The Director-General shall be responsible to the Conference and the Executive Council for the appointment of the staff and the organization and functioning of the Technical Secretariat. The paramount consideration in the employment of the staff and in the determination of the conditions of service shall be the necessity of securing the highest standards of efficiency, competence and integrity. Only citizens of States Parties shall serve as the Director-General, as inspectors or as other members of the professional and clerical staff. Due regard shall be paid to the importance of recruiting the staff on as wide a geographical basis as possible. Recruitment shall be guided by the principle that the staff shall be kept to a minimum necessary for the proper discharge of the responsibilities of the Technical Secretariat.

45. The Director-General shall be responsible for the organization and functioning of the Scientific Advisory Board referred to in paragraph 21 (h). The Director-General shall, in consultation with States Parties, appoint members of the Scientific Advisory Board, who shall serve in their individual capacity. The members of the Board shall be appointed on the basis of their expertise in the particular scientific fields relevant to the implementation of this Convention. The Director-General may also, as appropriate, in consultation with members of the Board, establish temporary working groups of scientific experts to provide recommendations on specific issues. In regard to the above, States Parties may submit lists of experts to the Director-General.

46. In the performance of their duties, the Director-General, the inspectors and the other members of the staff shall not seek or receive instructions from any Government or from any other source external to the Organization. They shall refrain from any action that might reflect on their positions as international officers responsible only to the Conference and the Executive Council.

47. Each State Party shall respect the exclusively international character of the responsibilities of the Director-General, the inspectors and the other members of the staff and not seek to influence them in the discharge of their responsibilities.

E. PRIVILEGES AND IMMUNITIES

48. The Organization shall enjoy on the territory and in any other place under the jurisdiction or control of a State Party such legal capacity and such privileges and immunities as are necessary for the exercise of its functions.

49. Delegates of States Parties, together with their alternates and advisers, representatives appointed to the Executive Council together with their alternates and advisers, the Director-General and the staff of the Organization shall enjoy such privileges and immunities as are necessary in

the independent exercise of their functions in connection with the Organization.

50. The legal capacity, privileges, and immunities referred to in this Article shall be defined in agreements between the Organization and the States Parties as well as in an agreement between the Organization and the State in which the headquarters of the Organization is seated. These agreements shall be considered and approved by the Conference pursuant to paragraph 21 (i).

51. Notwithstanding paragraphs 48 and 49, the privileges and immunities enjoyed by the Director-General and the staff of the Technical Secretariat during the conduct of verification activities shall be those set forth in Part II, Section B, of the Verification Annex.

ARTICLE IX

CONSULTATIONS, COOPERATION AND FACT-FINDING

1. States Parties shall consult and cooperate, directly among themselves, or through the Organization or other appropriate international procedures, including procedures within the framework of the United Nations and in accordance with its Charter, on any matter which may be raised relating to the object and purpose, or the implementation of the provisions, of this Convention.

2. Without prejudice to the right of any State Party to request a challenge inspection, States Parties should, whenever possible, first make every effort to clarify and resolve, through exchange of information and consultations among themselves, any matter which may cause doubt about compliance with this Convention, or which gives rise to concerns about a related matter which may be considered ambiguous. A State Party which receives a request from another State Party for clarification of any matter which the requesting State Party believes causes such a doubt or concern shall provide the requesting State Party as soon as possible, but in any case not later than 10 days after the request, with information sufficient to answer the doubt or concern raised along with an explanation of how the information provided resolves the matter. Nothing in this Convention shall affect the right of any two or more States Parties to arrange by mutual consent for inspections or any other procedures among themselves to clarify and resolve any matter which may cause doubt about compliance or gives rise to a concern about a related matter which may be considered ambiguous. Such arrangements shall not affect the rights and obligations of any State Party under other provisions of this Convention.

<u>Procedure for requesting clarification</u>

3. A State Party shall have the right to request the Executive Council to assist in clarifying any situation which may be considered ambiguous or which gives rise to a concern about the possible non-compliance of another State Party with this Convention. The Executive Council shall provide appropriate information in its possession relevant to such a concern.

4. A State Party shall have the right to request the Executive Council to obtain clarification from another State Party on any situation which may be considered ambiguous or which gives rise to a concern about its possible non-compliance with this Convention. In such a case, the following shall apply:

(a) The Executive Council shall forward the request for clarification to the State Party concerned through the Director-General not later than 24 hours after its receipt;

(b) The requested State Party shall provide the clarification to the Executive Council as soon as possible, but in any case not later than 10 days after the receipt of the request;

(c) The Executive Council shall take note of the clarification and forward it to the requesting State Party not later than 24 hours after its receipt;

(d) If the requesting State Party deems the clarification to be inadequate, it shall have the right to request the Executive Council to obtain from the requested State Party further clarification;

(e) For the purpose of obtaining further clarification requested under subparagraph (d), the Executive Council may call on the Director-General to establish a group of experts from the Technical Secretariat, or if appropriate staff are not available in the Technical Secretariat, from elsewhere, to examine all available information and data relevant to the situation causing the concern. The group of experts shall submit a factual report to the Executive Council on its findings;

(f) If the requesting State Party considers the clarification obtained under subparagraphs (d) and (e) to be unsatisfactory, it shall have the right to request a special session of the Executive Council in which States Parties involved that are not members of the Executive Council shall be entitled to take part. In such a special session, the Executive Council shall consider the matter and may recommend any measure it deems appropriate to resolve the situation.

5. A State Party shall also have the right to request the Executive Council to clarify any situation which has been considered ambiguous or has given

rise to a concern about its possible non-compliance with this Convention. The Executive Council shall respond by providing such assistance as appropriate.

6. The Executive Council shall inform the States Parties about any request for clarification provided in this Article.

7. If the doubt or concern of a State Party about a possible non-compliance has not been resolved within 60 days after the submission of the request for clarification to the Executive Council, or it believes its doubts warrant urgent consideration, notwithstanding its right to request a challenge inspection, it may request a special session of the Conference in accordance with Article VIII, paragraph 12 (c). At such a special session, the Conference shall consider the matter and may recommend any measure it deems appropriate to resolve the situation.

Procedures for challenge inspections

8. Each State Party has the right to request an on-site challenge inspection of any facility or location in the territory or in any other place under the jurisdiction or control of any other State Party for the sole purpose of clarifying and resolving any questions concerning possible non-compliance with the provisions of this Convention, and to have this inspection conducted anywhere without delay by an inspection team designated by the Director-General and in accordance with the Verification Annex.

9. Each State Party is under the obligation to keep the inspection request within the scope of this Convention and to provide in the inspection request all appropriate information on the basis of which a concern has arisen regarding possible non-compliance with this Convention as specified in the Verification Annex. Each State Party shall refrain from unfounded inspection requests, care being taken to avoid abuse. The challenge inspection shall be carried out for the sole purpose of determining facts relating to the possible non-compliance.

10. For the purpose of verifying compliance with the provisions of this Convention, each State Party shall permit the Technical Secretariat to conduct the on-site challenge inspection pursuant to paragraph 8.

11. Pursuant to a request for a challenge inspection of a facility or location, and in accordance with the procedures provided for in the Verification Annex, the inspected State Party shall have:

(a) The right and the obligation to make every reasonable effort to demonstrate its compliance with this Convention and, to this end, to enable the inspection team to fulfil its mandate;

(b) The obligation to provide access within the requested site for the sole purpose of establishing facts relevant to the concern regarding possible non-compliance; and

(c) The right to take measures to protect sensitive installations, and to prevent disclosure of confidential information and data, not related to this Convention.

12. With regard to an observer, the following shall apply:

(a) The requesting State Party may, subject to the agreement of the inspected State Party, send a representative who may be a national either of the requesting State Party or of a third State Party, to observe the conduct of the challenge inspection.

(b) The inspected State Party shall then grant access to the observer in accordance with the Verification Annex.

(c) The inspected State Party shall, as a rule, accept the proposed observer, but if the inspected State Party exercises a refusal, that fact shall be recorded in the final report.

13. The requesting State Party shall present an inspection request for an on-site challenge inspection to the Executive Council and at the same time to the Director-General for immediate processing.

14. The Director-General shall immediately ascertain that the inspection request meets the requirements specified in Part X, paragraph 4, of the Verification Annex, and, if necessary, assist the requesting State Party in filing the inspection request accordingly. When the inspection request fulfils the requirements, preparations for the challenge inspection shall begin.

15. The Director-General shall transmit the inspection request to the inspected State Party not less than 12 hours before the planned arrival of the inspection team at the point of entry.

16. After having received the inspection request, the Executive Council shall take cognizance of the Director-General's actions on the request and shall keep the case under its consideration throughout the inspection procedure. However, its deliberations shall not delay the inspection process.

17. The Executive Council may, not later than 12 hours after having received the inspection request, decide by a three-quarter majority of all its members against carrying out the challenge inspection, if it considers the inspection request to be frivolous, abusive or clearly beyond the scope of this Convention as described in paragraph 8. Neither the requesting nor the inspected State Party shall participate in such a decision. If the Executive

Council decides against the challenge inspection, preparations shall be stopped, no further action on the inspection request shall be taken, and the States Parties concerned shall be informed accordingly.

18. The Director-General shall issue an inspection mandate for the conduct of the challenge inspection. The inspection mandate shall be the inspection request referred to in paragraphs 8 and 9 put into operational terms, and shall conform with the inspection request.

19. The challenge inspection shall be conducted in accordance with Part X or, in the case of alleged use, in accordance with Part XI of the Verification Annex. The inspection team shall be guided by the principle of conducting the challenge inspection in the least intrusive manner possible, consistent with the effective and timely accomplishment of its mission.

20. The inspected State Party shall assist the inspection team throughout the challenge inspection and facilitate its task. If the inspected State Party proposes, pursuant to Part X, Section C, of the Verification Annex, arrangements to demonstrate compliance with this Convention, alternative to full and comprehensive access, it shall make every reasonable effort, through consultations with the inspection team, to reach agreement on the modalities for establishing the facts with the aim of demonstrating its compliance.

21. The final report shall contain the factual findings as well as an assessment by the inspection team of the degree and nature of access and cooperation granted for the satisfactory implementation of the challenge inspection. The Director-General shall promptly transmit the final report of the inspection team to the requesting State Party, to the inspected State Party, to the Executive Council and to all other States Parties. The Director-General shall further transmit promptly to the Executive Council the assessments of the requesting and of the inspected States Parties, as well as the views of other States Parties which may be conveyed to the Director-General for that purpose, and then provide them to all States Parties.

22. The Executive Council shall, in accordance with its powers and functions, review the final report of the inspection team as soon as it is presented, and address any concerns as to:

(a) Whether any non-compliance has occurred;

(b) Whether the request had been within the scope of this Convention; and

(c) Whether the right to request a challenge inspection had been abused.

23. If the Executive Council reaches the conclusion, in keeping with its powers and functions, that further action may be necessary with regard to paragraph 22, it shall take the appropriate measures to redress the situation and to ensure compliance with this Convention, including specific recommendations to the Conference. In the case of abuse, the Executive Council shall examine whether the requesting State Party should bear any of the financial implications of the challenge inspection.

24. The requesting State Party and the inspected State Party shall have the right to participate in the review process. The Executive Council shall inform the States Parties and the next session of the Conference of the outcome of the process.

25. If the Executive Council has made specific recommendations to the Conference, the Conference shall consider action in accordance with Article XII.

ARTICLE X

ASSISTANCE AND PROTECTION AGAINST CHEMICAL WEAPONS

1. For the purposes of this Article, "Assistance" means the coordination and delivery to States Parties of protection against chemical weapons, including, inter alia, the following: detection equipment and alarm systems; protective equipment; decontamination equipment and decontaminants; medical antidotes and treatments; and advice on any of these protective measures.

2. Nothing in this Convention shall be interpreted as impeding the right of any State Party to conduct research into, develop, produce, acquire, transfer or use means of protection against chemical weapons, for purposes not prohibited under this Convention.

3. Each State Party undertakes to facilitate, and shall have the right to participate in, the fullest possible exchange of equipment, material and scientific and technological information concerning means of protection against chemical weapons.

4. For the purposes of increasing the transparency of national programmes related to protective purposes, each State Party shall provide annually to the Technical Secretariat information on its programme, in accordance with procedures to be considered and approved by the Conference pursuant to Article VIII, paragraph 21 (i).

5. The Technical Secretariat shall establish, not later than 180 days after entry into force of this Convention and maintain, for the use of any requesting State Party, a data bank containing freely available information concerning

various means of protection against chemical weapons as well as such information as may be provided by States Parties.

The Technical Secretariat shall also, within the resources available to it, and at the request of a State Party, provide expert advice and assist the State Party in identifying how its programmes for the development and improvement of a protective capacity against chemical weapons could be implemented.

6. Nothing in this Convention shall be interpreted as impeding the right of States Parties to request and provide assistance bilaterally and to conclude individual agreements with other States Parties concerning the emergency procurement of assistance.

7. Each State Party undertakes to provide assistance through the Organization and to this end to elect to take one or more of the following measures:

(a) To contribute to the voluntary fund for assistance to be established by the Conference at its first session;

(b) To conclude, if possible not later than 180 days after this Convention enters into force for it, agreements with the Organization concerning the procurement, upon demand, of assistance;

(c) To declare, not later than 180 days after this Convention enters into force for it, the kind of assistance it might provide in response to an appeal by the Organization. If, however, a State Party subsequently is unable to provide the assistance envisaged in its declaration, it is still under the obligation to provide assistance in accordance with this paragraph.

8. Each State Party has the right to request and, subject to the procedures set forth in paragraphs 9, 10 and 11, to receive assistance and protection against the use or threat of use of chemical weapons if it considers that:

(a) Chemical weapons have been used against it;

(b) Riot control agents have been used against it as a method of warfare; or

(c) It is threatened by actions or activities of any State that are prohibited for States Parties by Article I.

9. The request, substantiated by relevant information, shall be submitted to the Director-General, who shall transmit it immediately to the Executive Council and to all States Parties. The Director-General shall immediately forward the request to States Parties which have volunteered, in accordance

with paragraphs 7 (b) and (c), to dispatch emergency assistance in case of use of chemical weapons or use of riot control agents as a method of warfare, or humanitarian assistance in case of serious threat of use of chemical weapons or serious threat of use of riot control agents as a method of warfare to the State Party concerned not later than 12 hours after receipt of the request. The Director-General shall initiate, not later than 24 hours after receipt of the request, an investigation in order to provide foundation for further action. He shall complete the investigation within 72 hours and forward a report to the Executive Council. If additional time is required for completion of the investigation, an interim report shall be submitted within the same time-frame. The additional time required for investigation shall not exceed 72 hours. It may, however, be further extended by similar periods. Reports at the end of each additional period shall be submitted to the Executive Council. The investigation shall, as appropriate and in conformity with the request and the information accompanying the request, establish relevant facts related to the request as well as the type and scope of supplementary assistance and protection needed.

10. The Executive Council shall meet not later than 24 hours after receiving an investigation report to consider the situation and shall take a decision by simple majority within the following 24 hours on whether to instruct the Technical Secretariat to provide supplementary assistance. The Technical Secretariat shall immediately transmit to all States Parties and relevant international organizations the investigation report and the decision taken by the Executive Council. When so decided by the Executive Council, the Director-General shall provide assistance immediately. For this purpose, the Director-General may cooperate with the requesting State Party, other States Parties and relevant international organizations. The States Parties shall make the fullest possible efforts to provide assistance.

11. If the information available from the ongoing investigation or other reliable sources would give sufficient proof that there are victims of use of chemical weapons and immediate action is indispensable, the Director-General shall notify all States Parties and shall take emergency measures of assistance, using the resources the Conference has placed at his disposal for such contingencies. The Director-General shall keep the Executive Council informed of actions undertaken pursuant to this paragraph.

ARTICLE XI

ECONOMIC AND TECHNOLOGICAL DEVELOPMENT

1. The provisions of this Convention shall be implemented in a manner which avoids hampering the economic or technological development of States Parties, and international cooperation in the field of chemical activities for purposes not prohibited under this Convention including the international

exchange of scientific and technical information and chemicals and equipment for the production, processing or use of chemicals for purposes not prohibited under this Convention.

2. Subject to the provisions of this Convention and without prejudice to the principles and applicable rules of international law, the States Parties shall:

(a) Have the right, individually or collectively, to conduct research with, to develop, produce, acquire, retain, transfer, and use chemicals;

(b) Undertake to facilitate, and have the right to participate in, the fullest possible exchange of chemicals, equipment and scientific and technical information relating to the development and application of chemistry for purposes not prohibited under this Convention;

(c) Not maintain among themselves any restrictions, including those in any international agreements, incompatible with the obligations undertaken under this Convention, which would restrict or impede trade and the development and promotion of scientific and technological knowledge in the field of chemistry for industrial, agricultural, research, medical, pharmaceutical or other peaceful purposes;

(d) Not use this Convention as grounds for applying any measures other than those provided for, or permitted, under this Convention nor use any other international agreement for pursuing an objective inconsistent with this Convention;

(e) Undertake to review their existing national regulations in the field of trade in chemicals in order to render them consistent with the object and purpose of this Convention.

ARTICLE XII

MEASURES TO REDRESS A SITUATION AND TO ENSURE COMPLIANCE, INCLUDING SANCTIONS

1. The Conference shall take the necessary measures, as set forth in paragraphs 2, 3 and 4, to ensure compliance with this Convention and to redress and remedy any situation which contravenes the provisions of this Convention. In considering action pursuant to this paragraph, the Conference shall take into account all information and recommendations on the issues submitted by the Executive Council.

2. In cases where a State Party has been requested by the Executive Council to take measures to redress a situation raising problems with regard to its compliance, and where the State Party fails to fulfil the request within the specified time, the Conference may, inter alia, upon the recommendation of the Executive Council, restrict or suspend the State Party's rights and privileges under this Convention until it undertakes the necessary action to conform with its obligations under this Convention.

3. In cases where serious damage to the object and purpose of this Convention may result from activities prohibited under this Convention, in particular by Article I, the Conference may recommend collective measures to States Parties in conformity with international law.

4. The Conference shall, in cases of particular gravity, bring the issue, including relevant information and conclusions, to the attention of the United Nations General Assembly and the United Nations Security Council.

ARTICLE XIII

RELATION TO OTHER INTERNATIONAL AGREEMENTS

Nothing in this Convention shall be interpreted as in any way limiting or detracting from the obligations assumed by any State under the Protocol for the Prohibition of the Use in War of Asphyxiating, Poisonous or Other Gases, and of Bacteriological Methods of Warfare, signed at Geneva on 17 June 1925, and under the Convention on the Prohibition of the Development, Production and Stockpiling of Bacteriological (Biological) and Toxin Weapons and on Their Destruction, signed at London, Moscow and Washington on 10 April 1972.

ARTICLE XIV

SETTLEMENT OF DISPUTES

1. Disputes that may arise concerning the application or the interpretation of this Convention shall be settled in accordance with the relevant provisions of this Convention and in conformity with the provisions of the Charter of the United Nations.

2. When a dispute arises between two or more States Parties, or between one or more States Parties and the Organization, relating to the interpretation or application of this Convention, the parties concerned shall consult together with a view to the expeditious settlement of the dispute by negotiation or by other peaceful means of the parties' choice, including recourse to

appropriate organs of this Convention and, by mutual consent, referral to the International Court of Justice in conformity with the Statute of the Court. The States Parties involved shall keep the Executive Council informed of actions being taken.

3. The Executive Council may contribute to the settlement of a dispute by whatever means it deems appropriate, including offering its good offices, calling upon the States Parties to a dispute to start the settlement process of their choice and recommending a time-limit for any agreed procedure.

4. The Conference shall consider questions related to disputes raised by States Parties or brought to its attention by the Executive Council. The Conference shall, as it finds necessary, establish or entrust organs with tasks related to the settlement of these disputes in conformity with Article VIII, paragraph 21 (f).

5. The Conference and the Executive Council are separately empowered, subject to authorization from the General Assembly of the United Nations, to request the International Court of Justice to give an advisory opinion on any legal question arising within the scope of the activities of the Organization. An agreement between the Organization and the United Nations shall be concluded for this purpose in accordance with Article VIII, paragraph 34 (a).

6. This Article is without prejudice to Article IX or to the provisions on measures to redress a situation and to ensure compliance, including sanctions.

ARTICLE XV

AMENDMENTS

1. Any State Party may propose amendments to this Convention. Any State Party may also propose changes, as specified in paragraph 4, to the Annexes of this Convention. Proposals for amendments shall be subject to the procedures in paragraphs 2 and 3. Proposals for changes, as specified in paragraph 4, shall be subject to the procedures in paragraph 5.

2. The text of a proposed amendment shall be submitted to the Director-General for circulation to all States Parties and to the Depositary. The proposed amendment shall be considered only by an Amendment Conference. Such an Amendment Conference shall be convened if one third or more of the States Parties notify the Director-General not later than 30 days after its circulation that they support further consideration of the proposal. The Amendment Conference shall be held immediately following a regular session of the Conference unless the requesting States Parties ask for an earlier meeting. In no case shall an Amendment

Conference be held less than 60 days after the circulation of the proposed amendment.

3. Amendments shall enter into force for all States Parties 30 days after deposit of the instruments of ratification or acceptance by all the States Parties referred to under subparagraph (b) below:

(a) When adopted by the Amendment Conference by a positive vote of a majority of all States Parties with no State Party casting a negative vote; and

(b) Ratified or accepted by all those States Parties casting a positive vote at the Amendment Conference.

4. In order to ensure the viability and the effectiveness of this Convention, provisions in the Annexes shall be subject to changes in accordance with paragraph 5, if proposed changes are related only to matters of an administrative or technical nature. All changes to the Annex on Chemicals shall be made in accordance with paragraph 5. Sections A and C of the Confidentiality Annex, Part X of the Verification Annex, and those definitions in Part I of the Verification Annex which relate exclusively to challenge inspections, shall not be subject to changes in accordance with paragraph 5.

5. Proposed changes referred to in paragraph 4 shall be made in accordance with the following procedures:

(a) The text of the proposed changes shall be transmitted together with the necessary information to the Director-General. Additional information for the evaluation of the proposal may be provided by any State Party and the Director-General. The Director-General shall promptly communicate any such proposals and information to all States Parties, the Executive Council and the Depositary;

(b) Not later than 60 days after its receipt, the Director-General shall evaluate the proposal to determine all its possible consequences for the provisions of this Convention and its implementation and shall communicate any such information to all States Parties and the Executive Council;

(c) The Executive Council shall examine the proposal in the light of all information available to it, including whether the proposal fulfils the requirements of paragraph 4. Not later than 90 days after its receipt, the Executive Council shall notify its recommendation, with appropriate explanations, to all States Parties for consideration. States Parties shall acknowledge receipt within 10 days;

(d) If the Executive Council recommends to all States Parties that the proposal be adopted, it shall be considered approved if no State Party objects to it within 90 days after receipt of the recommendation. If the Executive Council recommends that the proposal be rejected, it shall be considered rejected if no State Party objects to the rejection within 90 days after receipt of the recommendation;

(e) If a recommendation of the Executive Council does not meet with the acceptance required under subparagraph (d), a decision on the proposal, including whether it fulfils the requirements of paragraph 4, shall be taken as a matter of substance by the Conference at its next session;

(f) The Director-General shall notify all States Parties and the Depositary of any decision under this paragraph;

(g) Changes approved under this procedure shall enter into force for all States Parties 180 days after the date of notification by the Director-General of their approval unless another time period is recommended by the Executive Council or decided by the Conference.

ARTICLE XVI

DURATION AND WITHDRAWAL

1. This Convention shall be of unlimited duration.

2. Each State Party shall, in exercising its national sovereignty, have the right to withdraw from this Convention if it decides that extraordinary events, related to the subject-matter of this Convention, have jeopardized the supreme interests of its country. It shall give notice of such withdrawal 90 days in advance to all other States Parties, the Executive Council, the Depositary and the United Nations Security Council. Such notice shall include a statement of the extraordinary events it regards as having jeopardized its supreme interests.

3. The withdrawal of a State Party from this Convention shall not in any way affect the duty of States to continue fulfilling the obligations assumed under any relevant rules of international law, particularly the Geneva Protocol of 1925.

ARTICLE XVII

STATUS OF THE ANNEXES

The Annexes form an integral part of this Convention. Any reference to this Convention includes the Annexes.

ARTICLE XVIII

SIGNATURE

This Convention shall be open for signature for all States before its entry into force.

ARTICLE XIX

RATIFICATION

This Convention shall be subject to ratification by States Signatories according to their respective constitutional processes.

ARTICLE XX

ACCESSION

Any State which does not sign this Convention before its entry into force may accede to it at any time thereafter.

ARTICLE XXI

ENTRY INTO FORCE

1. This Convention shall enter into force 180 days after the date of the deposit of the 65th instrument of ratification, but in no case earlier than two years after its opening for signature.

2. For States whose instruments of ratification or accession are deposited subsequent to the entry into force of this Convention, it shall enter into force on the 30th day following the date of deposit of their instrument of ratification or accession.

ARTICLE XXII

RESERVATIONS

The Articles of this Convention shall not be subject to reservations. The Annexes of this Convention shall not be subject to reservations incompatible with its object and purpose.

ARTICLE XXIII

DEPOSITARY

The Secretary-General of the United Nations is hereby designated as the Depositary of this Convention and shall, inter alia:

(a) Promptly inform all signatory and acceding States of the date of each signature, the date of deposit of each instrument of ratification or accession and the date of the entry into force of this Convention, and of the receipt of other notices;

(b) Transmit duly certified copies of this Convention to the Governments of all signatory and acceding States; and

(c) Register this Convention pursuant to Article 102 of the Charter of the United Nations.

ARTICLE XXIV

AUTHENTIC TEXTS

This Convention, of which the Arabic, Chinese, English, French, Russian and Spanish texts are equally authentic, shall be deposited with the Secretary-General of the United Nations.

IN WITNESS WHEREOF the undersigned, being duly authorized to that effect, have signed this Convention.

Done at Paris on the thirteenth day of January, one thousand nine hundred and ninety-three.

- **ANNEX ON CHEMICALS**
- **VERIFICATION ANNEX**
- **CONFIDENTIALITY ANNEX**